Imperialism in East Africa

Volume 2: Imperialism and Integration

D. Wadada Nabudere

Dedicated to the leaders of the Working Class Movement in East Africa who contributed so greatly to the development and formation of the National Movement; and particularly to:

Abdul Wahid Sykes and Erika Fiah — Tanganyika
Chege Kibachia and Makhan Singh — Kenya
James Kivu and I.K. Musazi — Uganda

Zed Press, 57 Caledonian Road, London N1 9DN

Imperialism in East Africa, Volume 2 —
Imperialism and Integration, was first
published by Zed Press Ltd., 57 Caledonian
Road, London N1 9DN in 1982.

Copyright © Dan Wadada Nabudere, 1982

Copyedited by Beverley Brown
Proofread by Mark Gourlay
Cover design by Jan Brown
Typeset by Lyn Caldwell
Printed by Redwood Burn, Trowbridge,
Wiltshire

U.S. Distribution
Lawrence Hill and Co., 520 Riverside Avenue,
Westport, Conn. 06880, U.S.A.

**British Library Cataloguing in Publication Data
Data**

Nabudere, D. Wadada
   Imperialism in East Africa.
   Vol. 2: Imperialism and integration
   1. Africa, East — History
   I. Title
   967.6   DT365
   ISBN 0 905762 05 3

Contents

Preface

Every phase of imperialism over the last 400 years has been associated with particular mechanisms integrating the imperialist powers with the dominated peoples. The aim of this book is to analyse these various mechanisms in East Africa. We seek to provide a materialist explanation for the economic and political events of the exploited and oppressed countries of East Africa first, but only briefly, during the era of feudal merchant capital, which was the pre-history to industrial capitalism in Europe; and then, again briefly, with 'free trade' imperialism, which in the first half of the 19th Century characterized British hegemony in the world market based on capitalist production. This phase in East Africa was dominated by the Britain's struggle against slavery and slave trading, and for the establishment of 'legitimate trade'. This period in the 19th Century was the prelude to the scramble for the new British Empire in a period of modern imperialism, which was characterized by the rise of monopoly capitalism and finance capital and which marked the entry of Germany and the United States into the world market, each claiming a share of it, a phenomenon that overshadowed the struggle for the remaining uncolonized parts of the world for exports of capital for its extended reproduction.

In the period after the 1880s, the real stage of imperialist integration of the East African countries began to take place, initially in its 'bilateral' phase in which each imperialist power carved out its own sphere of 'influence' which it later colonized or exchanged for another area of colonization. The First World War shook this type of integration. The Second World War (all for the imperialist redivision of the world by the major imperialist powers) finished off the process as British imperialism gave way to another form of modern imperialism under U.S. hegemony.

Although up to 1919 Britain had accepted a reciprocal 'open door' colonialism under the Congo Basin Treaties with the other imperialist powers, in the 1920s she established a bilateral grip of her own on two countries (Kenya and Uganda) and then, after the First World War, on the entire area of her original acquisition, plus the conquered colony of German East African (Tanganyika).

Britain's apparent victory over the entire East African hinterland enabled her to establish a number of integrative institutions, both economic and political, all intended to tighten her grip over these countries in order to assure her industrial, financial, shipping and merchant monopolies a favourable competitive position in the world market against the monopolies of the other imperialist powers. But this grip was only possible at the cost of generating immense antagonisms with the exploited and oppressed peoples of East Africa, who increasingly strove to throw off this yoke and bondage. At the same time the other imperialist powers, for instance, Germany and Italy, were struggling to recapture lost territories in order to provide their own bulging monopolies with assured outlets for capital and industrial goods, which were having trouble competing in the world market. This process also produced its share of clashes with Britain.

The result of these intensified antagonisms on the world stage was the unleashing of another imperialist world war that signalled the demise of British hegemony in East Africa. Although Britain was victorious against Germany and Italy, her economy was soon superseded, along with the other European powers — victor and vanquished alike — by a new imperialist superpower, the United States of America. This change in the balance of forces in the world after 1945, (particularly the rise of the socialist camp) compelled a redivision of the *remaining* colonized world which had to adjust and compromise at the political level with the forces of national liberation. Rapidly there developed a new system of arrangements in the world imperialist system, which for the sake of specificity and concreteness we have called 'multilateral imperialism'.

Under this new phase of imperialism, the former British colonies in East Africa underwent a political transformation, in which they were turned into neo-colonies under the benevolent eye of U.S. imperialism. This was not a contrived arrangement but a response to the growing national movements opposed to colonialism and imperialism. However, the weakness of the national movements lay in their leadership by a vaccilating 'national' bourgeoisie and the results were clear in terms of a compromised independence and neo-colonialism. With these changed conditions, new forms of integration suited to multilateral imperialism quietly began to take root, thereby increasing the pressures on the already shaky bilateral integrative mechanisms created by British imperialism. These new integrative mechanisms were based on an intensified monopolistic competition of giant transnational monopoly corporations, many of them new to the area (particularly U.S., German and Japanese). These new monopolistic competitive conditions also interacted with neo-colonial politics, bringing out into the open the political rivalry of monopoly groups which used the local comprador bourgeoisie and petty bourgeoisie.

The use of the local leadership by monopoly capital was made possible through 'aid', bribery, corruption by the monopolies. The surplus cash came from the super-profits they made by means of their grip on the neo-colonial states. There thus arose petty-bourgeois rivalries in economics and politics, intensifying the secondary contradictions among the people of East Africa. This comprador bourgeoisie enabled multilateral imperialism to manipulate the national economies, thereby creating the conditions for further vertical integration, this time on a multilateral basis, with the entire imperialist world. Bilaterally inherited institutional arrangements, such as the East African Community, collapsed, giving way to newer forms of integration assisted by institutional arrangements like the World Bank, the International Monetary Fund, the General Agreement on Trade and Tariffs, the Lome Convention, etc.

These new integrative arrangements were but a reflection of the still growing tendency of capital to concentrate on a world scale as a counter-action to the ever pressing tendency of the rate of profit to fall. The transnational corporate strategy was therefore nothing but a monopolistic rearrangement of the capitalist enterprise on a world scale, taking full advantage of the economies of scale that the ever narrowing – but still large world market – still provided. The transnational companies had a single global decision-making point, they spread production and marketing activities all over the world; they developed their organizational tentacles which included foreign affiliates, subsidiaries, branches, joint ventures, licences, distributors and agents. These made it possible for the monopoly enterprises to make larger than average profits – making a loss here but making greater profits there, on global scale. All of these devices were used in East Africa as new integrative mechanisms which vertically integrated the region with monopoly enterprise.

In our view, it is this materialist approach which can give us a solid basis for analysing the developments in the economic, social and political fields of these three East African countries (Kenya, Uganda and Tanzania). The tight compartments of the bourgeois social sciences, 'political science' or 'economic history', are based on an idealist world outlook and cannot take us to reality. It is only a synthetic analysis, based on historical materialism and using the dialectical materialist world outlook, that enables us to analyse the totality of the situation, grappling with the reality, and helping to indicate the way forward for the people of East Africa, who alone are qualified and entitled to put a stop to the exploitative and oppressive system that has ravaged and continues to dominate the three East African countries, exploiting the working people and oppressing all the national forces.

In this study therefore we shall, in Part One, focus on the bilateral integrative mechanisms adopted by British and German imperialism over their respective areas during the first phase of modern colonialism. Here we examine theoretically the underlying forces behind the new type of imperialism that arose during the 1880s, in which Germany, originally without any colonies of her own, found herself caught up in the new scramble for territory, alongside the more longstanding imperialists – Britain, France, Belgium, Portugal, Italy and Spain. The economic basis of these struggles is examined and the politics of division and redivision discussed so as to let the two explain each other, with the economic providing the overall basis. Various institutional changes, whether economic, political or legal, are analysed in the context of the class forces at work both globally and regionally.

Here it will be noted that a section of British finance capital, particularly that linked to the old landed interests, pursued an economic line aimed at introducing a white settler agricultural economy and, in alliance with the local white settler bourgeoisie, engaged in large estate farming in the Kenya High-lands and to some extent in the Tanganyika Highlands of Kilimanjaro (now under British 'Mandate'). They also pursued a policy of a political federation for the East African and Central African territories. This line was to some extent not supported by the industrial and financial sections of British capital normally associated with the Manchester and Liverpool textile monopolies who preferred peasant production to settler agriculture. Despite the fact that such a policy failed, British interests were still advanced by such common institutions as were created to further their joint interests. The East African people's opposition to colonialism, together with the intra-imperialist rivalries and working-class struggles at home in Britain, all contributed to the collapse of British colonialism and the integrative mechanisms it had created, and to their replacement by the new neo-colonial mechanism.

These we analyse in Part Two of the book. Here we begin to show the forces that were responsible for putting the U.S. in a hegemonic position globally, and the means by which it used this hegemony in its entry into East Africa. We then look concretely at the transnational corporate strategies which the U.S. monopolies, in particular, used to penetrate new areas not under their control. These strategies were soon forced on the other monopoly groups, particularly the British, who had to resort to them to defend their existing markets. These strategies included encouraging import substitution in each of the three territories which they had previously controlled as a single market. But now, with the political transformations and competitive rivalries that were being forced on them by the new monopolies from the U.S., Germany, Japan, etc. they adopted a new strategy globally. We look at the institutional frame-work, based on multilateral imperialism, which now began to fashion the policies of the neo-colonial states to advance this new type of monopolistic competition, and show how this monopolistic competition first fashioned and determined the individual neo-colonial economies and then created the conflicts which dealt a blow to Pan African aspirations (which were behind the drive to the establishment of an East African Federation).

Having inevitably failed in their efforts to federate, the neo-colonial states now concentrated on how best to run the neo-colonial economies on the basis of existing regional and territorial structures, modified to suit the neo-colonial situation. It is at this point that we examine the Treaty for East African Co-operation which created the East African Community, hailed at the time as evidence of the unity of the East African people. We look at the structures and institutions which were established to oversee the common market and common services which were expected to operate for the benefit of the entire region. We then examine the actual economics of the co-operative effort, and argue that such regional arrangements could only collapse due to: (1) the uneven economic development of the territories, (2) the new dominant forces of competition operating in this environment and (3) the petty rivalries implied by a small propertied local competition between the weak East African 'national' bourgeoisies and petty bourgeoisies, (itself an aspect and a product of monopolistic competition).

The collapse of the East African Community gave way to segmented economies in which the transnational monopoly corporations (given all the protection and guarantees they desired) still continued to integrate the national economies with their operations on a global basis. I shall argue further that transnational corporate integration, in modern conditions of intensified monopolistic rivalries and the still rising national anti-imperialist movement, is inconsistent with regional integration as such, since all the production activities of these monopolies are vertical rather than horizontal (in the geographical sense). I also look at the neo-colonial politics of such integration and the collapse of the East African Community. Finally I examine the new vertical institutional forms that continue to assist the new process of corporate integration. The book ends with the conclusion in which these new forms of exploitation and domination are shown to be facing resistance: and indeed this new form of imperialism must be opposed by new forms of political organization in which the working class is galvanized as the central force for rallying all the national forces against it in a new democratic revolution.

I argue further that regional integration has no advantage over development on the national level, as far as economic development is concerned. On the contrary, the nation-state still remains the only revolutionary unit not only for resolving class struggles but also for removing uneven economic and social development between peoples and nations. This is the only basis on which the full potential of a people can be mobilized into a revolutionary force for socialist reconstruction of society. Only *mutual assistance* between states embarked on socialist construction is permissible, even for socialist states. Any arguments about an 'international socialist division of labour' is nothing but social imperialist rhetoric. Equally any argument that economic development can be achieved on a regional basis under conditions of neo-colonialism is demonstrably hollow. The only solution to national development lies in new struggles for a new democratic society — a transition to a socialist society, and here the independent nation-state is still the most revolutionary instrument for achieving victory.

Part One
Integration Under Bilateral Imperialism

1. The Colonization of East Africa

In Volume One, Chapter One, the various stages through which East Africa was integrated into the world capitalist system were shown. In the first phase mercantalist imperialism was interested in exporting slaves to the 'New World' to work for the emergent merchant bourgeoisie with the aim of producing exotic products in the East Indies and for the settler colonists in America. What made this system possible was the British social structure in transition from feudalism to capitalism. The colonization of East Africa by Portuguese merchants, although restricted to the coastal outposts where slaves were collected and ships reprovisioned, had a devastating impact on the societies of East Africa. It reduced the population of the region, emptied it of the most able-bodied men and women, created warfare among the various societies and led to famine in many parts. As a result the productive power of the region was irreprably weakened.

The second stage consisted in the attempts of British imperialism to establish a system based on free trade rather than slavery. This was not so much a belated altruism as an act of rivalry against the other imperialist powers in the Indian Ocean. This rivalry itself was due to domestic pressures. The new forces of production in the English economy demanded new colonial outlets for the productive capitalist relations that were becoming hegemonic at home. Subsequently, the rise of monopolies in the next stage compelled a new rivalry and a division of the world, and it was in this later stage that East Africa found herself truly colonized in the modern sense, as a base of production for raw materials and food products for export to the metropolitan countries and as a market for its products based on the incomes that were earned by its exports. This development introduced entirely new relations of production in the region and led increasingly to the intensified exploitation of the peasantry and other working people.

The Methods Used

Whether German or British, imperialism adopted the same methods: first by forcibly annexing the territories and lands of the indigenous peoples of East Africa and then turning these people into labourers for the imperialist bourgeoisie. In order to achieve this objective, a colonial state machine was set up to supervise productive activities and to ensure the requisite 'order and peace', which operated in conjunction with the local recruitment of comprador chiefs.

In Uganda this strategy was carried out by fomenting a civil war in Buganda between the various factions of the ruling class. Although represented as a 'religious' civil war between the local people, in fact the Imperial British East Africa Company) (I.B.E.A.C.), with its charter from the British Foreign Office to keep the country under British control, intervened in these wars, fuelled them, and at last, when all the parties were worn down by the strife, gave support to the winning faction and strengthened it to become its effective agent in Uganda. With this victorious *Ba-Ingleza* faction it signed the Uganda Agreement, distributing the land of the peasantry to these chiefs as reward and designating the remainder, amounting to about 50% of the land, British Crown Lands.[1] On this basis it was then possible to mount a campaign, led by some of these agents, in order to bring the rest of the country under British control. Uganda's colonization was sealed when it was declared a 'Protectorate' in 1893 and officially became part of the British Empire.

The colonial system of administration was organized on the basis of districts and local authorities. Under a Native Authority Ordinance and a Native Courts Ordinance, the local authorities were given powers, making use of locally acceptable native customs, to punish those who did not comply with the rule of British imperialism. A colonial state was created and colonial state institution were constituted throughout the country, with agents and district commissioners appointed to supervise the work of chiefs in order to ensure orderly administration.[2]

In Kenya the British imperialists declared a Protectorate in 1895 over what they called British East Africa, in fact a small part of the present region. As colonists settled, the area was expanded to include the Kenya Highlands, most of which at this time lay in the Uganda Protectorate. Local 'headmen' and chiefs were recruited to install British authority. In this case, however, the British imperialists were not so sure that they could establish a self-sufficient colony. The first Commissioner, Eliot, had reported to the Colonial Office that unlike Uganda, the whole Kenyan people and area was unproductive It was a 'barren wilderness' which merely 'hampered' communication with Uganda, at this time considered by the British imperialists as its main prize.[3]

Taking this into account, efforts were now made to recruit settlers to manage and perform the production, beginning with India where it was thought a relatively cheap peasant labour force could be obtained to settle and produce in the colony. This failed, as did further efforts to recruit Zionists and even Finns. Finally, it was decided to bring in settlers from South Africa and Britain to settle in the colony and make it productive for British imperialism. It was in these circumstances that land was forcibly taken from the indigenous people. In 1921 the greater part of the Protectorate was declared a colony in order to make it easier for capital to be raised for the state and for settler agriculture under the Colonial Stocks Act of 1914. The colonial state machine now tightened its grip on the colony and, using the same methods as the Native Authority system in a more direct way, the British imperialists increasingly brought the country under control.

In the south the German imperialists, having manoeuvred Britain into accepting their control over this part of the region through the Treaty of Heligoland in 1890, also set about establishing a colonial state. Through the agency of the German East African Company, under the command of Carl Peters, the first elements of colonial power were established. Unable to quell all the revolts of the people against it, the German imperialists sent in a contingent of the navy.[4] In all, the process of suppression took eight years, 1888 to 1906. Supremacy once achieved, a colonial economic administration was set up using the former agents of the Sultan on the Coastal areas: the *Liwalis,* the *Jumbes* and the *Akidas* in the villages.

German rule was not to last long. Due to the colonial rivalries that were building up between the imperialist powers in Europe, an imperialist war broke out, as a result of which German East Africa passed to British and Belgian 'mandate'. The British took control of Tanganyika and, working on the model of Uganda and Kenya as well as the experience of indirect rule in Nigeria, they instituted a system of local authorities, using the Native Authorities Ordinance which they soon introduced as a law in the country.[5] Having consolidated their control over the country, they also soon started to put the colony to production.

The System of Production

The type of production activities that British imperialism encouraged, and which we have analysed at greater length in Part One of Volume One, were aimed at making each part of the territories sustain themselves as a colonial economy. In Uganda they had little difficulty in coercing the peasant labour force by means of taxes and other measures. Within a few years the colony was not only self-financing but had itself become vital to supporting Britain's East Africa venture as a whole. When Kenya's high-cost settler agriculture ran into difficulties, surcharges on Ugandan production provided the subsidies to prop it up. It was the regional colonial economy which was self-sufficient, not the individual units. Hence, regional colonial infrastructures, such as the Ugandan Railways, attained a particular importance, as we shall see in the next chapter.

In Tanganyika, the strategy involved the deployment of a 'dual economy' of peasant production and settler plantation agriculture. Inherited from the days of German rule, the policy had guaranteed the monopolies the highest return on their colonial investment. As maintained by the first British Governors, especially Cameron, Tanganyikan production occupied a position mid-way between the Ugandan and Kenyan systems of colonial production.

The difficulties experienced by the Kenyan type of colonial production were neither accidental nor, finally, ameliorable. In the end it very much

11

hastened the collapse of the colonial system in the region, for it introduced secondary and antagonistic contradictions. Indeed the repeated attempts to recruit Indian, Zionist and Finnish settlers can be seen as a recogntion of the problems attending the implantation of British settlement. Once this was unavoidable, it was only a matter of delaying actions. To be sure, the acquisition of land and the transformation of peasants into labourers for the settler and plantation capitalists at first succeeded in discouraging peasant production in the country. Efforts were made to reserve certain 'economic' crops, such as coffee, only for settler capitalists. In fact it was peasant production, both directly and in the form of government revenue, which sustained the colonial state. But this source of subsidy was constantly denied and undermined by the massive deprivation of land and productive facilities from Africans who were forced to labour at very low rates of pay for the white settler capitalist farmers. The sharp antagonisms this produced at the level of race relations were so intense that what was in fact the economic and institutional basis of colonial exploitation was itself taken to be evidence of racism.

How was it possible for the settler economy to both depend on and deny the existence of peasant production? One answer lies in the person of the 'squatter'. Rendered landless, the peasant laboured free of charge or for very low wages for the settler capitalist farmer, in return for a small piece of land which had in fact been originally stolen from him. On this land, subsistence and cash crops were grown. Since, by law, cash crops were not officially allowed to Africans, they could be sold only to the landlord. However, this type of peasant production on settler farms became fairly profitable for the peasants and later was to give them certain freedoms. Where, say, a middle-level farmer needed money badly, the squatter peasant could pay rent instead of labour. It was not these small and restricted advantages, however, which were important so much as the overall effect of the success and increase in this kind of peasant production. That it constituted a threat to settler capitalist production can be seen in the rigorous legal measures that were finally taken to control peasant production, measures which were an important factor in the Mau Mau uprising in the Abadares in the 1950s.

This type of colonial production, so heavily based on peasant or semi-peasant as well as working-class labour, proved very profitable for the British imperialism in general. The effects can be seen in Tables 1 to 3, which show that by 1907 very little development had taken place in the region. Exports amounted barely to £1 million, while net imports amounted to nearly £2.5 million. Revenue amounted to £10 million and expenditure to £1.6 million. All this indicates that some money capital was still being exported to East Africa from Britain and Germany either as grants-in-aid to revenue or for private investment. But by 1928 the picture had changed considerably. Exports were now valued at some £11 million while net imports had also gone up to some £12.5 million. Revenue to the colonial states had increased to £6.5 million and expenditure had also increased to £6.1 million. Thus the region was already self-sufficient and already providing a solid base of

exploitation for British finance capital. By 1952 the picture had 'improved'
by some 400% over all for British imperialism.

British East African colonial policy essentially operated within these
developments. The dual policy in production meant that the peasant producer
should be given a place to produce on his own, and also that the settler
capitalist should be given the opportunity to engage in production on the
basis of cheap labour available in the region. Thus it was no surprise that
peasant production in Uganda went on side by side with settler capitalist
agriculture in Kenya in which the peasant was turned increasingly into a
labourer for the settler farmer, while production in Tanganyika was a hybrid
of the two. The communication system established in the region tied the
economies together and it was emphasized from time to time (as we shall see
in the next chapter) that such common services as railways and harbours, as
well as other inter-territorial institutions, were absolutely necessary for the
exploitation of the region as an economic entity to the greatest possible
extent.

But such hopes were bought at the cost of creating antagonisms within
each of the colonial economies: at the level of production was created a
politics of resistance and forms of competition which threatened to pull the
system apart. Depriving the peasants of land was to place them face to face
with their exploiters in relations of wage-labour or squatting. Beyond the
individual exploiter there was the colonial state with its taxes and restrictions.
The antagonisms at both levels focused on the grievances and resistance of
the peasants, workers and new middle classes emerging in the interstices of the
colonial economy.

Not only were there antagonisms within the separate units of the region,
but there was also a degree of competition between the three colonial
bourgeoisies in commerce, agriculture and industry. And, at the level of the
territories, conflicts arose between the colonial bureaucracies. This followed
naturally upon the nature of capitalist relations for, while the interests of
imperialism in general saw no conflict in the interests of the various strata of
the bourgeoisie and their colonial states, competition at the level of the firm
necessarily produced rivalries. Thus, despite the inter-territorial institutions
and structures that were being encouraged in the region by British imperialism
and certain local classes, the territorial units in each case played the important
role of regulating relations and assisting the competitive power of individual
enterprises. The same duality characterized the relationships between the
bureaucracies of each territorial unit. Each saw itself as being in charge of
a particular territory and therefore of its interests. Each was under pressure
to raise revenue for the maintenance of the colonial state structures and this
tended to create conflicts which required British imperialism to regulate from
the centre — as we shall see in the next chapter.

References

1. H.W. West, *Land Policy in Buganda,* (Nairobi, East Africa Publishing House, 1972.)
2. A.D. Low, 'The Protectorate, 1894-1919' in Harlow, Chilver and Smith (eds.), *History of East Africa,* (London, Oxford University Press, 1965). Vol. II.
3. M.P.K. Sorrenson, *Land Policy in Kenya, 1895-1945,* in Harlow, Chilver and Smith, op. cit., p.672.
4. J. Illife, *Tanganyika under German Rule, 1905-1912,* (Nairobi, East Africa Publishing House, 1973).
5. K. Ingham, 'Tanganyika: The Mandate and Cameron 1919-31' in Harlow, Chilver and Smith, op. cit.

Table 1
Kenya: Exports/Imports, Revenue and Expenditure, 1907-53

	1907	1928	1931	1938	1946	1952	1953
Domestic Imports (£m.)	0.2	3.3	2.3	3.8	7.1	25.8	19.5
Non-Mineral Exports (est.)(£m.)	0.2	3.0	2.1	3.2	6.4	24.4	18.6
As a % Total Domestic Export	100	90	91	83	90	95	95
Mineral Exports (est.) (£m.)	N.A.	0.3	0.2	0.6	0.7	1.4	0.9
As % Total Domestic Export	—	10.0(d)	9.0(c)	17.0	10.0	5.0	5.0
Selected Exports							
Maize (£m.)	N.A.	0.3	0.4	0.3	0.2	2.4	0.3
As % Total Domestic Export	—	9	18	9	2	9	2
Volume ('000 cwt.)	N.A.	892	1,859	N.A.	348	1,365	215
Sisal (£m.)	N.A.	90.5	180.2	90.4	20.9	94.5	22.5
As % Total Domestic Export	—	16	10	11	12	17	13
Volume ('000 tons)	N.A.	16	16	28	24	35	35
Coffee (£m.)	N.A.	1.1	1.0	0.8	0.9	7.1	6.7
As % Total Domesic Export	—	34	42	20	13	28	34
Volume ('000 cwt.)	N.A.	212	246	339	191	338	296
Imports (£m.)	0.9(g)(c)	8.5(g)(c)	4.5(g)(c)	6.4	16.4	59.3	51.7
Revenue (£m.)	0.5	3.0	3.0	3.8	9.0	20.5	21.3
Expenditure	0.7	2.8	3.2	3.6	7.7	18.8	22.8

Source: *East African Royal Commission Report, 1953-55,* pp.460-1.

Notes
  (a) Domestic exports for 1952 and 1953 are East African products exported to countries outside the East African territories. Estimates between 1907 and 1946 inclusive, relate to trade between Tanganyika on the one hand, and Kenya and Uganda on the other, as overseas trade and in consequence include these transactions.

Table 2
Uganda: Exports/Imports, Revenue and Expenditure, 1907-53

	1907	1928	1931	1938	1946	1952	1953
Domestic Imports (£m.)	0.1	3.4	2.0	4.7	9.6	47.2	33.4
Non-Mineral Exports (est.) (£m.)	0.1	3.4	2.0	4.5	9.5	47.0	33.2
As a % Total Domestic Export	100	100	100	95	99	99	99
Mineral Exports (est.) (£m.)	N.	N.	N.	0.2	0.1	0.2	0.2
As a % Total Domestic Export	—	—	—(e)	5.0	1.0	0.4	0.5
Selected Exports							
Cotton (£m.)	0.5	0.5	1.7	3.4	5.7	29.9	16.8
As % Total Domestic Export	35	35	83	73	59	63	50
Volume ('000 400 lb bales)	4	138	189	432	219	378	334
Sisal (£m.)	N.A.	N.	N.	N.	N.	N.	N.
As a % Total Domestic Export	—	—	—	—	—	—	—
Volume ('000 cwt.)	N.A.	N.	N.	N.	N.	N.	N.
Coffee (£m.)	N.A.	0.2	0.2	0.3	1.8	12.3	11.5
As a % Total Domestic Export	—	6	10	7	18	26	35
Volume ('000 cwt.)	N.A.	40	70	280	611	789	714
Imports (£m.)	—(e)	—(e)	—(e)	2.5	5.3	24.3	25.7
Revenue (£m.)	0.1	1.5	1.4	1.9	4.0	17.3	17.7
Expenditure	0.2	1.4	1.4	2.0	3.6	15.9	17.4

Source: *East African Royal Commission Report, 1953-55*, pp.460-1.

Table 3
Tanganyika: Exports/Imports, Revenue and Expenditure, 1907-53

	1907	1928	1931	1938	1946	1952	1953
Domestic Imports (£m.)	0.6	3.9	1.6	3.7	8.8	47.0	34.5
Non-Mineral Exports (est.) (£m.)	0.6	3.9	1.6	3.1	7.4	40.8	30.9
As a % Total Domestic Export	100	100	100	83	83	87	90
Mineral Exports (est.) (£m.)	N.A.	N.A.	N.A.	0.6	1.4	6.2	3.6
As a % Total Domestic Export	—	—	—	17.0	17.0	13.0	10.0
Selected Exports							
Cotton (£m.)	N.A.	0.5	0.1	0.4	0.4	4.7	4.7
As a % Total Domestic Export	—	13	7	10	4	10	14
Volume ('000 400 lb bales)	N.A.	27	13	49	22	62	80
Sisal (£m.)	N.A.	1.1	0.7	1.4	3.9	21.7	14.7
As a % Total Domestic Export	—	29	43	38	44	46	37
Volume ('000 cwt.)	N.A.	36	56	101	111	158	171
Coffee (£m.)	N.A.	0.7	0.2	0.4	0.7	5.5	5.8
As a % Total Domestic Export	—	19	15	10	8	12	17
Volume ('000 cwt.)	N.A.	209	185	274	200	372	305
Imports (£m.)	1.2(g)	3.7(g)	2.5(g)	3.4	8.1	37.5	28.4
Revenue (£m)	0.4	2.0	2.5	2.1	5.1	16.4	14.7
Expenditure	0.7	1.9	1.8	2.2	5.1	15.8	14.7

Source: *East African Royal Commission Report, 1953-55*, pp.460-1.

(b) These figures are estimates based on calculation of the value of the principal exports of the territories.

(c) Kenya and Uganda combined.

(d) Kenya and Uganda combined for the year 1929.

(e) The Uganda contribution is included under Kenya.

(f) Net imports for 1952 and 1953 are imports received direct from countries outside East Africa, plus imported goods transferred from another East African territory minus imported goods transferred to another East African territory. Some goods which will subsequently be re-exported are included under net imports.

(g) Merchandise imports only.

(h) For 1946, 1952, and 1953, Kenya revenue and expenditure excludes the development budget. The Tanganyika estimates also exclude their development plan. In the case of Uganda it is not possible to separate development from other expenditure.

General

Figures have been rounded off and the use of decimal points does not indicate that degree of accuracy.

N. = Nil or neglibible.

N.A. = Not available.

General Statistical Note

This table is designed to show some of the basic data of the economic development and structure of the three East African territories. Certain years have been chosen to illustrate the growth and fluctuations of the economies. Statistics for 1907 indicate the very limited development that had taken place in the course of the first decade of this century; the peak that was reached before the impact of the Depression is illustrated by the year 1928; the effect of the Depression can be seen from the 1931 figures; the year 1938 shows to what extent a recovery had been made before the outbreak of the Second World War; and the rapid rise in money values in the immediate aftermath of that war can be judged by comparing the 1946 statistics with those of 1952. Statistics for 1953 have made apparent again the vulnerability of the East African economies to changes in world prices.

Unfortunately, the comparison of East African statistics over a time span of nearly half a century cannot be made with complete accuracy. For example, domestic exports for 1952 and 1953 are the values of Kenyan, Ugandan and Tanganyikan products exported to countries *outside* East Africa. Thus interterritorial trade is excluded. But in the other years, although exports between Kenya and Uganda do not appear in their respective estimates of domestic exports, their exports to Tanganyika are regarded as a part of total domestic exports. Similarly, Tanganyika's domestic exports for 1952 and 1953 do not include trade with Kenya and Uganda, although for the other years in the table exports to these territories are included. Discrepancies also exist in the other columns, but the table has not been constructed to convey small variations, but the overall picture. And so as not to detract from the broad picture it is intended to present qualifying footnotes and minor statistical adjustments have been reduced to a minimum.

2. Closer Union or Dual Policy?

Having sketched the process of bilateral integration of East Africa, we now want to show how important it was that this was achieved in the absence of political 'closer union' between the East African territories, despite a long struggle by certain political forces both in Britain itself and among a section of Kenyan and Tanganyikan settlers. At this period of history, as far as British imperialism in general was concerned, closer union of the East African territories was to be achieved only through the metropolitan link and, despite local conflicts, its interests were served very well by this arrangement.

So long as the colonies paid their way and produced what the British monopolies required in order to compete in the world market and so long as they provided a market for their manufactures, this bilateral arrangement was adequate. Thus the question of a closer political union did not present itself as a burning issue to British imperialism. Nor could Britain, even had it wanted to, have forced the issue beyond certain limits, for the international political situation at this time was generally not in its favour. In order to appreciate this point, it is therefore important to consider the general international forces surrounding British imperialism as well as the specific forces which were operating in the region.

British Policy on Federations

The stance of British imperialism on the question of federation, or closer links with its Empire, has seen three main phases, each manifesting a stage of crisis and further evolution of capitalism in its path of growth.

The first period is associated with the mercantalist imperialism of the 16th and 17th Centuries, in which colonization took place under charters issued by the absolute monarch to merchants engaged in long-distance trade. This type of licensing embraced the thirteen colonies of America, the Cape of Good Hope, India, the East Indies and the Caribbean. Settlers' rights were essentially those of being able to make representations, under a colonial constitution, to the imperial power. Imperial interest thus remained supreme in that the colony was a possession of the imperial power. These were 'Crown Colonies'.

The second type of imperial link with colonies came into being in the 19th Century with the rapid expansion of the population in Europe and consequent increase in migration to new lands. The same contradictory forces in capitalist development which in Europe meant that it could not contain its increased population also dictated that these settlements be integrated by a new free trade imperialism. Although the status of Crown Colony still applied until the 1840s, the interests of the now consolidated industrial bourgeoisie resulted in a pressure to 'enfranchise' these colonies. Apart from anything else, the cost of protecting them in time of war was proving prohibitive.

In working out a solution for 'responsible government', for these newly self-ruling entities, Lord Durham in his Report of 1839 proposed a separation between British interests and those of the colonists. According 'responsible government' to Canada and Nova Scotia in 1867 and British Columbia in 1871, marked this as the 'era of colonial nationalism',[1] a stage which was followed by a new concept of colonial rule known as 'federation'.

In the third stage, this federation concept was worked out by Chamberlain to contain growing 'nationalism' in the colonies of white settlement in the early stages of modern imperialism. The implications of federation were spelled out in a new phase in the development of capitalism into monopoly capital, a phase which Knowles calls a stage of 'nationhood', the 'sloughing off of the colonial attitude', and the beginning of a 'new economic policy of national development for each region carried out by its own government.'[2]

In fact this policy helped to hold the colonies within the Empire, and 'in a period of growing international tension and vast continental armaments [it was anticipated that] they might share the cost of the British Navy, and supply manpower for the British Army.'[3] The Imperial Federation League formed in 1884 advocated this policy for the white settler colonies and indeed its success in Australia, New Zealand and South Africa, earned Chamberlain fame as 'the enlarger and strengthener of the Empire'. Instead of utilizing Britain's difficulties in their own interests, instead of seeking to loosen their ties with Britain, 'as pessimists had predicted, all the colonies, without exception most warmly supported Great Britain's struggle' against the Boers in South Africa.[4]

In this phase emphasis is on the extraction of *cheap raw materials* – and the creation of colonial superstructures to make this possible – in order to bolster up the otherwise sagging economy of the British Empire, caught between the over-production of capital, on the one hand, and contracting markets, on the other. A further consideration was the establishment of local markets.[5] The economic role of the indigenous population is clearly defined as producers of food and raw materials while their political status as part of a Crown Colony is one of subordination. A further feature of the new colonies is the presence of substantial minority of white settlers, as we have seen.

This, then, was the type of setting in which Lord Milner and his 'kindergarten' of young men in the British civil service applied the new idea of federation. Unfortunately for Milner and Amery and the 'kindergarten', the idea was already out of date and unsuited to the new type of colony, such as the East African colonies, which was emerging in this period. Remember that this was after 1917; it was the era of the proletarian revolution in Russia and of a new type of nationalism which fought against imperialism (i.e. monopoly capital). Why such a policy was pursued can nevertheless be explained by analysing the specific interests in East Africa which saw a prospect of gain.

Social and Class Forces

We have seen how the white settlement of Kenya and to some extent of Tanganyika was motivated partly by a fear that otherwise the colonies would not pay and make themselves self-sufficient. In fact the arrival of these settlers had a radical effect on the whole orientation of British colonial policy in East Africa.

But who were these settlers and what was their class composition? It can be argued that it is in the context of class differentiation that the stance of Kenya, and indeed of the whole region, on the 'closer union' issue is to be understood. This includes class differentiation not only among the white population but amongst the African population as well, and among the Asians and Arabs, whose economic interests were also at issue during this period.

The British financial oligarchy had a definite but general interest – to make the colony produce certain products as cheaply as possible. Otherwise they simply did not care who did it. If one section of producers proved unsuccessful, they could simply be dismissed or subsidized by the cheapest of the other groups.

Within this general economic constraint, the various classes and groups of classes articulated themselves so as to advance their individual interests. In intervening in this play of forces, the British financial oligarchy merely sought a minimum 'neutral' position which balanced these interests while maintaining final control. In this way the working class and the poor peasantry – the real producers – were set upon and exploited to the maximum.

The African population of East Africa was composed of an aristocracy concentrated in a number of areas where there existed a feudal and/or semi-feudal form of social organization. Here the real producing class was the peasant serf and/or slave who produced a surplus for the aristocratic ruling class in areas like Buganda, Bunyoro, Ankole, Kigezi, Toro, Buhaya and Barwanda-Burundi.

It was fairly easy for the colonialists to ally themselves with the African aristocrats and form colonial administrative structures around them – the strategy of 'indirect rule'. In the later stages these erstwhile allies were stripped of the economic advantages they had claimed as a former ruling class and were slowly turned into paid administrators of British and German imperialism. Thus alongside the fundamental antagonism between imperialism and the peasantry and the rising working class, there was also a secondary contradiction with the old feudal aristocracy.

In the other groups, like the Lango, Lugbara, Nyamwezi, Ngoni, Luo and among the Kikuyu, where neither feudalism nor slavery existed, there was the mass of undifferentiated peasantry at the one end of the spectrum and an as yet unelected leadership under an emerging military commander and his retinue at the other. This was in areas in which the communal formation was in the process of evolution to what Engels calls the higher barbaric stage of a heroic age. The advent of colonialism meant that in this group of societies the peasantry were either turned into commodity producers for the imperialist markets or were dispossessed of their lands and turned into a labouring class for the white immigrant capitalist class.

In Zanzibar and on the coast at Mombasa, the Arab feudal-cum-slave-owning and trading class existed but, with the onset of colonialism, despite its earlier alliance with British, French and German imperialism, this class too was routed and turned into a subject, but still allied, people within East Africa. The Indian merchant class which had operated from Zanzibar for a long period, albeit under British domination, continued to function within the interstices of the British colonial economy. To them was added a working class in the shape of coolie labourers brought in by the British to construct the Uganda Railway. Many of these died, and many returned home, but a small number were left who continued to work as labourers, artisans, carpenters, gardeners, and soldiers, and even as policemen and clerks within the colonial administrations in the territories.

To these were now added a differentiated class of European settlers. Among these were the colonial civil servants who manned the state machine for the monopolist ruling class in Britain who 'owned' the colony. These civil servants were a petty bourgeoisie and not a ruling class, as Brett would like us to believe.[6] Another petty bourgeoisie staffed the banks, commercial, insurance, and shipping companies operating from East Africa.

Nor was the agricultural settler bourgeoisie itself a homogenous group, for it was made up of individuals from aristocratic, middle-class and even working-class and lumpenproletariat origins, (some of the soldiers who came in under the Soldiers Settlement Scheme in 1919).

The first lot of settlers — Lord Delamere, Captain Grogan, the Earl of Enniskillen, Galbraith and Berkeley Cole were 'aristocratic misfits' looking for adventure.[7] They constituted the upper stratum of the settler bourgeoisie, which also included a number of lesser English and Anglo-Irish nobility and gentry, impoverished by the fall in land rents and 'bored with the life of a country gentleman or a peacetime cavalry officer'.[8]

Many of them had their own financial resources either inherited or acquired through various nefarious and adventurist activities. For instance, Lord Delamere who travelled to Kenya through Ethiopia and Somaliland, acquired on the way, according to Sir Harry Johnston, £14,000 worth of ivory to set himself up on arrival.[9] Others had little capital, if any. Wealthy or not, this aristocratic crust naturally had great influence on British policies, particularly through the Conservative Party at home.

These roving adventurers were joined by other 'restless spirits'[10] from Natal in South Africa. Invited by Eliot, the first Governor of Kenya, this group of 80 Boer families formed the core of the middle stratum of the settler bourgeoisie.

There were also a number of medium-small farmers from England and South Africa at the bottom of the ladder. Taking up the 640-acre or even 160-acre homesteads, this type of settler could neither plant coffee nor sisal, nor engage in sheep and cattle breeding, which all required a large outlay of initial capital. Limited to small-scale market gardening, they came up against considerable competition from the African farmer. With this competition from the very class they had expected to employ, and without the means to do so anyway, by 1908 it was becoming clear that East Africa, unlike South Africa, 'was not a place for a small European farmer.'[11]

To this basic formation should be added 545 families settled under the Soldier Settlement Scheme in 1919. These were mainly low-ranking commissioned officers, 'men without substantial capital',[12] as well as a number of soldiers in the lower ranks.

This motley of class forces was blurred by racial organization, but even so, many organizational forms coincided with class interests. Still, the overwhelming contradiction between imperialism and the African population, exploited not only as workers but also nationally oppressed, still manifested itself in types of organizations that apparently cut across class interest. For instance, the Young Baganda Association, the Young Kikuyu Association and the Bukoba-Bahaya Union in the 1920s — the first manifestations of African political organization — represented peasants, workers, and the intellectual petty bourgeoisie. Even organizations of chiefs like the Kikuyu Association of 1920 actually represented peasant interests in that the Association focused attention on the burning question of land. The Young Baganda Association was supported by members of the Buganda Government like Apollo Kagwa, himself a comprador of British imperialism. This type of cohesion reflected the common grievance of all classes against national oppression and domination.

Later, more class-oriented movements would emerge as classes became more differentiated. The trade unions and poor peasants associations are examples of this. On the whole they would unite under umbrella national movements such as the movements that emerged in the 1950s.

European organizations also expressed the interests of different strata among the settlers, although at a certain level these too converged. For instance, among the agricultural settlers the distinction between the large farmers — 'the Colonists', and the medium and small ones — 'the Pastoralists' — was at times a sharp one. The Pastoralists condemned the 'dummying' of land (i.e., illegal acquisition of land by using the names of dependants), practised by large farmers like Delamere. They also objected to the Colonists' attempts to control the Legislature. The Colonists were led by Delamere and later Grogan, while the Pastoralists found a leader in Robert Chamberlain. On his arrival in the colony Chamberlain formed his Association in Nakuru as a platform of protest against the Colonists.[13] Later, a number of other small associations sprang up, reflecting the dispersed character of settler interests.

To co-ordinate their general interests, a Convention of Associations, dubbed the 'Settlers Parliament', was formed in 1910, and it obtained representation at the Imperial Conference in 1911. Through such organizations the settlers could advance their general claims against competitive groups within their own class. It is at this point that the element of race was used by them both against Asians who wanted land in the Highlands and against the African majority whom they feared because of their national cause against imperialism in general and the land and labour question in particular.

The Indians, too, were organized on both class and on common interest levels. There were commercial capitalists with relatively large enterprises, for instance, people like A.M. Jeevanjee, who, with others, owned a firm of contractors, some ships, and a general merchant company. In 1901, he started the *African Standard*, in Mombasa, which was later acquired by the Europeans in 1903, and in 1905 renamed the *East African Standard*.

There were also middle and small Indian traders whose interests were expressed through the Indian Association at Nairobi and Mombasa. At this time there were also 28 Indian farmers in the Kenya Highlands, and later in the 1950s many Asians acquired large estates for sisal and sugar as well as tea. In 1914 the Indian working class found unity in the Indian Trades Union and organized strikes jointly with African workers to oppose the Poll Tax.[14]

The more general Indian struggle against British imperialism, which still oppressed and dominated India itself, was manifested in East Africa in the Indian Congress. In many cases Indian interests converged with those of the Africans, and Indian representatives in the colony's legislature, such as Isher Dass, voiced African grievances against the colonialists. Indeed as Bennett has noted, 'Such indirect representation by an Indian provided the only means for the African political associations to be heard' at this time.[15]

These organizations sometimes cut across territorial boundaries and drew together European settler interests, Indian interests, and at times African national interests – as in the case of the East African Association formed by Harry Thuku in 1921 to unite the struggle of the African people in East Africa. This is also true of the Indian Association of East Africa and the Settler Conferences.

In the metropole, the various class interests converged in the three major parties – the Conservative Party, representing the former landed gentry and established merchants and shipowners; the Labour Party, representing mainly middle-class and petty-bourgeois interests but with a large working class support; and the Liberal Party, representing the industrial bourgeoisie and some middle-class interests.

The Conservatives supported the idea of Empire as a broad political integration in a form of federation with those colonies where white settlement was present. The Labour Party took a line of 'respect for native interests', and, along with the Liberals and the Manchester Group, tended to encourage and support cheap African agriculture as against settler agriculture. This line of policy was also supported by 'humanitarian' organizations. Despite all these differences, all the parties nevertheless stood for the interests of British finance capital at home and in the colonies. The small Communist Party in Britain supported the struggle of the colonial peoples against British imperialism and therefore represented the internationalist proletarian position which threateningly reminded British imperialism of the politics of the new era of the proletarian revolution after 1917 and its joint cause with the new national movements in the colonies and semi-colonies.

But while the imperialist state and the colonial state represented the interests of the bourgeoisie as the ruling class in general and that of the financial oligarchy in particular, the conflicting claims within the class tended to create a lack of cohesion, which affected the politics of closer union. Commercial and industrial interests sometimes conflicted or their metropolitan organizations acted out of concert with one another; for instance, the Chambers of Commerce representing industry and commerce in Liverpool and London had separate organizations in East Africa. There was also the British East African Corporation which represented textile interests. In order to contain and adjudicate between such interests, the Joint East African Board was formed in London in 1923. It was to represent 'those sections of the British community which are actively interested in the agricultural, commercial, financial and industrial development of East Africa.'[16] On the Board were represented the Chambers of Commerce of London, Liverpool and Manchester, the Uganda Planters Association, the Kenya Convention of Associations and settler interests in Tanganyika, as well as local chambers of commerce — but not any Asian or African organizations. Not all interests relied on the Board for representation, however. Banks and other big businesses, for instance, had direct contact with the Colonial Office, 'where the more important of them were assured of a sympathetic hearing'.[17] In a letter to the Kenya Convention, the Board Chairman, Sydney Henn (himself with farming interests in Uganda and Kenya), expressed clearly its projected role:

> So far from wishing to run East Africa from this end, the main aim of the Board (so far as I am concerned) is to strengthen local interests out there by fighting their battles with the Colonial Office on the one hand and the public on the other, until they are able to achieve complete independence, which can only come when the country is sufficiently developed to yield revenue proportionate to its needs.[18]

Thus Conservative opinion and local settler interests, who saw in East Africa and Central Africa the idea of a federation on the lines of Canada, Australia or New Zealand, were well organized in pushing for the idea of closer union within East and Central Africa, using such common forums as the Board.

Closer Union in East Africa

The idea that there should be a closer political union and/or federation in East and Central Africa was brought to the public arena by no other person than the same Sydney Henn, himself an M.P. in the British Parliament. In a motion in the House of Commons on 8 April 1924, Henn pointed to the 'desirability of unity of policy both in administration and development' of Kenya, Uganda and Tanganyika, Zanzibar, Nyasaland and Northern Rhodesia. He expressed the belief that federation of East Africa was a policy most likely to 'conduce to its future welfare', arguing that the attempt to implant the principle of self-determination, 'which had led to the disintegration of Europe' and resulted in the erection of tariff walls — 'a veritable repetition of the story of the Tower of Babel' would be equally disastrous in East Africa.

Without heed to history, he pointed to the example of the 'greatest of all federations', the United States, a federation in which there was 'free trade within an encircling barrier that embraces a whole continent'. But within the British Empire, he continued, Canada, Australia and South Africa offered recent examples 'of the great advantage of federation', which could be taken as models even in the widely different areas of the 'progressive colony of Kenya' and the undeveloped mandated territory of Tanganyika.[19]

The debate led to the setting up of a commission of inquiry, the Ormsby-Gore Commission, which was sent out to East Africa in 1924. It came to the conclusion, however, that 'the day is still far off when such co-operation could be brought about by the imposition of federal government over the whole of the territories' finding 'little, if any, support in East Africa for the idea of immediate federation, and in some quarters we found definite, hostility.'[20] Nor was there much support for the idea among the Africans. The Kabaka of Buganda was against the idea but so, apparently, were the majority of the European settlers who, according to the Commission, had received the idea 'with more than a suspicion'. Indeed the Report found opposition expressed 'by all sections of the European opinion in Kenya',[21] noting further that all 'shades of opinion in Zanzibar were hostile to federation' as well as the various Indian Associations 'throughout the northern territories' (i.e. Kenya, Uganda and Tanganyika).

But why was the proposal made? What were the interests behind it? It is clear that the initial step was taken by the Milner and Amery clique in the Colonial Office who were members of the Conservative Party and known supporters of white settlement in Kenya. Amery had appointed Grigg as Governor in Kenya in 1919, a known sympathiser with the idea of closer union on South African lines, regarding it as a necessity for 'effective growth' This drive was itself part of an even more grandiose scheme to create an 'Organic Imperial Union' uniting the entire British Empire under a British Imperial Government, which was to be constitutionally responsible to the while electors within all the countries of the Empire.[23] As for the less ambitious idea of a federation encompassing just Central and East Africa, with the defeat of Germany in the War, the existence of German East Africa was removed as an obstacle and it was now possible to advance and work for its realization.

Milner's and Amery's ideas were being supported on the spot in Kenya mainly by the upper stratum of the Kenya settlers, particularly Lord Delamer and Grogan and their Colonists' Association. The medium and small farmer at this time was more concerned with the pressing need for credit and labour, and the related demand for majority representation in the Kenya Legislature. For, as Captain Cooney of the Pastoralists had declared at a public meeting in February 1926, 'You will never solve the labour problem until you have control of the country – when you have that, you will immediately solve the problem.'[24] The Pastoralists were agitating for the importing of Indian and Chinese indentured labour, opposed by Delamere and his group who nevertheless conceded a possibility of bringing in Italians. It was left to Grigg to tie up both these arguments by suggesting closer settlement by Europeans, bringing in Europeans 'of all classes' to build up a white state and ending the dependence on 'native' labour.[25]

Thus the white agricultural settler bourgeoisie agreed on the need to achieve a representative majority in the Legislative Council as the real first step to control in Kenya: 'Then self-government would follow, whereas for many settlers, agitatedly concerned about labour, it was simply associated as a solution of that problem.'[26] For this reason Grigg was already prepared to have an Official majority terminated in favour of the settlers' elected representatives, as a condition of attaining the grand design; and even when the settlers went as far as demanding a majority of European 'elected members', he expressed sympathy; but the 'fault' in not realizing the first step, as Amery later recounted, was not due to Grigg. It lay, he argued, 'in the course of events',[27] and these events increasingly made it impossible for the grand design to be realized, as we shall see.

Working well ahead of time after the War, the Milner 'kindergarten' had included the idea of federation in East Africa in the League of Nations Mandate over the territory. Amery at the Colonial Office had the project of federation in East Africa 'very much at heart' and persuaded Milner, his boss, to let him do something about the Mandate. Amery states: 'He let me draft a clause in the Tanganyika Mandate expressly providing for federation with the neighbouring territories, but was inclined to let things in East Africa settle down before taking action.'[28] The first step had already been taken with the appointment of the Ormsby-Gore Commission.

Delamere now turned to the settlers in Tanganyika, where the idea was at first coldly received. However, a problem had arisen which was to make them more amenable to federation. This was the right of Africans to grow coffee in the Arusha and Moshi districts, a right allowed under the German 'dual policy' and maintained by the first two British Governors. With the failure of plantations during the War and the advent of a new group of white settlers, demands were made to give the settlers exclusive rights to coffee-growing. Delamere was able to play on this in order to encourage the settler bourgeoisie to demand transfer of the coffee-growing areas to Kenya, a demand that was refused. Opinion was beginning to shift, to oppose the domination by Kenyan settlers among East African commercial interests.

The President of the Dar es Salaam Chamber of Commerce warned its members of this possibility, and before the Ormsby-Gore Commission had come, the *Dar es Salaam Times,* attacked 'the campaign in Kenya for the transfer of Kilimanjaro area' to Kenya.[29] After the Report of the Ormsby-Gore Commission, opposition to the scheme in Tanganyika declined among the settler bourgeoisie as the same problems over labour supply and the demand for protection against African cultivation of economic crops affected all of them.

The precariousness of the settlers' position produced an awareness of convergence of interests which was very much encouraged by the settler conferences held at the invitation of Delamere at Tukuyu, Livingstone and Nairobi in 1925, 1926, 1927. The Governor of Kenya lent his support, through the administrative means of the Governors' Conference (set up in 1926), by trying to produce agreement on closer union, in the words of Grigg himself, 'by conference and discussion'.[30]

These pressures within the local administrative structures to accept the grand design still did not go unopposed. Cameron, now Governor of Tanganyika, was committed to dual policy as the only realistic basis for exploiting the area. It was Cameron who had dismissed the Ormsby-Gore Commission's observations on the importance of Kenya white settler agriculture as 'station gossip', and now in 1927 he was equally opposed to Amery's renewed initiative, the draft proposal on closer union submitted to the Governors' Conference.[31]

This initiative having failed, Amery attempted to enlist Cabinet support for sending out another Commission to East Africa, to inquire into 'how' a federation should be brought into being. While agreeing to the Commission, the Cabinet wanted it to inquire into 'whether', either by federation or 'some other form of closer union', more effective co-operation between the different territories could be secured 'more particularly in regard to the development of transport and communications, customs tariffs and customs administration, scientific research and defence'. In particular, it insisted that the Commission examine how the dual policy recommended by the Conference of East African Governors could 'best be progressively applied in the political as well as the economic sphere'.[32]

In other words, it was the more practical aspects of economic integration that were of immediate interest to British imperialism, particularly in the area of communication and a common market. For this reason the dual policy was stressed throughout the terms of reference to the various Commissions. Consistent with this, the Hilton Young Commission, which came to East Africa in 1927, in recommending a three-stage plan for union, culminating in the appointment of a Governor-General for the region, nevertheless underlined the retention of both native and the dual policy.

In the words of the Colonial Office, the Commission gave 'a very full and weighty exposition of the general principles of native policy, not only as regards East Africa but as regards the British Empire at large, with particular reference to the principles which should govern the relationships between native and immigrant races.'[33] The editorial of *The Times* of London of 25 February 1929 also reiterated that the Commission's Report was one 'which affects the future of the Empire as a whole', as it touched 'decisively the principles that guide the administration of subject races under the Imperial Government in more than one continent and the chief task with which the present century confronts the British race.' As these 'weighty expositions' were supported by the majority of the members of the Commission except the Chairman, and since the expositions aroused 'great interest and criticism' in both East Africa — where the Kenya settlers received them with 'shock'.[34] — and in Britain and since obviously they reflected a more clear articulation of a new policy on these matters, it is well for us to examine them and assess them.

The majority report, clearly ventilating the politics of the British imperialist bourgeoisie, hypothesized that the 'chief need' in Eastern and Central Africa 'today' was that there should be applied 'throughout the territories as a whole', continuously and 'without vacillation' a 'native policy', which while adapted to the varying conditions of different tribes and different localities, was consistent 'in its principles'. 'The whole nature' of the Commission's recommendations, had, they claimed, been influenced by this hypothesis, whether in the economic, social and/or political fields. 'Thus on both counts we are brought back to the necessity for defining the guiding principles of the native policy, and an attempt at such definition has been made the main feature of our report.'[35]

The Commission began from the Devonshire Declaration on African interests contained in the White Paper of 1923 on Indians in Kenya:

> Primarily Kenya is an African territory and His Majesty's Government thinks it necessary definitely to record their considered opinion that the interests of the African natives must be paramount and that if and when these interests and the interests of the migrant races should conflict the former shall prevail . . . . In the administration of Kenya His Majesty's Government regard themselves as exercising a trust on behalf of the African population and they are unable to delegate or share this trust, the object of which may be defined as the protection and advancement of native races.[36]

Although softened by another declaration made in 1927 to reassure the settlers who objected to this outright statement of British policy, it was understood generally that the 'paramountcy of African interests' and the obligation to uphold this remained the cornerstone of British rule in Kenya.

In its Report, the Hilton Young Commission pointed out that contact between the white and black races in Africa constituted 'one of the great problems of the twentieth century'. It was a problem whose solution demanded a 'consistent policy carefully thought out, rather than emergency action designed to meet particular difficulties only'.[37]

In the economic field, the Commission warned that 'whatever view may be taken of the extent and rate of the progress of the native people', *they constituted, notwithstanding their present backwardness, 'the dominant*

27

factor in the territories ' (emphasis added). Moreover the Commission emphasized that the greater part of the territory was not suited to white settlement, and *'throughout this area the production of most crops must be in the main native'* (emphasis added). This would necessarily be so 'even where European settlement is possible, [for] non-native enterprise must always to a large extent be dependent on native labour.'

It followed that the economic development of these vast areas could be brought about only by the united efforts of the whole population, 'of which the natives constitute the overwhelming majority'. Their progress in every direction was necessary, and they must — to go back to the words of the earlier Ormsby-Gore Report — be induced 'to become willing and increasingly intelligent co-operators in development, and here European civilization had a role to play creating a duality of interest.'[38] The Commission stressed the 'complementary development of native and non-native communties', insisting that: 'The essential principle involved in the acceptance of the 'Dual Policy' is that native interests must be regarded as an end in themselves; i.e. that the natives cannot be treated as a mere accessory to immigrant communities.'[39]

The dual economic policy was in fact the best possible policy for British finance capital, which was at the time primarily interested in the production of cheap food and raw materials to give its already sagging economy a leverage in international monopolistic competition. It was thus not interested in grandiose federation schemes which — as such — had no immediate practical use. This singlemindedness was necessary given the unfavourable international situation.

The Hilton Young Commission went on to point out that Kenya would be the most difficult area for applying this policy 'where permanent settlers are present in considerable numbers', although it was also necessary to consider the territories where such settlement was a small factor like Uganda. The principle of 'paramountcy of native interests' laid down for Kenya 'must be taken as applying *a fortiori* to Uganda, Tanganyika and Nyasaland' it added.

Reiterating the principle that the administration of these territories was based on the exercise by the British Government of 'a trust on behalf of the African population',[40] the Commission argued that the only alternative would be a policy of 'consistent and perpetual repression' which would 'be doomed to failure in East Africa and Central Africa'.

It is at this point that the dual policy was put forward as the only viable political as well as economic strategy. Economic development was bound to continue and involve the 'natives'; this would entail contact with the white population, which in turn would lead to a process of education, 'which again must lead to political demands'. It continued: 'This process would go on whether the Government itself initiated a system of native education or not, but, without any proper system of education, it would be infinitely more dangerous.'[41]

Since the British Government was already committed to a policy 'other than repression', and since the policies applied to a number of territories throughout the Empire represented 'the very antithesis of repression', it would be 'impossible, even if it was desired by anybody to do so, to apply a completely contrary policy in any contiguous area under British administration'. 'Processes have indeed started which cannot be stopped and which must inevitably lead to a stage when native people will demand some voice in the management of their own affairs.'

Thus, already sensitive to the danger of nationalism, the Commission began to erect barrages to contain it. It advised in the circumstances that 'wise statesmanship' must therefore prevail to lead the 'natives' on a course of 'steady mental and moral [*sic*] advancement, so that when they realise their power they may be prepared to use it'.

> The strongest foundation, however, of Western Civilization and British rule does not lie in the size of the white community, which must always remain a relatively small island in the midst of a greatly preponderant black population, but in the establishment of a rule of justice which will enlist the loyalty of the native people, and strengthen their confidence in British rule . . . .
>
> It should be stated that, apart from moral issues, repression is not a possible course, not only because it is contrary to the declared policy of His Majesty's Government, but because *conditions are such today* that any attempt to persist in such policy is doomed to failure. [42]

This insouciant conception of Kenyans' 'confidence in British rule' was repeated much more recently on the occasion of the death of Kenya's leader. Jomo Kenyatta, originally described as a 'leader into darkness' for his alleged activities in the Mau Mau movement was now priased by the British Prime Minister, Jim Callaghan, as a 'great friend of Britain'. [43]

The sharply expressed and concrete proposals of the Hilton Young Commission were quite different from the haziness of the Ormsby-Gore approach. When the earlier Commission had spoken of trusteeship, it referred to an abstract moral duty rather than a concrete economic necessity, although it was not above taking Lugard's Dual Mandate to authorize the proposition that 'we [i.e. the white race] have a duty to humanity to develop the vast economic resources of a great continent'. The Ormsby-Gore concept of trusteeship was so general as to include not only the responsibility of government but also missionaries, and finally the 'shoulders of every man and woman of European race in Africa'. It had closed on a note of exalted, almost natural, responsibility: 'It is in very truth a white man's burden and all Europeans in Africa must share in the work. . . . The Europeans in East Africa have the position, and therefore the dangers and responsibilities, of an aristocracy.' [44]

It was sheer economic necessity which produced the shift in tone we find in the later Commission. The Hilton Young redefinition of trusteeship pitted the interests of the settler against those of the African peasant, indicating clearly that *in general* it regarded the native peasant as preferable on economic grounds:

According to our view the paramountcy of native interests is to be interpreted in the sense that the creation and the preservation of a field for the development of native life is a first charge on any territory, and that the government having created this field has the duty to devote all available resources to assisting the natives to develop within it. But if, after having settled what is necessary for the above purpose, there appears to be room for immigrant settlers — still more if these are likely to assist the advancement of the natives — then immigration can be permitted and even encouraged. Once this has been done, the immigrants also deserve consideration and it is equally a duty for the Government to protect their interests, provided that their needs do not involve any interference with the development of the natives in the field that has been created for them.

What therefore is required is, first, to define what are the essential nati interests; secondly, to settle what are the conditions that must be created and preserved in order to give those interests a fair field in which to start and an adequate measure of protection and assistance for their develop- ment, and thirdly to allow nothing to interfere with those conditions subject to these requirements the government must do all in its power to help the immigrant communities. [45]

This apparently exalted policy position of the British imperialists was neither the result of 'wise statemanship', nor of the 'trusteeship' reposed in it for the good of the 'native', and indeed the policy of dual development was the only economic policy that British imperialism as a whole could support. But we can see that it marks a considerable departure from the earlier policy (which we observed in Volume I Chapter Four) in Kenya in 1900 wherein it was declared by the Crown Law Officers that all the lands occupied by the 'native' people 'who are practically savages', was effectively vacant and could be declared 'crown lands' to be given to any tenant other than the 'natives'. This change in fortune of the contradictions of capitalism and imperialism is immediately traceable to the precarious situation resulting from inter-imperia- list rivalry. The policy of trusteeship was a response to the unfavourable inter- national political atmosphere created by War, itself the result of imperialist rivalry, and, even more important, the arrival on the world scene of the first socialist state in 1917 at the end of the First World War.

The International Situation

We have already outlined the evolution of British policy on the question of responsible government and federation. Fieldhouse states that by 1872 Britain invariably granted the status of responsible government to any colony 'which had sufficient Europeans to run it', and was financially self-sufficient. He adds that a 'large non-European population was no bar' to this policy. These principles, he states, operated until 1923 'when they were applied for the last time to Southern Rhodesia'.

> Thereafter British policy changed, as 'trusteeship' principles gained acceptance. Kenya, whose considerable minority of white settlers were anxious to obtain at least representative, if not 'full' responsible government, was refused both, on the principle that African interests must remain 'paramount.' No other colony with a white minority could qualify where Kenya did not.[46]

Why did Southern Rhodesia become the exception to the new general rule? Hailey attributes the difference to the fact that in Rhodesia the white population was given a referendum to decide between incorporation into the Union of South Africa or separate responsible government.[47] But this is no explanation since we have to enquire why the referendum had the outcome it did. Unlike all other colonial possessions, the two Rhodesian territories were in 1918 still under the administration of the British South African Company, with its head office at 2 London Wall Buildings, London E.C.2, and which governed these territories under its board of directors, appointed in the usual way by its shareholders. In the case of Southern Rhodesia, the Company on the spot appointed administrators, assisted by an advisory council elected by the white settlers. There was also an Imperial Resident Commissioner, appointed by the Governor-General of South Africa, who represented the Colonial Office. For both Northern and Southern Rhodesia the situation was short-term: the settlers and the Colonial Office both regarded company rule as unsatisfactory, its charter was due to expire in 1923, and the Company itself had no wish to renew it. However, since there was a large white, mostly South African population in the southern part, the referendum was suggested; in Northern Rhodesia there was only a small minority of whites and so it became an ordinary colony with a Governor appointed from London.

The vote in the plebiscite 'went the wrong way' insofar as the whites decided against joining South Africa, and since under company rule they had already been entitled to an elected council, it was decided as a special case to give the colony responsible government, but with the British Government retaining final control.[48] But when the Kenya settlers demanded to be given the same terms, 'the British Government showed that it was no longer prepared to accept as a rule of practice' the procedure it had followed in Southern Rhodesia.[49] The reasons for this are given in Fieldhouse's account. He accurately indicates that after the War had 'resolved the deadlock which had checked the expansion of the colonial Empire', there also developed a marked and increasing suspicion of the justifications of the 'old-fashioned' imperialist system, and an adoption of the principle of trusteeship 'for the good of the inhabitants.'[50] But less credence can be given to his remark that the War 'seemed to have exhausted imperialist instincts', or the following:

> Confidence in the moral justification of imposing alien rule was waning; socialist ideology eroded nationalist enthusiasm. The elimination of

Germany, the renewed isolationism of the United States and the internal preoccupation of Bolshevik Russia combined to destroy the political tensions which had previously stimulated expansion. No colonial power thought seriously of emancipating its colonies, but neither did it show any desire to acquire new ones. This was an age of imperial consolidation, of high-minded concepts of trusteeship and economic development. Empire seemed to have reached its plateau.[51]

The decline in credibility of moral justifications for alien rule must be sought elsewhere. Counterposing socialism and the possibility of nationalism is not so simple — indeed 'nationalism' was soon to reappear as a form of competition against foreign-dumped goods in the drive for 'national self-sufficiency' a few years later. That no imperialist power thought seriously of emancipating its colonies is true, but that they showed no desire to acquire new ones is false as the next war was to show. That this was the age of consolidation was true, but that this generated 'high-minded concepts' of trusteeship is a myth.

First of all, the concept of trusteeship had been an aspect of British colonial policy before the 1920s while a form of dual policy was already being pursued by the British imperialists in places like Nigeria. What compelled Britain to adopt it as a universal policy, particularly in the white-settled areas as well, was the rise in nationalist sentiment and its *strengthening by socialist ideology of the proletariat,* which in 1917 demanded the right of self-determination for the colonies.

The demand, contained in the Soviet Decree on Peace of 1917, required all the territories in Europe and elsewhere which had been annexed by force to be granted the right to their independence. By extending the principle to the colonies, the Bolsheviks widened the scope of the national question from the limited question of combating national oppression in Europe to the general question of emancipating oppressed peoples, colonies and semi-colonies from imperialism in general.[52]

When the U.S. President Woodrow Wilson put forward his 14 Points in 1918, he recognized the ideological content of the Soviet demand and its implication for world-imperialism. Point 4 included the need to apply the principle of right of peoples to self-determination to the world as a whole and to safeguard this right by creating the League of Nations.[53] Whether or not these measures can be taken at face value, it is quite clear that the 'Bolshevik menace' — which, in the words of Lloyd George, had filled the 'whole of Europe with the spirit of revolution', creating 'everywhere a deep sense of discontent, anger and revolt', threatening 'the whole existing order in its political, social and economic aspects', — was having an impact on the imperialists' relationships with their colonies. No longer would old prescriptions apply in a world of change. It is self-evident that these were the changes that the Hilton Young Commission recognized when it warned that 'the conditions are such today' that any long-term policy based on repression *per se* 'was doomed to failure'.

And there were good grounds for this conclusion in East Africa itself. In Kenya national consciousness was already in evidence by the 1920s. The

Kikuyu Association, led by Chief Koinange, had been formed in 1919 with a membership of chiefs and headmen in Kikuyu country and was already posing the agrarian and peasant question to the colonialists, demanding that their peoples' lands be returned to them. The *East African Standard* had noted that 'the country will watch with unfeigned interest the progress or otherwise of this first attempt at organization among the natives of Kenya'. But this was just the beginning. In 1921, the formation of the Young Kikuyu Association, led by Harry Thuku, a telephone operator in the Treasury, with the objective of fighting the pass system *(Kipande),* and the one-third reduction in wages caused by the financial crisis, as well as other labour abuses, brought to the fore even more sharply the national question in Kenya. More important, the industrial workers' struggle was increasingly linking up with the agrarian issue.

Thuku's meetings drew huge crowds from all sections of the African population, and, as the agitation gained momentum, the government began to lose its nerve. On 7 July 1921 the settlers' newspaper, *The Leader,* drew attention to the 'native contamination' that was taking root in the country. It pointed out that according to the evidence available 'the natives of the country, supported by the better organized Buganda political section' had moved towards building its own political and industrial organization. This, the paper warned, was the direct outcome of the 'recent much debated and more or less self-efficient action of the Kenya employer' fanned by 'the unmeasured agitation of the Indian Community for equal political rights'. It continued that, while there was no reason to take native associations too seriously, *'yet a new situation has arisen and it would be foolish to ignore it.'* (emphasis added). As far as the native claims in industrial matters were concerned, they were only doing 'what they have been told by their masters', which was unfortunate. But with regard to native political aspirations, 'British and official pandering to the Asiatic claims' was responsible for the precocious movement. It noted: 'there is no doubt that the Asiatic claims as a right to political equality may be advanced with better reason by the Africans. If the political test be educational then the Africans have the same right as the Asiatic.' But the paper did not stop there. It went on to link this agitation with the ideology behind the dual policy itself. Apparently the spread of the 'Bolshevik Menace' was overspilling the geographical bounds of Europe, and the Bolshevik Decree on Peace, which put forward the proletarian position on the right of colonial peoples to self-determination was producing a 'red scare' in Kenya as well. The article continued: *'We want neither Czar nor Lenin in Kenya. This territory demands British rule ....* Those in England or in Kenya who play with the principle of political equality when no racial equality exists are playing with fire with risk of grave disaster'.[54] (emphasis added)

But this was the reaction of small property owners in Kenya who did not yet understand that their interests under British imperialism were advanced just as well under the changes in official policy, or, more accurately, that it was only under these conditions that they could survive. Therefore it was not the British imperialists who were 'pandering to the Asiatic claims' and 'playing with fire with the risk of grave disaster'. In arguing against 'too much' repression the imperialists were registering the 'Bolshevik Menace' that had announced itself on the world scene, and the risk it represented of graver disaster to British imperialism and to their bourgeois interests.

But this does not mean that the British imperialists were putting forward a new and universal anti-repressive policy. Repression was merely reserved as a weapon of last resort. And when the justifiable activities of the new organizations became too threatening, then repression was the order of the day. For example, the Kavirondo Association held a meeting at Lunda, Gem Location, called by the teacher Jonathan Okwiri and attended by about 8,000 peasants on 23 December 1921, at which the following demands were made:

1) That the meeting requests the Government to be good enough to grant us council;
2) That this meeting requests the Government to be good enough as to alter the 'Hut tax' and to pay the 'Poll tax' instead;
3) That this meeting is strongly opposed against the native registration ordinance, which has convicted more than thousand of us;
4) That the meeting requests the Government to be good enough as to spread the high education for the natives in the country;
5) That the meeting are strongly opposed to the use of the word 'colony';
6) That the meeting are strongly opposed against work done in the reserve in respect of the Government (and that it) be paid (for) accordingly;
7) That this meeting is opposed against the definition of officers 1922, 'who are stationed in every Chief's location in the reserves',
8) That the meeting requests the Government to be good enough to grant us title deeds.

These legitimate national demands attracted the wrath of the colonial representatives. *The Leader* reproduced the demands followed by a report that a newly arrived Assistant District Commissioner had immediately proceeded to the meeting with a force of policemen! 'The sight of the police infuriated the natives and bloodshed might have resulted had not an elder D.C. from another District turned up and his wisdom prevented anything in the way of exhibition of force.'[55] *The Leader* itself now cautioned: 'The native has a right to petition and to ask. But the ultimate decision must be left to his mentors — the Government.'

Another example of repression concerns a different association, the East African Association, formed by Harry Thuku, as a general workers and political organization. As Makhan Singh has vividly observed: 'They considered the East African Association and its leaders as the greatest threat to the colonial regime not only in Kenya but in the whole of East Africa. They struck the blow.'[56] Harry Thuku was arrested on 14 March 1922 and deported to a remote part of Kenya. After petitions by Johnstone (later Jomo) Kenyatta (who was the Association's Propaganda Secretary) to the Acting Governor failed to get him released, a general strike and demonstration by the workers provoked the full force of the K.A.R., with armoured cars and machine guns. They fired on a peaceful, praying crowd carrying white flags and demanding their leader's release, killing, according to *The Leader,* 27 people and wounding 24 but, according to the *Manchester Guardian,* killing 100 people and wounding a much larger number.[57]

Thus the Hilton Young Commission knew what it meant by 'native trust'. Still this formula succeeded not only in putting across a new line but in at least laying out the future policy for the emergence of a bureaucrat/comprador agent class in East Africa. Because of its emphasis on the 'native way', it was able to brush aside the Harry Thuku type of leadership as not being representative of the people. Instead it sought native leadership in the traditional institutions, reviving the old principle of Indirect Rule — which in fact meant nothing but direct rule. Thus the dual policy and 'trusteeship' took the form of a politics of creating and/or restructuring the earlier alliance with the former ruling classes or institutions, such as the *Akidas* and the *Jumbes* in Tanganyika, the *Lukikos* in Uganda, and the comprador chiefs.

It will be remembered that in Uganda Lugard had struck an alliance with the former Ba-Ingleza faction led by Apollo Kagwa, and was thus able to subdue the other factions and establish British rule. The 1900 Uganda Agreement granted more than half of the entire land in Buganda to this faction as a freehold with the other half going to the Crown. Now in 1927, under the Envujjo and Busulu Law, the Ba-Ingleza were to be deprived of their traditional right to free labour from the peasantry whom the dual policy now required to produce directly for the market. The *Katikiro,* Apollo Kagwa, and his clique were still to occupy administrative positions but now were employed directly, and paid, by the British colonial government.

In Tanganyika, Governor Cameron was busy restructuring the administrative structure created by the Germans. Under the Native Authority Ordinance of 1926 he energetically set out to create indigenous authorities throughout the territory to which administrative, judicial, and executive functions were then passed. And in Kenya, the Hilton Young Commission insisted that since traditional institutions were either non-existent or very weak efforts should be made to create them! In this way, a basis was laid for the consolidation of a new bureaucrat/capitalist agent or comprador class within East African society who were to play a very important role for British imperialism in assisting it to fight the national movement.

As we have seen already, the Kenyan agricultural bourgeoisie were 'shocked' by the findings. But not the commercial interests. As one writer has noted:

> Whereas the commercial interests accepted the majority report, the farming community vehemently rejected it. Business placed hope of profit above racial fears. Seeing economic gain in any form of closer union, they held a meeting of the East African Chambers of Commerce

in which they agreed to support the recommendations of the majority.[58]

It was this *economic interest* which the British monopolies, represented by these commercial interests, were most interested in, arguring for closer union of the region to create a large market.

The Last Effort

Back at the Colonial Office, Amery and the 'kindergarten' were unhappy about the Hilton Young Report on the ground that its recommendations 'did not seem . . . altogether practical'. Instead of confining themselves to the 'economic issues where a single development policy was needed', the Commission had instead 'aimed at the much more difficult and doubtful object of unifying native policy, where local conditions differed so widely not only between the three territories, but within those territories themselves.'[59]

Amery now, 'despite the imminence of a general election', attempted to 'salvage something of his federation plan'.[60] He sent out his right-hand man Sir Samuel Wilson, who, after several months of Cabinet wrangle over Amery's instructions to him, went out to discuss the Hilton Young recommendations with the governments concerned and with individuals representing the various interests, 'with a view to seeing how far it may be possible to find a basis of general agreement'.[61]

But by the time Wilson had gone out, conducted his negotiations and by his 'wisdom and tact' secured complete agreement from 'all' — all, that is, except the Indians and Africans — the 1929 British election was in progress. Sir Samuel Wilson's solution was to replace the three stages which the Hilton Young Commission recommended for the appointment of a Governor-General for East Africa, with the immediate creation of a High Commissioner, who was to have legislative and administrative responsibilities for certain services, and who, as Chairman of the Governors' Conference, would have advisory function in all matters of common interest, and keep the Secretary of State informed.[62] As regards native policy, he argued that the conditions in each territory were different and hence no uniform policy was possible; the control of such a policy should be left in the hands of the Governors of the three territories. On both counts this solution was acceptable to the European immigrant (mainly agricultural) classes and of course opposed by the Kikuyu Central Association and the Indian Associations.

The Wilson Report was, however, too late for Amery. The election had seen him replaced by Sidney Webb (Lord Passfield) of the Labour Party. Amery records bitterly that Webb 'immediately scrapped [Wilson's recommendations] and produced a dogmatic White Paper which completely upset European opinion, both in East and Central Africa and coupled with the subsequent economic depression, postponed all possibility of federation indefinitely.'[63] What actually happened is that, in 1930, the Labour Government published *two* White Papers. In one, closer union was proposed, with a High Commissioner to supervise the territories by power of suspension and initiation of legislation within them. [64] The High Commissioner was also to administer and legislate with the assistance of a council on technical matters. There was to be a change in the representation in the Kenya Legislative Council of both the African and European groups and a common roll for Whites and Indians. 'Responsible government' was recognized as applicable elsewhere, the White Paper stated, but this was on the basis of an electorate in which every section of the population had been assured an adequate voice; in Kenya, in contrast, responsible government was not immediately possible since only 1% of the population was enfranchised.

The Labour Government also produced another White Paper entitled a *Memorandum on Native Policy in East Africa,* which the settlers referred to cynically as the 'Black Paper'. In it was spelt out British policy on trusteeship in East Africa: it pointed out that trusteeship must rest with His Majesty's Government 'alone', which must therefore have the ultimate responsibility for decision and final control, even if it were to be decided later that the Official majorities in the Legislative Councils were to be abandoned. The political development of the native people, it added, should take place through the Native Councils 'until they could share in the government of the territory'. [65]

This led to a new storm from a section of the white settlers in Kenya and their supporters in England. In an angry telegram to the Colonial Office Delamere denounced the idea of whites being referred to as 'immigrant races', and poured scorn on the idea of equality with Indians! 'East Africa colonists stand on the principle that the white race is the only people which has proved its capacity to govern mixed races.' [66]

In the meantime, Labour lost an election and a coalition government was formed with the Conservatives. The settler agricultrual interests in East Africa were unanimous in opposing the two White Papers. Also some organizations in Britain itself opposed the whole concept of 'native paramountcy' as spelt out in the *Memorandum.* A Joint Select Committee of both Houses of Parliament which came out to East Africa in 1931 looked into the matter of federation again and reviewed the two White Papers. It listened to the settlers and this time to a number of African and Indian representatives, who opposed the federation. The Joint Select Committee, in its three volumes of evidence, proceedings and conclusions, came to the conclusion that the time was not ripe for closer union, a view, according to Ingham, 'hastened by the imminent fall of the Labour Government', while the world-wide economic crisis 'pushed the issue into the background so far as interest in Britain itself was concerned'. [67] The Committee stated:

> There has undoubtedly been a certain reaction against the whole idea of closer Union in East Africa. Witnesses, almost without exception, expressed the view that the time for giving effect to any far-reaching scheme in East Africa was inopportune .... These circumstances ... make it clear to the Committee that this is not the time for taking

any far-reaching step in the direction of formal Union.[68]

The Joint Select Committee also agreed to increase nominated representation of the Africans. It reaffirmed the principle of trusteeship and that this 'must remain' the function of His Majesty's Government, but added that the 'assistance' of the non-native communities 'in carrying out this obligation' be encouraged 'to an increasing extent'. It added: 'Further association in the responsibility of trusteeship is, however, not necessarily synonymous with increased political control in native affairs.'[69] It went on to approve the dual policy in the sense of 'complementary development' of the native and non-native communities.[70]

Implicit in this statement were the abandonment of the Devonshire Declaration's assertion of paramountcy of African interests in favour of a greater emphasis on the economic aspects of dual policy. The paramountcy doctrine was now held to have been occasioned by the circumstances of 1923 and to some extent 1930, of 'particular cases' which arose and could arise where conflict over land and labour were the central issue. The doctrine was now to be reconciled with the strategy of dual policy:

> The Committee consider that the matter can be summed up briefly by saying that the doctrine of paramountcy means no more than that the interests of the overwhelming majority of the indigenous population should not be subordinated to those of a minority belonging to another race, however important in itself.[71]

It, therefore, no longer was to mean holding African interests above those of other races or above the political control of native affairs by white settlers. The new Secretary of State, the Conservative Cunliffe-Lister, could now tidy up the situation. British colonial policy had been summed up in a way satisfactory to the demands of finance capital for production on the basis of native labour. The disputes of the 1920s about closer union were 'quietly dropped'. Certain that policy statements and the ensuing controversies had been the bane of the recent past, he sought to make 'action not talk the motto of the Colonial Office'.[72] Cunliffe-Lister may have been as wise as Solomon but this does not explain why the idea of federation could be 'quietly dropped' in favour of dual policy.

Clearly the answer lies in the economy. Closer union was the policy of an outmoded settler agriculture. Where the crisis of the Great Depression spelt doom for settler agriculture in Kenya and Tanganyika, in Uganda peasant production remained buoyant and resilient and even increased during the crisis. In Tanganyika after an initial drop in peasant production in the same period, output was ultimately restored by this same peasant with the 'Grow More Crops Campaign' initiated by the colonial regime with very satisfactory results. Settler agriculture survived but only on the back of African labour whose wages dropped from Shs. 36 to Shs. 10 a month. Even in Kenya itself, while small settler agriculture collapsed entirely, African peasant production, although hindered and restricted by settler pressure, began to pick up.

The Hilton Young Commission was vindicated and the dual policy, although modified a little showed itself to be the only viable one for British imperialism. It is in this context that the Hilton Young Commission's observations on the role of African peasant production begin to make economic sense:

> It is important to realize, especially when weight is placed on the economic considerations for determining policy, what wide variations in suitable methods of economic exploitation are possible. Thus there are some areas which can produce the best economic results from a system of cultivation by natives each working a small holding on his own account. . . . All that the native requires is instruction and supervision from agricultural inspectors and the provision of the machinery of trade. A good example . . . is afforded by the development of cotton growing in Uganda . . . . Similar conditions suitable for small native cultivators prevail in large parts of Tanganyika and in such areas as the Kavirondo reserves in Kenya.[73]

In short, by 1939, British imperialism found that it could only survive on the basis of peasant production.

White settler short-term interest in a political federation which they could dominate made such an economic policy hard to achieve. White settler demands in this direction had to be dropped. And they were. Even when the Conservative Colonial Secretary, Lyttelton, tried to revive the whole issue of an East African Federation in 1953, it caused such renewed protest that it was dropped indefinitely. The demand was now as dead as the dodo – only to be revived eventually by the *African* petty bourgeoisie as a Pan African ideal for East Africa. In the era of heightened monopolistic competition under multilateral imperialism, this effort also failed as we shall see in Chapter Nine. In the meantime production on these lines continued.

Despite a whole variety of imperial pressures, which had included Sydney Henn in London, the Milner/Amery 'kindergarten', and Delamere and Grigg, the idea of a federation of all three territories failed. These three groups represented three vital elements of the imperialist thrust – finance and trading capital in London, political imperial authority and settler capitalism in East Africa; an apparently unassailable trio – yet they failed.

As we have shown, there was widespread opposition from the peasantry, wherever they had a voice. The local administration in Tanganyika likewise felt threatened. But neither were enough to defeat the forces of imperial interest. What was behind the equivocation of the British was the overriding impact of the Russian Revolution, and the underlying fear of revolt in the colonies. The East African Federation could only have been brought into being against the wishes of the African people, by repression. By the 1920s and 1930s British imperial authority had lost the confidence and the aggression to push through such a policy. It tried to compromise, and prepared the ground for neo-colonialism.

References

1. L.C.A. Knowles, *The Economic Development of the British Overseas Empire* (London, Routledge, 1924).
2. Ibid., pp.23-5, p.15.
3. D.K. Fieldhouse, *The Colonial Empires* (London, Weidenfeld, 1966) p.266.
4. A certain Wirth, quoted in V.I. Lenin, *Notebooks on Imperialism, Collected Works* (London, Lawrence and Wishart), Vol. 39, p.522.
5. Knowles, pp.15, 23.
6. E.A. Brett, *Colonialism and Underdevelopment in East Africa. The Politics of Economic Change, 1919-39* (London, Heinemann, 1973), pp.41-2, 55-6.
7. See G. Bennett, *'Settlers and Politics in Kenya'*, Harlow, Chilver and Smith (eds.) *History of East Africa* (London, Oxford University Press, 1965), Vol. II, p.268.
8. C.C. Wrigley, 'Kenya: The Patterns of Economic Life 1902-1945', in Harlow, Chilver and Smith, op. cit., p.217.
9. Bennett, op. cit., p.268.
10. Ibid., pp.216-7.
11. Amery, quoted in Brett, op. cit., p.17.
12. Bennett, op. cit., p.283.
13. Makhansing, *History of Kenya's Trade Union Movement to 1952* (Nairobi, E.A.P.H., 1969).
14. Bennett, op. cit., p.328.
15. Quoted in Brett, op. cit., p.63.
16. Brett, op. cit., p.65.
17. Quoted in Brett, op. cit., p.64.
18. Quoted in D. Rothchild, (ed.) *Politics of Integration: An East African Documentary*, (Nairobi, E.A.P.H., 1968) pp.21-2.
19. *Report of the East African Commission* (London, H.M.S.O., 1925) p.7, hereinafter 'the Ormsby-Gore Report'.
20. Ormsby-Gore Report, p.7.
21. Bennett, op. cit., p.301.
22. R. van Zwanenberg and A. King, *An Economic History of Kenya and Uganda, 1800-1970* (Nairobi, E.A.P.H., 1975), p.234.
23. Quoted in Bennett op. cit., p.303.
24. Bennett, op. cit., p.303.
25. Ibid.
26. L.S. Amery, *My Political Life,* (London, Hutchinson, 1953), Vol. II, p.361.
27. Ibid., p.360.
28. K. Ingham, 'Tanganyika: The Mandate and Cameron, 1919-31' in Harlow, Chilver and Smith, op. cit., pp.563-6.
29. Lord Altrincham, *Kenya's Opportunity,* (London, Faber and Faber, 1953), p.71.
30. Ingham, op. cit., p.589.

31. Terms of Reference to the Hilton Young Commission 1927.
32. Colonial Office: *Conclusions on Closer Union in East Africa,* Cmd. 3574 (London, H.M.S.O., 1930), p.11.
33. Bennett, op. cit., p.310.
34. *Report of the Commission on Closer Union of The Dependencies in East and Central Africa,* (London, H.M.S.O., 1929) p.7, (hereafter the Hilton Young Report).
35. Colonial Office, *Indians in Kenya,* Cmd. 1922.
36. The Hilton Young Report, p.9.
37. Ibid., pp.15-20.
38. Ormsby-Gore Report, pp.22-3.
39. Hilton Young Report, p.37.
40. Ibid., p.39.
41. Ibid., p.39 (emphasis added).
42. Ibid., p.39 (emphasis added).
43. *Daily News,* Dar es Salaam, 22 August 1978, p.1.
44. Ormsby-Gore Report, pp.21-3.
45. Hilton Young Report, pp.40-1.
46. Fieldhouse, op. cit., p.261.
47. Lord Hailey, *African Survey,* (OUP 1956), p.190.
48. C. Cross, *The Fall of the British Empire* (London, Paladin, 1970), pp.98-100.
49. Lord Hailey, op. cit., p.190.
50. Fieldhouse, op. cit., p.235.
51. Ibid., pp.237-8.
52. J.V. Stalin, *The October Revolution and the National Question, Collected Works* (London, Lawrence and Wishart) Vol. IV.
53. G. Schulz, *Revolutions and Peace Treaties* (London, Methuen, 1967).
54. Quoted in Singh, op. cit., p.12.
55. Ibid., p.14.
56. Ibid., p.15.
57. Ibid., pp.15-16
58. R.G. Gregory, *Sydney Webb and East Africa: Labour's Experiment with the Doctrine of Native Paramountcy* (Los Angeles, University of California Press, 1962), p.74.
59. Amery, op. cit., p.362.
60. Bennett, op. cit., p.310.
61. Amery, op. cit., p.362.
62. *Report of Sir Samuel Wilson,* Cmd. 3378 (London, H.M.S.O., 1929).
63. Amery, op. cit., p.362.
64. *Statement of Conclusions of His Majesty's Government in the United Kingdom, as regards closer Union in East Africa,* Cmd. 3574 (London, H.M.S.O., 1930), pp.4-6.
65. *Memorandum on Native Policy in East Africa,* Cmd. 3573, (London, H.M.S.O., 1930) pp.4-6.
66. Quoted in Bennett, op. cit., p.314.
67. Ingham, op. cit., p.592.
68. Joint Select Committee, *Report,* (London, HMSO, 1931), pp.14-5.
69. Ibid., p.28.
70. Ibid., pp.24-5.

71.   Ibid., p.31.
72.   Bennett, op. cit., p.318.
73.   Hilton Young Report, p.134.

3. Institutional Arrangements Under Bilateral Imperialism

The purpose of this chapter is to explain the actual political and economic institutional arrangements through which Britain integrated the three territories of East Africa. We are concerned with the content and the logic of these arrangements, generated by British bilateral imperialism in the 1920s and 1930s. We shall therefore be examining the institutions which connected Britain to the territories and the territories to each other — the administrative and consultative structures, the institutions for a customs union and common market, the currency and monetary institutions, institutions co-ordinating the transport and communications systems, legislative institutions and the very important scientific research institutes — all of which were tied to the imperial institutions directly or indirectly.

The analysis we have carried out in the last two chapters clearly indicates that the power behind these institutional arrangements was British finance capital and British imperialism. But this was not just British imperialism in general, but British imperialism of a particular period, which we have characterized as British bilateral imperialism. And this form of imperialism had its own specific characteristics, and also a degree of power that we find lacking at the end of the period and more so in the next stage of U.S. led multilateral imperialism. And while it is tempting to talk as some have done, of the origin and shaping of East Africa's integrative institutions as having been 'programmatic', and the arrangements as having been a 'functional association',[1] or as having grown 'out of accidents', and/or having been created by '*ad hoc* administrative collective decisions',[2] yet all this is looking at legal formalities. While no doubt law had to do with the question, and indeed while it is true that the colonial legal draftsman enjoyed a 'prestige and latitude'[3] in the matter, yet that law, as we have seen over the land question, and any prestige the legal draftsman might have enjoyed were themselves only an element of the underlying logic that fashioned the system to serve that end.

The power of British bilateral imperialism lay precisely in its capacity to integrate with itself the region we refer to as East Africa. It has been argued that this integration was made possible by its *legal* commitments under the Congo Basin Treaty.[4] But the Treaty obligations were to keep the area as a 'free trade' zone for the joint enjoyment of all the signatories; it was British finance capital's power to work *against* this obligation which marked its character.

This overwhelming power of British capital was of course very much assisted by law, yet the beauty of it all is that the arrangement worked without any formal East African legislative mechanism but through the bureaucratic power of colonial officialdom. If it appears at times as if this officialdom advanced the interests of the white farming bourgeoisie, as is generally claimed, these *were* the very interests of British imperialism itself. British bilateral imperialism designed, advanced, and put into effect an informal institutional arrangement in East Africa that served to advance the competitive position of its monopoly capital vis-a-vis that of its imperialist rival, Germany. But, in order to do so, it had to integrate these countries economically and politically with its own imperial system. Already by 1939, as one writer has observed, the East African market was dominated by British manufacturing exports and import-export trade by British firms.[5]

Although there existed no supra-territorial legal entity in East Africa to run this system of institutions, and to moderate the conflicts, this gap was filled by the institution of the British imperialist state itself. From the centre it oversaw the whole system and directed its operations, overruling and, underwriting those on the spot in order to advance the 'common good'. i.e. those interests common to British finance capital. This political authority came direct from the Colonial Office which acted as the nerve centre of the entire colonial system, and this nerve centre was in turn linked to another centre, the City of London, itself the financial hub of British finance capital and the heart of the system.

Administrative and Consultative Institutions

The Secretary of State

Although it has been claimed that the whole integrative mechanism was a purely administrative convenience, it was in fact necessary to facilitate the economic and political integration of the region. It enabled British imperialism to withstand and keep out of the region the monopolies of the other imperialist powers. At the head of this administrative machine was the Secretary of State with overall supervisory powers for the colonies, and therefore able to handle all queries as to what was going on in the colonies in the British Parliament, and also to direct the activities of the colonial Governors individually and *inter se* whenever need arose.

In the case of East Africa, where there was an informal consultative body for co-ordinating affairs of common interest, the role of the Secretary of State was vital, as arbitrator and final authority in issues which could not be resolved, particularly in cases of conflict of territorial interest. In relation to economic activities in the colonies, he was also the real voice of the British Treasury and the City of London's financial experts. These financial and industrial sharks were also represented by strong pressure groups like the Joint East African Board, the British Cotton Growing Association, the East

African Corporation, and other imperial organizations of bankers, shipping lines and huge merchandising firms. 'The banks and many trading and manufacturing concerns treated East Africa as a unified area, and their territorial boundaries as commercially irrelevant.'[6]

The Secretary of State had the final say over financial projects proposed in the colonies and in that way he also wielded considerable authority. He was responsible on behalf of the British Government for all the political affairs of the colonies in the British Parliament, particularly as concerned 'native interests'. He advised on the appointment of commissions of inquiry, proposed policy and directed the Governors in carrying it out. Under the Secretary of State there were various Advisory Committees responsible for reviewing colonial affairs in their various fields and advising the Secretary of State; these were: the Colonial Advisory Medical and Sanitary Committee, the Colonial Survey Committee, the Advisory Committee on Native Education, the Colonial Medical Research Committee, and the Colonial Advisory Agricultural Committee. These were linked to the similarly specialized, bigger imperial bureaux overseeing the Empire's affairs as a whole, bodies such as the Imperial Bureau of Entomology, the Imperial Bureau of Mycology and the Bureau of Hygiene and Tropical Diseases etc. Through this set of institutions, the Secretary of State was the vital link with the institutions that were established in East Africa.

Insofar as he was responsible for the drafting of legislation for all the colonies, he was able to impose a certain unifromity on them. In East Africa, in particular, these legislative functions enabled uniform provisions in commercial law, based on the English Companies legislation, as well as an identical Sale of Goods law, Bills of Exchange law, etc. Although other statutes were not entirely unifrom, they nevertheless had 'substantial uniformity': these were laws regulating arbitration, trade marks, patents, drugs and poisons; the law of contract, as well as family law, including the British common law and procedural rules.[7]

A Court of Appeal for the entire area, set up in 1902 on the basis of an Order-in-Council, ensured more or less uniform application of the law. All this was facilitated by the co-ordinating and supervisory hand of the Secretary of State, backed by the full authority of the British imperialist state, which ultimately explains why the system operated despite the conflicts which were at work in the period of bilateral imperialism.

The Governors' Conference

In the three territories, the co-ordination between the two Governors at first, and then the three after the incorporation of Tanganyika within the Empire, was *ad hoc* and in many cases uneasy, particularly over matters of revenue-sharing from common services like customs, and benefits and obligations arising from institutions like the railways. In those issues which required a common policy, the Secretary of State would rule one way or the other, and where financial disputes were concerned a grant-in-aid would be found from the Treasury to prop up the aggrieved territory. Such issues as how much of the customs revenue collected by Kenya on Uganda-destined goods should be paid over to Uganda were burning issues before the formation of the Customs Union, and even after. In all these situations the solution came from London with a grant-in-aid to Uganda.

The need to make the relationships more orderly had already compelled the setting up of consultative meetings. But after the Ormsby-Gore Commission of 1925 had looked into the question of the need to secure closer policy co-ordination on transport, cotton-growing, and the control of human, animal, and plant diseases in order to accelerate the general economic development of the region,[8] the issue of administrative and consultative organizations arose with a new force. After consultations in East Africa, the Commission had come to the conclusion that any attempt at federation was premature, and that, in order to avoid impairing the individual rights and interests of each of the territories, a looser arrangement should be worked out. They therefore recommended co-ordination by conference:

> We suggest that there should be regular periodic conferences of Governors and also of the responsible officials of the various departments. The territories might be selected in turn for the holding of the conferences and a start might be made forthwith in the holding of a Governors conference to be attended by the Governors of Kenya, Uganda, Tanganyika, and Northern Rhodesia, and the Resident of Zanzibar.[9]

The Report further suggested that the Governor in whose territory the conference was held should make all the secretarial arrangements and collect the subjects for discussion from the others; these would comprise matters of common interest to all the territories, such as native administration, communications, taxation, land policy, labour etc. It added: 'Questions relating to the recruitment of labour and the care of labour engaged in work outside its own territory can only be satisfactorily dealt with by such conferences'.

The Report also recommended the regular holding of conferences on technical issues such as agriculture, education, and health and others in which the technical staff in the colonies could exchange experiences and work out a common strategy in their areas of competence. It is in this way that, at least for the moment, co-ordination and co-operation were to be achieved without impairing in the least the individual rights and interests of the territories concerned. On presentation of the Report to the British Government, the Secretary of State established the Governors' Conference by administrative directive.

The first of these conferences was held in 1926, and thereafter irregularly until 1929. In 1929-30 the Hilton Young Commission worked out further proposals and recommended the setting up of a Central Authority which would be the supervising body over broad policies of the territories and also a link with the 'general staff' in London, in the guidance of policy.[10] As we saw in the last chapter, this was not immediately implemented and the

Wilson Report which reviewed the Hilton Young recommendations instead advocated the establishment of a High Commission with a High Commissioner assisted by a Central Council to have 'full control (including legislation) of certain common services — Customs, Railways and Harbours, Posts and Telegraphs, and Fundamental Research'.[11]

At the same time the Joint Select Committee of both Houses of the British Parliament was sent out again by the Labour Government to seek the views of all communities on the federation issues before any action could be taken on the Hilton Young Report. They recommended, contrary to Wilson, the regularization of the Governors' Conference, with at least one meeting every two years, with extraordinary sessions when necessary, and to include the Governors from Northern Rhodesia and Nyasaland and the British Resident in Zanzibar. The small secretariat which had been established in 1926 to service the first Conference was to be expanded and turned into a permanent central secretariat for the Conference.[12] This was still a fairly loose arrangement for regular consultation and co-operation, with the Secretary of State as the last voice. This loose arrangement continued, as we shall see in the next chapter, because of the failure to implement an East African federation, due to various social forces at work.

When the time came to recommend once more a High Commission as a post-war necessity to co-ordinate the various bodies that had emerged in the war period (bodies to co-ordinate, on a regional basis, defence, production, supply, and industry), there were in all 20 councils, boards, committees, and directorates, 'which covered subjects from control of prices to control of locusts'.[13] It was decided that the Governors' Conference was an inadequate instrument and, now that general imperialist interest demanded it, a High Commission was set up by Order-in-Council. The inadequacy of the Conference was explained by the Secretary of State himself in these terms:

> The Governors' Conference is a body which was established by admin-istrative direction of the Secretary of State and which has no juridical or constitutional basis. It functions without public debate or discussion and its decisions are normally based on material available only to the government concerned and not to the general public. In practice it is frequently necessary for the Governors, having agreed in the Governors' Conference to a certain course of action, only to present their Executive and the Legislative Councils with what amounts to a fait accompli. By its nature the Conference is not well designed to enlist the support of public opinion and to take full advantage of the considerable body of expert knowledge and experience which is available within East Africa.[14]

This spurt of wisdom had nothing to do with the availability or non-avail-ability of expertise, nor with the need or lack of democracy as such, for this arrangement did not envisage consultation with the people at large but with the local propertied classes, specially those of expatriate extraction, who were already being consulted in the existing Legislative Councils in the three territories. What was involved, as we shall see later, was the legalization, to the extent possible, of a machinery to handle all those bodies that had sprung up as a result of the wartime period's exigencies and which had now to be continued for the needs of British finance capital, given that federation was already a dead letter as early as 1931. But this new administrative machinery, loose as it was, did adequately co-ordinate all the services that had existed before the War as well as those which sprang up during the War. We now look at some of these bodies and institutions.

The So-called Customs Union and Common Market
It has been suggested, as we noted earlier, that the history of the regional tariffs essentially grew 'out of accidents', and that it was also partly the result of the Congo Basin Treaties' stipulation that trade in the countries east of the Congo should be free and non-discriminatory.[15] In our view, the creation of these structures — misnamed as the Customs Union and Common Market — was not haphazard but the result of the need to maintain British monopolistic competition in the three territories. They were mainly aimed at a monopolistic integration of the territories, in order to consolidate Britain's regional position against other imperialist countries' demand for free trade as stipulated in the treaties.

Nor is it even factually correct to say that Kenya and Uganda 'agreed' to merge 'their' customs authorities in 1917, and that this involved the creation of 'free trade' in local products as well as in imported goods. The creation of the tariff structures between Kenya and Uganda come through a directive and an Act of the British Government which saw value in such an arrangement, and indeed led to one-sided 'free trade' between the two territories, with the more advanced colony utilizing the tariff to concentrate development in its area, a characteristic of capitalism in general — a law of uneven development.

The cross-subsidization of Kenyan high-cost production by Uganda peasant production and later by Tanganyika's 'dual' economy was a requirement on the part of British imperialism itself, since it could not exist in the circumstances it had created in Kenya without such protection and support. Our aim in this analysis has been to try to separate and distinguish imperialist interests and settler interests which, though not entirely identical, essentially merged at crucial points.

It is also wrong to say that the Governors' Conference formed the basis for the existence of the Common Market,[16] for such basis lay not in institutions but in the British-dictated production regimen imposed on East Africa. This explains why, despite the non-existence of a supra-territorial authority to determine the level of tariff, a common tariff nonetheless operated and was observed. The hand of the Secretary of State, which represented such production needs, was adequate to this purpose and had no need of the Governors' Conference, which merely facilitated the process.

The first tariff to be levied in the region was in 1900 by Uganda on all goods entering the Protectorate.[17] The British East Africa Protectorate

(Kenya) and German East Africa also had their own systems. Most of Uganda's goods, however, at this time passed through German East Africa via Lake Victoria. But while the goods coming in through the German colony destined for Uganda incurred no duty while passing through German territory, with Uganda collecting the custom duty at its own customs posts, similar goods passing through Mombasa were charged duty at Mombasa by the Kenyan authorities and none of this duty was transferred by these authorities in Kenya to Uganda. This did not unduly worry the revenue-conscious Uganda Government so long as the bulk of her imports passed through the German territory, but this situation changed in 1902 the moment the Uganda Railway was completed. As a result, all Uganda's imports now had to pass through Mombasa, and customs revenue decreased although her imports increased.

An open conflict was averted precisely because the British Treasury continued to pay a grant-in-aid to Uganda to make up for this loss until 1915. It was only in 1909 that Kenya agreed to release some of the customs revenue to Uganda on the directive of the Secretary of State. This improved her revenues and meant that she was able to pay her own way by 1915. The amount paid to Uganda was 25% of the revenue collected, later raised to 33% in 1919 but, before the increase, Uganda's revenue earned in this way was still not adequate. For this reason, the two customs services of Kenya and Uganda were merged in 1917 creating a 'Customs Union' between the two countries.

From that moment a 'free trade' area was set up between the two countries in both locally produced and imported products. In fact, even on the basis of bourgeois economic theory, this was a free trade area in a formal sense only, since there was very little complementarity in the production of the two countries, and very little or no specialization as such within the region. Since the two territories both produced essentially for export to the imperialist countries, this was effectively ruled out. We see, therefore, the increasing use of the customs arrangement for either protecting Kenyan high-cost settler agriculture or British industry in Kenya.

The first such open support to settler agriculture occurred with the 1918-21 crisis in Kenyan agriculture. This crisis demanded protection of existing agricultural production in Kenya, but this protection was also required in order to strengthen a certain level of semi-processing and pro- cessing of some of the temperate food products for the local market and for export. In 1922 a committee appointed by the Kenya Government recom- mended an increase in duty on the import of such products. But this was at a time when Uganda would have benefited by their *decrease* in order to cheapen her imports, in view of the increased rail rates (which had been raised to protect Kenyan production).

The new tariff was established in 1922 with high protective duties on butter, ham, ghee, timber, sugar, and wheat and other grains. The net result, as one writer has observed, was that: 'There can be no doubt that these duties did prove to be highly successful in encouraging a number of Kenya's industries in a period when world economic conditions were far from con- ducive to agricultural development.'[18] This was certainly true of agriculture.

But the fact is that these measures required the approval of the British Government, and the interest of British imperialism, and not of the settlers as such, required that this should be so. In this way the roots of uneven development in the two territories were being laid within the East African political economy, a development that was to bring the system increasingly under stress in the era of bilateral integration and in the next phase under multilateral imperialism. But this was not all.

Talk about a free trade area was just as banal as the Customs Union. As Kenya's industrialization proceeded, its products found a ready outlet in the captive markets of the other two territories which, as we have already noted, were themselves being discouraged from engaging in any kind of industrialization. The high degree of protection granted to the industrial capitalists in Kenya 'allowed' consumers in the three territories to 'freely' buy products from them. Moreover, there was in fact no 'comparative advantage' in Kenya engaging in this manufacturing to justify the ideology of free trade, since the three economies were by no means complementary. They were merely colonial enclaves all serving the interests of British imperialism. The notion of a Customs Union could hardly be applied to such an arrangement. Indeed Kenya could be called highly 'disadvantaged' in one sense in that it required a high level of protection for its agriculture in order to enable manufacturing to go on at all. It is not even that Kenya imported the agricultural products it needed from the other two territories and so justify any claim of advantage and being an efficient producer. The logic of it was simply domination and monopoly perpetrated by British imperialism.

It is not surprising, therefore, that, even within the system, the bureaucracy itself should have seen the 'unfairness' of the arrangement. The local commercial interests desiring 'free trade' insisted that the arrangement was unduly advantageous to their Kenyan counterparts. The Ginners Association and the Planters Association, as well as the Uganda Chamber of Commerce, joined with the Uganda Government in sending a delegation to Kenya to protest against the protective tariff, and even threatened to withdraw from the Customs Union, but all to no avail.[19] Clearly, it was not in the interests of British imperialism to comply with these demands since these interests desired an integrated market in the whole region. Tanganyika came onto the scene later, after the German defeat. British imperialist interests clearly had this in mind when they insisted on the insertion of Clause 10 in the Mandate of the territory, under which Britain was empowered to 'constitute the territory into a customs, fiscal and administrative union or federation with the adjacent territories under [its] sovereignty or control', subject to the Mandate. Despite the fact that the Territories Treasurer and Comptroller of Customs had officially advised *against* a customs union between Kenya, Uganda and Tanganyika on the grounds that it would make Tanganyika a 'satellite of Kenya' and help to 'subordinate Tanganyika to Kenya influence', the British Secretary of State overruled this advice and directed that the introduction of a complete customs union 'should no longer be delayed'.[20]

As a result Tanganyika was finally brought under the Customs Union in

1927. Her earlier involvement in the Union from 1923 had been only in local products and the 1927 solution meant that she, too, would be subject to the common external tariff and therefore to the high protectionist rates imposed for the benefit of Kenyan agriculture and manufactures. Although under the earlier relative freedom Tanganyika had been able to renounce the protective duty on butter in 1925, under the new arrangement she found herself increasingly giving in to the protection of Kenya-based products. Despite the fact that a one-man mission[21] to look into the finances of the Territory had very biting things to say about the customs arrangement as regards Tanganyika and world trade,[22] these appeals — which tended to contradict British interests in the region as a whole — were rejected.

Thus all the economistic arguments about the benefits of a customs union, about specialization, free movement of factors of production, rational allocation of resources, and comparative advantage were just ideological trappings to justify an exploitative and oppressive arrangement. Comparative advantage, in any case, was never even true of the Ricardian example of England and Portugal, particularly in the period under review when monopoly capital negated all the essentials of pure (free) competition. In the 1930s British imperialism was increasingly in crisis and could not afford the luxury of free trade in the colonies. It is not surprising that, because the East African customs arrangement was based on no more than voluntary agreement, the Hilton Young Commission should have insisted that the voluntary agreement should be formalized into a completely unified service of customs collection in all the three territories. But despite the unified service of a Customs Union which had been imposed in 1927, there was no unified administration of the system as a whole. This was not achieved immediately due to the conflicts between 1926 and 1931 over the politics of federation. And then there was the crisis that led to the War. But the need for a unified administration remained and was finally imposed in 1949 on all the three areas which now came under one customs management.

One of the instrumentalities for maintaining the Common Market in manufacturing after World War II was the system of industrial licensing which was operated under the Industrial Licensing Ordinance. This law came into force in 1948 in order to stimulate industrial undertakings and thus save Britain from spending dollars purchasing similar products in other markets. But such undertakings had to be assured of the entire East African market and by this licensing mechanism any such enterprise was granted a monopoly, thus permitting it to invest a relatively large amount in the industry. It is for this reason that the law required the potential investor to have, among other things, the capital, technical skill and raw materials for the industry before being granted a licence. This type of arrangement was suitable for maintaining British hegemony over industrial development in East Africa and was tailored to discourage too much competition in manufacturing in the region. It also intensified uneven development between the different parts of the region..

By the outbreak of the Second World War, the East African region was well integrated as a result of the Customs Union. This level of integration was highly beneficial to British monopolies both at home and locally. The economies of scale were due, in fact, to the monopolies and 'free trade' meant precisely the integration of the region to achieve their ends. The War intensified the integrative movement in East Africa, and this integration reflected the concentration of British capital at home. The attendant tendency for the rate of profit to fall increasingly compelled the counter-active maintenance of an integrated region to cheapen the elements of constant and variable capital. But the deepening of these exploitative and oppressive arrangements throughout the British Empire led in turn to resistance, in particular, the growth of national liberation movements. In East Africa, as we shall see, these nationalist movements were to lead to the downfall of Britain's finance capital from a hegemonic position, and to the disintegration of the Customs Union under neo-colonialism.

Transport and Communications

The role of a system of communications as an integrative mechanism was explicitly noted by the imperialists. Almost all the commissions of enquiry that came out to East Africa in connection with the closer union affair were asked to look into the prospects of co-ordination in transport and communications as a lever to economic development and integration in the region. The East African Commission put the point bluntly: 'Where there are railways today, there is development. There is really no effective substitute for railways.' The development in those commodities required by the British financial oligarchy was what justified a railway. Indeed the very purpose of the Uganda Railway had been to open up the area to such development, as we have already noted.

But the building of such a railway could not have been financed by private capital, since the area was still undeveloped and no immediate return could be expected. This is why construction of the railway was almost wholly funded by the British State. Of the £7,200,000 of the total cost, £5,502,592 came out of parliamentary grants and £1,155,520 out of subsequent state loans. A further loan of £3½ million had been raised in 1924 for the Soroti extension in order to open up that area to cotton production.[24]

This state-backed activity to create the necessary external economies for British finance capital in the region was supported by the Ormsby-Gore Commission of 1925. Preaching to the converted, it emphasized:

> After investigating this matter on the spot and giving considerable thought to it, we are convinced that railways in East Africa should be owned by the state and their management should be under the effective control of Government. Private ownership and administration of railways really postulates some element of competition and, in the circumstances of tropical Africa, railways must for some time to come be free from competition and monopolistic in character. They should

be managed and run primarily in the interests of the economic development of the country, and, even if it were desirable to hand over a
concession of such monopolies to a company of private shareholders,
it is more than doubtful whether any private company would undertake the task without a Government guarantee, together with grants
of land and mineral concessions. . . . We are therefore driven to the
conclusion that, if transportation facilities are to be provided for East
Africa, they must be provided in the future, as in the main they have
been provided in the past, by Government enterprise and Government
finance.[25]

This elaborate argument was in fact unnecessary since there was no doubt
whatsoever that the railways, even in Europe, were becoming a public utility
run by the state. The argumentation was important all the same in that it
demonstrates that, without such state control of the communications systems,
integration in East Africa could never have taken place in the way it did. This
underlines our concern here with the institutional arrangements, such as
transport and communications, which facilitated British bilateral integration
of East Africa, not merely by physically connecting the territories but as an
institutional lever to cohesion.

The Uganda Railway could be perhaps best summed up in the term
'lunatic express',[26] were it not a more serious matter. This 'magnificent saga
of how the white man changed Africa', is itself a magnificent saga of robbery
and exploitation. Held out both at the time and since then by the ideologues
of the system as a 'strategic' project in which 'political' considerations were
paramount, actually it simply advanced the exploitation of the region by
British imperialism. In its initial stages up to 1921 the railway was run as
part of the Kenya Protectorate and Colony with all the revenues of Uganda
Railways being paid into the treasury of the Kenya colony.

Indeed it is safe to say that the whole settlement project in Kenya was
connected with the progress of the railway; we have already noted the
allocation of land for homesteads by Eliot within the one mile railway
corridor acquired. But it is also known that Kenya had no revenue of its own
at the time because productive activity could not be initiated without adequate settlement. Thus Uganda Railways became a department of Kenya and
all the revenues were appropriated by it.

This was possible simply because the Colonial Office accepted it. The
surcharges and then supercharges imposed for its use all went to drain surpluses from Uganda's peasant production, so much so that even those who
never produced at all in Uganda were heard to complain about this
'indefensible tax'[27] from which neither Uganda nor the Railways received
any benefit. The surcharges were over and above the railway rates, paid direct
to the Kenya Treasury with the railway being used as tax collector. But such
complaints coming from Uganda and later from Tanganyika represented
merely *particular* interests which had to be subordinated to the *general*
interests of British imperialism in the region as a whole.

We have seen how the inflation and financial crises of 1919-21 led to a policy of utilizing railway rates to give protection to Kenya-produced food products. In 1921, for instance, rates on the transportation of maize and sisal were lowered, while those on cotton and coffee as well as rubber (mainly produced in Uganda) were raised by the new management, in order to support Kenyan agriculture. Furthermore, the costs of running the Busoga spur line and the Port Bell-Kampala line were being subsidized by the Uganda Government when they should have been debited to the Railways out of these funds.

All these abuses caused an outcry in Uganda among commercial and plantation interests, The Secretary of State responded by ruling that branch-line costs should be borne by the Railways and not the Uganda Government. Despite this intervention, other increases in railway rates to assist agricultural production in Kenya were retained and indeed stepped up in 1923 and 1929. The Uganda planters, led by Stafford, asserted that the Uganda Railways was a 'system of loot, robbing Uganda to pay the debts of East Africa [i.e. Kenya]'[28] But British imperialism would hear nothing of such particularist arguments.

What happened instead was that the conflict of interest was used to justify further integration at the institutional level. Indeed 1921 became the occasion for bringing discipline to the railway system. In that year the Secretary of State appointed a Special Commissioner in the person of Lieut-Colonel Hammond to devise a plan for the complete reorganization and unification of the East African communications system. (By this time Tanganyika Railways was already under the control of the British.) As the official history of the East African Railways has it:

> The crux of the argument was whether the Railway's policy should be guided by strict 'railway economics' or by the wider consideration that it was a major instrument of development. Unfortunately, the lack of an East African authority made it difficult to pursue an East African economic policy. In the absence of any arbiter nearer and more accessible than the Secretary of State, there was a tendency to overstate the gravity of the several rather petty disputes arising from a conflict of interests between Kenya and Uganda.[29]

After Hammond had submitted his report, the next step was the Ormsby-Gore Commission which was sent out to East Africa in 1924. The real immediate reason for examining the closer union issue was in fact the Railways. As the Official History states, the closer union issue 'kept cropping up, and the Railway was the principal cause of its periodic emergence'. It adds:

> The proposals for the control of the Railways in the Hammond Report drew attention to the need for some common authority over Kenya and Uganda. As the railway crossed the Uasin Gishu Plateau and crept closer to Uganda, the need increased. The arguments about the Voi-Kahe line raised an issue in respect of Kenya and Tanganyika; and the project

of the Tanganyika Railways to build a branch line to Mwanza, on the southern part of Lake Victoria, stressed the issue.[30]

Such a line to Mwanza, it was argued, would compete with the Uganda line for the traffic of the Lake Region, 'and there appeared to be a battle of freight rates'.[31] Hammond had pointed out that the issue of the Railways had forced a union on South Africa, 'and they were doing so in East Africa'.[32] In both cases this is to overstate the case, since there were wider issues involved. But the point is well made in relation to what happened, namely that the closer integration of the railway system in East Africa was vital to the *economic needs* of British imperialism. But this did not necessarily imply a political federation, as we shall see in Chapter Four.

The speech of Sydney Henn, who moved the motion in the British Parliament for closer union in East Africa, was actually a plea for the unification of the railway systems serving Kenya and Uganda, Tanganyika and Nyasaland. He stated: 'These three systems serve a continuous block of a million square miles containing 12,000,000 people, and the railway construction in each of these territories cannot possibly be regarded as an isolated problem to be dealt with as local interest and rival jealousies suggest.'[33] What was required, he argued, was a co-ordinated system for the broader interest of British imperialism.

The Ormsby-Gore Commission dealt with the issue of railways, harbours and marine services in general from the point of view of responsibility for financing. As a result of the Commission's visit, later consultations were held in East Africa and an Order-in-Council was agreed, changing the name of the Uganda Railway to 'Kenya and Uganda Railway'. From 3 February 1926, control, management and working of all railway, port, harbour, wharf and steamship services were vested in the High Commissioner for Transport — who was the Governor of Kenya. A new Kenya and Uganda Advisory Council was established in place of the earlier Inter-Colonial Railway Council, thus bringing the system under a single authority, with separate funds and with power to set rates for approval by the Governments.

The integration of Tanganyika presented its own problems connected with German rule and the War; basically, it was acquired by the British at the end of the War on the cheap. The issue that arose in connection with co-ordination of services was over the Voi-Kahe line which had been built during the War to link the two systems. Colonel Hammond was commissioned to investigate the position as regards this line and to advise whether (1) the line should be bought from the War Office; (2) whether it should be maintained as the route from Moshi to Mombasa, in which case the upper Tanga-Kahe line was to be abandoned; or (3) whether the track should be used to improve the Tanga-Moshi railway.[34]

Hammond recommended that the Voi-Kahe line should be acquired and developed to connect the two systems and thus enable Kilindini (Mombasa) to be used for the Kilimanjaro traffic. To use Tanga as the outlet for this traffic, as the Tanganyika Government desired, and which would have required the Voi-Kahe line being dismantled, would be to suit only the immediate needs of the Tanganyika Treasury, he pointed out, and would be detrimental to 'wider interests'. Hammond was 'not impressed' by the argument that Tanganyika was a mandated territory. To use Tanga port would entail the development of two deep-water ports within 70 miles of each other, 'and the chief purpose of the second port, Tanga, would be merely to tap an area which could be equally served by Kilindini'. He strongly advised the retention of the line, for it to be realigned, and that the cost of doing so should fall on Tanganyika as 'the chief beneficiary'.[35]

As Tanganyika did not agree, and because of the Mandate issue, but most importantly because of political reasons, the Secretary of State rejected the advice and accepted Governor Byatt's view that Tanga should be developed into a modern and well-equipped port. The new General Manager of the Uganda Railway protested against the ruling, but to no avail. Later the new Governor of Kenya, Coryndon, 'persuaded' Governor Byatt of the necessity to retain the line 'and the battle was won'.[36] The Government of Kenya bought the line, reconditioned it, and re-opened it to traffic in 1924, and it very 'soon paid its way'.[37] This line took 75% of the Kilimanjaro coffee to Kilindini and took 30% of its 'up' traffic to Moshi, causing continuous complaints from Tanganyika: 'There were many such complaints during the twenty five years (1923-1948) needed to bring about the amalgamation of the two systems, which was the only sound solution of this and several other economic problems.'[38]

In this roundabout manner the British imperialists had by 1949 integrated the two systems, not in the interests of the Kenya settlers as has sometimes been claimed,[39] but of British imperialism in general. It is true that railway rates were used to protect Kenyan settler agriculture and to some extent manufacturing; and also that more branch lines were built into settler areas, etc. but it must be emphasized that this was done not because of the settlers' 'minority economic interests [with their] strong commitments, good social contacts, and effective place representation'[40] as such. No doubt colour, race and even influence played a part in all this, just as certain other local, not settler farming interests — but also commercial, financial, and other interests — were served.

It is, in our view, inadequate merely to leave the argument at this level of understanding, or to declare in general that imperialist interest was at the back of it all. We shall endeavour to follow through the argument in the course of the analysis. It is only after we have grasped the logic behind this force as a whole that we can explain why certain apparently contradictory policies in fact reflected the same interests. We shall maintain this also despite the conflict that we see reflected, say, in the opposition coming from the Staffords in Uganda or even Governor Byatt of Tanganyika. All these voices represented imperialist interests, which alone explains why, despite the fact that the Colonial Office had ruled in favour of Tanganyika on the Voi-Kahe issue, it was still possible for Byatt to agree in the end with the logic of finance capital as a whole. The fact that the initiative for this acceptance came from

Kenya is irrelevant from this point of view. Thus the logic behind integration reflected this *general* logic of British finance capital which, despite the conflicting claims, nevertheless had a unity of purpose to serve that general interest.

Before we conclude this examination of communications, it is important to refer to the role played by the postal and telegraphic services. These services between Kenya and Uganda were amalgamated very early, in 1911, into a Postal Union. In 1932, despite counter-arguments, Tanganyika was brought into the Union. Dr. Schnee, the last German Governor of the Territory, claimed that such integration would contravene the Mandate and Article 22 of the Covenant of the League of Nations, but he was rebutted by Stewart Symes, the British representative at the League of Nations, as 'too rigid' an interpretation of the Mandate that would lead to the erection of an 'ideological Chinese wall that would hinder the country's development'.[41]

A promise by the British Government that the Territory 'could readily assume separate control of the Post Office Department if circumstances should warrant such a course',[42] was soon forgotten as the logic of the integrating force of British finance capital continued in intensity. On the contrary, the postal services remained integrated with the other two territories until 1949 when a joint administration was worked out with a Postmaster-General running a number of services including a savings bank, control of radio and international communications with a British monopoly, Cable & Wireless.

The East African Currency Board

The strings that tied together British finance capital in East Africa were clearly shown in the East African Currency Board arrangement. The three major private banks in the region had been established as far back as 1893 at Zanzibar, then the trading and financial centre for East Africa. As soon as Kenya was declared a colony, a branch of the National Bank of India (a British-owned bank) was established in Mombasa in 1896, and also in Uganda at Kampala, Entebbe and Jinja. This was followed by the establishment of the Standard Bank of South Africa (also a British Bank) in 1910. The National Bank of South Africa (later called Barclays Bank, Dominion, Colonial and Overseas — also a British Bank) soon followed in 1914. All had their headquarters in London.

In German East Africa, the two German banks and an official savings bank, were replaced by these British 'Big Three' by 1923. These banks provided most of the finance required for the raw material trade, and to a lesser extent, for the importation of manufactured products. The latter worked more on the basis of the international credit system, with local banks operating only as collecting agents at the consumption end.

Through development corporations, the same banks also financed some industrial and mining activities. Where finance capital was not able to enter, as in the field of the infrastructure, state capital (itself a branch of finance capital) came in to the benefit of the imperialist bourgeoisie. The banks made the integration of East Africa tighter insofar as they tied the economic structures together. They were assisted in this by the fact that the currency used throughout the area was the Indian rupee, a sub-currency of Britain's in the Indian subcontinent where these banks had been established for some time.

So long as British finance capital was hegemonic in the region, it made sense to use this currency which had roots in the earlier slave trade. But very soon, as production in East Africa attained its own momentum and because of the rupee's dependent relationship to the British pound, the values of the two currencies began to diverge. This was brought about by developments in the British competitive position which led to an increase in the money supply unrelated to actual production. This inevitably led to an inflationary trend in Britain which was reflected in the Indian rupee, with the result that sterling declined in its purchasing power by 40% between 1914 and 1920.[43]

Since, from 1914, the Indian silver rupee ceased to be tied to gold and sterling, the divergence in production conditions in the two parts of the Empire necessarily led to a divergence in currency values. East Africa produced raw materials primarily for Britain but some of these were exported to the Indian market; the resulting conflict meant that the only rational decision was to create a local East African currency based on sterling. But this then led to a large fall of between 300 and 800% in the prices of primary products in East Africa, with the result that settler agriculture went into crisis.

The creation of the East African Currency Board was intended to solve this problem. In 1921 the British Government declared the Indian rupee no longer legal tender in East Africa. The Currency Board had been set up in April 1920 to supervise the monetary system in East Africa and therefore permit greater co-ordination in the monetary and fiscal policies of the three parts of the region. It was now charged with the function of organizing the changeover from the rupee-based currency to the shilling-based one by buying up all the existing notes in circulation. It was then to issue East African notes and coin against sterling at the rate of 20 shs. to the pound sterling; and to obtain British and colonial securities for the sterling it collected from the exchange.

In this way the shilling was tied to sterling and moved along with it, with a portion of the Currency Board's assets invested in Britain and other parts of the Empire and with locally created currency operating to facilitate production and exchange on the spot. Not all the currency was backed in this way but the fact that the system operated under the general monetary and fiscal discipline imposed by the Bank of England through the commercial banks allowed it to carry out all its functions efficiently.

At first the Board had its headquarters in Britain. An advisory board operated from Nairobi with colonial officials and the general managers of the 'Big Three' banks as the directors of the Board in East Africa. In this way the interests of the British financial oligarchy were well looked after.

Thus a system was established in the region which ensured not only the stability of the currency but also the institutions for mobilizing and centralizing any money capital which was not being utilized locally. This could then be used in Britain and other parts of the Empire in various production activities. The record of the mobilizing activities of the three banks and their lending record, at least up to the 1950s, reveals that in fact the bulk of the money deposits (money capital) was not invested locally but, on the contrary, were exported to London headquarters and there to investment in Britain or other parts of the world on short-term and medium-term basis. This is reflected in the fact that, as the banks moved into their second phase of accepting deposits rather than merely financing the trade in raw materials, a large proportion of these deposits, 60% in 1938, was sent as reserves to the banks' headquarters. This high level of reserves, as against local lending, continued throughout and indeed increased during the war period (to 88%).[44]

Although this increase is blamed by Newlyn on the 'lack of expansion due to the War',[45] it is quite evident that the reserves which were kept in London during these years went to the benefit of the British economy during the War and thereafter, and indeed that this was the whole point of having a colonial banking system. Indeed Newlyn himself acknowledges that this 'was an essential characteristic of the banking institutions of East Africa; that they [were] extensions of the financial system in the United Kingdom and that the credit base of the system [was] in the London market just as the credit base of the United Kingdom banking system was in London.'[46] And all this was facilitated by the Currency Board, for Newlyn again states: 'This operation of banks across national boundaries was only possible because of the existence of the Currency Board system which ensured the maintenance of the parity between the East African shilling and the pound.'[47] For this reason, he continues, a number of British banks were able to operate in various Sterling Area countries using some of their assets kept in Britain, 'only because it involved no exchange risks'.[48]

This explains why after the War there was an 'over-expansion' of productive activity and a decline in the ludicrously high ratio of reserves to loans began to take place. It was occasioned by the interests of the British monopolies and not because the banks had attained a capacity for activating a 'spontaneous banking cycle' as such. Indeed this flow back of funds to the East African branches was despite an on-going outflow of the savings of individual local capitalists who were frightened by the increasing resistance activities of the national movement. This was manifested in a fall in deposits in the East African banks following the Lancaster House constitutional talks in 1959. In Kenya, deposits at one stage fell by £6.6 million despite an increase in advances to production of £4.5 million. In Uganda, the World Bank Mission noted that, between 1954 and 1960, £5 million were repatriated in this way 'due to lack of investment opportunity'. Another writer has estimated that, between 1960 and 1963, the overall capital outflow was in the order of £20-35 million.[49] In Tanganyika, in 1960 alone, shs. 55 million left the country in this way.

Since the effect of the increase in advances, all other things being equal (which they were not!), should have entailed a similar increase in deposits,

Newlyn concludes that 'the implication was that there was a net outflow of money equal to the sum of these two figures, that is to say, £11.1 million.'[50] The net effect of the expansion in credit facilities in East Africa plus these capital flights resulted in an expansion of nearly £80 million in local earning assets and a fall of £55 million in reserves overseas between 1953 and 1964. But this expansion in local lending increasingly went to the Governments and to expatriate firms from Britain for the purpose of increasing local production and thus reducing imports from the dollar area and other hard currency areas. This move would help relieve Britain of her balance of payments problems, particularly with the U.S., which was slowly but surely encroaching on its markets in the era of multilateral imperialism that began after 1947.

This shift in investment patterns was partly made possible by a change in the Currency Board regulations in 1955 to permit domestic money creation through a fiduciary issue, a mechanism whereby East African Governments on the basis of their own Treasury Bills or other security, could borrow East African Shillings in order to purchase sterling. These purchases then permitted the East African Governments to import stores and services[51] from Britain for local development, once again helping out Britain's trade and balance of payments.

Fiduciary issues were an indirect way of utilizing earlier colonial surpluses which Britain had accumulated during the War and turned into British securities (to conserve dollars for the War effort and for repayments to the U.S.). This accumulation was achieved through the bulk-purchasing schemes employed during the War, and by the establishment of Marketing Boards after the War in all the colonies. These Boards allowed British imperialists to set the prices of peasant products below world market prices, and thus to accumulate the surplus in British securities paying very low rates of interest of 0.5% before 1950 and 2 to 4% after 1952.[52] The fiduciary issue mechanism was essentially a way of utilizing these surplus balances on British goods 'which would not otherwise have been spendable'.[53]

However, the level of the fiduciary issue was restricted to £20 million in 1957, with the result that the three territories had access only in proportion to British monetary and financial needs. Thus the Board acted as an 'automatic regulating' instrument in the balance-of-payments position of the three territories vis-a-vis the British Empire. Most important of all, on the local front it enabled the flow of funds across territorial boundaries, particularly when the crop peak periods, and hence the need for funding, varied across the three areas. This was important in rationalizing the use of money resources for the region as a whole.

The break-up in the unity of the entire East African economy, which the Currency Board brought about in the 1960s (and which culminated in 1965, demonstrated the power of the Board. The regional economy suffered stress at first, and finally collapse as an integrated entity.

Research Institutes

Imperialism saw another means to achieve co-ordination and that was scientific research. The Ormsby-Gore Commission even hailed it as being of 'greater importance [than communications] to the development of the East African territories'.[54] The Commission recommended concentrating on areas of immediate and long-term economic interest, studies such as those concerning rainfall, crop production, and 'the relation of crops to soil and climate', as well as in the fields of animal husbandry, exploitation of minerals and forests, the conservation of water supplies, the improvement of existing industries, and the development of new ones, the elimination of pests and insects harmful to crops and life.

The Commission also suggested to the Colonial Office 'the possibilities of formulating a scheme whereby research workers from Great Britain would be encouraged to spend some time in original investigations in the laboratories in East Africa'.[55] The German-established Institute at Amani was praised and its abandonment since the British takeover deplored. Drawing attention to how much the Germans had been able to accomplish, particularly in the field of industrial research and production, during the first 18 months of the War, it argued for greater commitment to the Institute.

This concern for scientific research in colonial production was not surprising, particularly after the War. Scientific research by the state and by industry in the imperialist countries themselves had become a major factor in monopolistic competition. According to Bernal, the 'turning-point' in the history of science occurred with the First World War: 'The War differed from all previous wars in that it involved whole nations and not only armies drawn from them. Agriculture and industry were drawn into direct war service.'[56]

The Colonial Office was not slow to take up this matter in a number of circulars to the colonial Governors, particularly after the First World War. In Circular A dated 11 June 1919, addressed to all colonial Governors, the Colonial Secretary pointed out that the 'depletion of raw materials' and the 'vast financial responsibilities' following the four years of war, had, even more than before, imposed on the Empire the need 'that the economic resources of the Empire in general be developed to the utmost', and that for these reasons it was 'particularly opportune' to review the activities carried on by the Governments in the field of 'scientific research and economic exploitation'. The Circular continued:

> It is becoming more and more clear that there is scarcely any industry which can develop or even maintain its position without the aid of scientific research, and that it is sound policy that research should be liberally provided for in the budgets of the firms engaged, although it is frequently necessary that those firms should combine to finance a central research association. . . . But the usual method in the colonies is for research to be carried on by the scientific departments of the government, and financed out of the ordinary revenues and out of

taxes on the particular industries.[57]

The Circular directed that particular attention should be paid to the raw materials required 'for imperial trade or defence which are produced within the Empire either in inadequate quantities or not at all'.

As we have already noted, the Governors in East Africa had already considered this problem and some amount of scientific work was already going on which the Ormsby-Gore Report had noted at length in his report.[58] The Governors' Conference had addressed itself to co-ordinating these activities as part of the integration of the region. Nevertheless the British Government was now looking at the problem in a wider context in view of the increasing needs of the Empire, and the Hilton Young Commission's concern with the closer union issue drew attention to the 'co-ordination of scientific research into matters affecting the economic development and administration of the territories of the British Empire [which] is at present under consideration by the Imperial authorities, and far-reaching schemes [which] are being worked out for the organization of a common effort'.[59] The Commission called for co-ordination of activities on an even wider basis, encompassing the whole of Eastern and Central Africa 'as a group in relation to an Imperial research organization [rather] than as separate units', and for this they thought a central (political) authority was desirable.

On the spot, however, various research organizations were being set up and run on an East African basis embracing medical, agricultural, forestry, fisheries, meteorological, industrial, and locust control, as well as various other scientific research units, all organized under co-ordinating councils or institutes, so that by 1945 there were in all ten such organizations, consolidated from time to time. (Some of them arose out of the war effort.) These were: 1) East African Agricultural and Forestry Organization (Muguga, Kenya); 2) East African Fisheries Research Organization (Jinja, Uganda); 3) East African Marine Fisheries Research Organization (Zanzibar); 4) East African Veterinary Research Organization (Muguga, Kenya); 5) East African Trypanosomiasis Research Organization (Tororo, Uganda); 6) East African Institute for Medical Research (Mwanza, Tanganyika); 7) East African Institute of Malaria and Vector-borne Disease (Amani, Tanganyika); 8) East African Virus Research Institute (Entebbe, Uganda); 9) East African Leprosy Research Centre (Alupe, Kenya); 10) East African Industrial Research Organization (Nairobi, Kenya).

In addition, there were the research departments, established under the East African High Commission when it was set up in 1945 such as the East African Meteorological Department. The finances for all these research services came partly from imperial sources and partly from local sources.

The East African High Commission

Many efforts at integrating East Africa as a unit were made by the British imperialists during periods of peace, but most were hastened and consolidated by the requirements of wars. It is for this reason that the need for co-operation between the territories in regard to economic matters, research and communications were recognized as matters of urgency after the 1914-18 War and again during the Second World War when the East African territories 'were obliged to pool their resources for the war effort'.[60] Actually, this was a decision of the British imperialists and had nothing to do with the wishes of the territories as such. The need to pool resources was a general imperialist strategy connected with monopoly capitalism as a form of concentration of capital in order to sustain production on a 'rational' scale.

The imperialist state was increasingly becoming an instrument of the monopoly bourgeoisie on whose behalf the colonies were carved out and on whose behalf wars of colonial oppression were being waged. It is not surprising that many of the institutions for pooling resources in East Africa in order to further the British war effort were very much a mechanism for integrating the region. Exploitation of the region could thereby be retained and the area kept safe from German attempts to regain what they had lost to the British during the First World War.

After the Second World War, it became clear just why such institutions had been created, and why they therefore needed to be more clearly organized in some legal form for their continuation in peace time. As the Colonial Office proposal put it:

> The War having ended, it is now necessary to consider the future of the inter-territorial organizations which were created in East Africa to co-ordinate and direct the joint war effort of Kenya, Uganda and Tanganyika (which has involved the pooling of resources in production and manpower and the common use of transport, shipping and supplies) and also the inter-territorial services which existed before the War and which will inevitably expand in the future.[61]

The proposals advanced by the Colonial Office for this rearrangement were based on the 'assumption that as a result of the twenty years' corroboration in the Governors' Conference and the developments that have been brought about by the War', it was considered necessary to 'establish a constitutional and juridical framework for the inter-territorial services, including a joint legislature, in order to provide effective means of doing what needs to be done.'[62]

As we have already noted, the Governors' Conference had come under criticism for not having been amenable to public consultation, and the proposal now was to enable some kind of representation in order to utlize local experience. So it was suggested that the legislature should comprise, apart from the Official representation, equal numbers of members representing the three major racial groups. But the Colonial Office warned that this would not imply that the British Government had accepted the idea of closer union or federation for the region. In the new arrangement the Governor of Kenya would continue to be a 'standing chairman' and Nairobi would operate as the seat for a central secretariat. The proposal for equal representation was opposed by the settlers in Kenya and, in deference to this opposition, the Colonial Office revised its proposals in 1947 and now agreed to give more representation to whites, as opposed to Asians and Africans, But, trying to be 'equal to all men' and thus to appease Asian and African opinion, the Colonial Office now decided to reduce the powers of the proposed Legislature.[63] Seven powers which had been spelt out as falling within the ambit of the Central Legislative Assembly were relegated back to the territorial legislatures (which meant nothing in fact since, here too, white settler or Official representation predominated). It is interesting to note at this stage that one of the areas relegated to the three territories was industrial licensing. This power which was excluded from the Central Legislative Assembly — as well as powers over tariff rates, road transport and commercial legislation — influenced later the development under the East African Common Services Organization and East African Community of growing industrial non-complementarity.

Finally, an East African High Commission was set up and proclaimed by an Order-in-Council despite the objections that were still being voiced in East Africa. Imperial power was exercised, thus creating the High Commission as a centre-piece consisting of the three Governors sitting in conference. The powers conferred upon the Commission were those of a 'colonial government' in respect of the services entrusted to it, with a permanent executive consisting of Officials. The experiment was to work for a trial period of four years from 1 January 1948.[64]

The Commission was to be a body corporate, again with the Governor of Kenya as its Chairman. The Commission was to meet three times a year, but when not in conference the Chairman had power to act on behalf of the Commission except in matters which the High Commission itself had agreed should not be dealt with without prior reference to the two other members. The Chairman could also, subject to the agreement of the other two members, delegate to the Administrator certain powers of the Chairman to facilitate an easy administration of the Commission.

The Central Legislative Assembly consisted of a Speaker, appointed by the High Commission, 7 *ex officio* members, 6 nominated members and 20 unofficial members, with power to legislate on matters outlined in the Third Schedule to the Order. The High Commission was then to be responsible for the running of common services and a Common Market in East Africa. The services included, in particular, transport and communications; revenue collection; economic and statistical services; scientific research; specific services like a literature bureau, locust control, survey work, a hides and leather bureau; and the general administrative services of the High Commission

Some of the services that require special mention here are those connected with economic co-ordination and industrial licensing, which we shall deal with later. Suffice it to say that all these services were financed from contributions from the territorial revenues, since the High Commission itself commanded no revenues of its own. The 'self-contained services', such as transport and communications, paid for themselves out of their own revenues, whereas the 'non-self-contained services' had to be financed from contributions and grants from the British Government under the Colonial Development and Welfare Acts or direct exchequer grants. For the year 1953, for instance, the £3,310,816 budget was made up of £968,949 from Kenya, £651,672 from Tanganyika and £537,003 from Uganda. The British Government contributed £784,639.[65]

Within this arrangement the Common Market became increasingly an area of conflict between the three territories, and it is here that the Commission was to find most of its problems. This conflict was manifested in Kenya's becoming more industrialized than the other two. Yet, despite these problems of 'unequal distribution of benefits' of the Market and the tensions and strains they generated, they must finally be regarded as disguising the real issue underlying the conflicts. This underlying cause was the dominant exploitative and oppressive activities of British imperialism that had been going on since the onset of colonialism. And it is this exploitation, and not the idea of regional co-operation, that the people of East Africa fought. We shall examine these stresses and strains in Chapter Six.

As the 1950s approached with the crisis of bilateral imperialism, the struggle intensified throughout the entire area. And as various reforms were made, concessions also followed concerning the right institutional arrangements to accommodate them. It was in the latter part of this period that the future of the Commission was reviewed because of the approaching sovereign status of Tanganyika (itself one of the nails in the coffin of bilateral imperialism at the political level). Independence was fixed for 28 December 1961. At a conference held in London in June 1961 to assess the adjustments this would entail it was agreed among the representatives of each of the territories (including the nationalist leaders of Kenya and Uganda) that it was 'in the interests of all the territories to ensure that, whatever constitutional changes might take place in the future in East Africa, common services at present provided by the East African High Commission should continue to be provided on an East African basis.'[66] The High Commission was to be renamed the East African Common Services Organization (EACSO) with a Secretary-General as the principal executive officer of the organization, headed by the East African Common Services Authority. The latter was to be constituted by the 'principal elected Minister' responsible to the legislature in each of the three territories, thus ensuring 'a popular support of the East African people'.[67] The Authority was to be supplemented by four councils or 'triumvirates', each consisting of one Minister from each of the territories, each responsible for the activities of the five councils in their respective territories covering communications, finance, commercial and industrial co-ordination, social and research services. There was also to be a legislature, this time consisting of the Ministers in the 'triumvirates' and elected members from the legislatures of the three territories.[68] In this way, British imperialism calculated that its economic interests, and those of the other imperialist powers, could best be served in the changed circumstances in which it found itself. At the same time the nationalist forces were hoping they could create a new unity based on the idea of Pan Africanism. Of this we will have more to say later.

References

1. Thomas M. Franck, *East African Unity through Law* (New Haven, Yale U.P., 1964), pp.20, 26.
2. T.A. Kennedy, 'The East African Customs Union: Some Features of its History and Operation', *Makerere Journal,* No. 3, 1959, p.19.
3. T.M. Franck, op. cit., pp.4-5.
4. T.A. Kennedy, op. cit., p.22.
5. E.A. Brett, *Colonialism and Underdevelopment in East Africa: The Politics of Economic Change, 1919-39* (London, Heinemann, 1973), p.268.
6. A. Hazelwood, *Economic Integration: The East African Experience* (London, Heinemann, 1975), p.28.
7. Y. Ghai, 'Some Legal Aspects of an East African Federation' in C. Leys, and P. Robson, *Federation in East Africa: Opportunities and Problems* (London, Oxford University Press, 1965), pp.179-82.
8. Terms of reference of the East African Commission 1924.
9. *Report of the East Africa Commission 1925* p.9, hereinafter referred to as the Ormsby-Gore Report.
10. *Report of the Commission on Closer Union of the Dependencies in Eastern and Central Africa,* (London, H.M.S.O., 1920) pp.141-2. hereinafter referred to as the Hilton Young Report.
11. *Report of Sir Samuel Wilson on His Visit to East Africa,* 1929, Cmd. 3378 (London, H.M.S.O., 1929) pp.15-16.
12. *Report of the Joint Select Committee on Closer Union in East Africa, 1931* (London, H.M.S.O., 1931), pp.14-15.
13. Franck, op. cit., p.42.
14. *Inter-Territorial Organisation in Africa,* 1945, Colonial No. 191 (London, H.M.S.O.) 1945, p.2.
15. Kennedy, op. cit., p.19.
16. Ibid.
17. Despite his weaknesses on basic issues, Kennedy nevertheless gives a good historical account of the Customs Union, from which most of the historical material is borrowed.
18. Ibid., p.24.
19. Uganda Government, *Report of the Customs Tariff and Railway Rates Committee* (Entebbe, Government Printer, 1929).
20. F.J. Peddler, *Customs Arrangements with Kenya and Uganda,* 1934.
21. *Report by Sir Sydney Armitage-Smith, K.B.E., C.B. on Financial Mission to Tanganyika.*
22. C. Leubuscher, *Tanganyika Territory* (Oxford, Clarendon, 1944), Ch. ix.
23. Ormsby-Gore Report, p.11.
24. M.F. Hill, *The Permanent Way: The Story of the Kenya and Uganda Railway* (Nairobi, E.A.R.& H., 1961), p.422.

25.   Ormsby-Gore Report, p.19.
26.   C. Miller, *The Lunatic Express* (London, Macdonald, 1971).
27.   Hill, op. cit., p.373.
28.   Ibid., pp.403-4
29.   Ibid., p.441.
30.   Ibid., p.444.
31.   Ibid.
32.   Ibid.,
33.   Quoted in Hill, op. cit., p.444.
34.   Hill, op. cit., Vol. II, 'The History of the Tanganyika Railway', (Nairobi, E.A.R. & H., 1957), p.185
35.   Ibid., p.190.
36.   Ibid., p.191.
37.   Ibid.
38.   Ibid.
39.   See, for instance, Brett, op. cit., pp.91-9.
40.   K. Ingham, 'Tanganyika: Slump and Short-Term Governors' in Harlow, Chilver and Smith,(eds.) *History of East Africa* (London, Oxford University Press, 1965), Vol. II, p.606.
41.   S. Symes, League of Nations.
42.   *Report on Administration of Tanganyika Territory for the Year 1932*, Colonial No. 81 (London, H.M.S.O., 1933) p.115.
43.   R. van Zwanenberg and A. King, *An Economic History of Kenya and Uganda, 1800-1970* (Nairobi, E.A.P.H., 1975), pp.281-2.
44.   Ibid.,p.222.
45.   W.T. Newlyn, *Money in an African Context* (Nairobi, Oxford University Press, 1965), p.47.
46.   Ibid.,p.48.
47.   Ibid., pp.45-6.
48.   Ibid., p.46.
49.   I.B.R.D., *The Economic Development of Uganda* p.30; B.A. Blomstrom in T.J. Taxer (ed.), *Financing African Development* (Boston, M.I.T., 1965) p.201.
50.   Newlyn, op. cit., pp.48-9.
51.   M. Yaffey, *Balance of Payments Problems of a Developing Country: Tanzania* (Munich, Welt Forum Verlag, 1968) p.66.
52.   Fitch and Openheimer, *Ghana: End of an Illusion* (New York, Monthly Review Press, 1966), pp.43-4.
53.   Yaffey, op. cit., p.66.
54.   Ormsby-Gore Report, p.80.
55.   Ibid., p.82.
56.   J.D. Bernal, *The Social Function of Science* (Boston, M.I.T., 1964),p.139.
57.   Circular A to the Colonial Governors from the Secretary of State for the Colonies, annexed as Appendix 1 to a Report to the Conference of East African Governors entitled *Report on a Fiscal Survey of Kenya, Uganda and Tanganyika* by Sir W. Wood, dated 12 August 1946, p.158.
58.   Ormsby-Gore Report, pp.80-94.
59.   Hilton Young Report, p.133.
60.   East Africa, *Report of the Economic Fiscal Commission 1961,* Cmd. 1279.

61.   Colonial Office, *Inter-Territorial Organisation in East Africa*, Colonial No. 191, 1945 (London, H.M.S.O., 1945).
62.   Ibid., p.5.
63.   Colonial Office, *Inter-Territorial Organisation in East Africa: Revised Proposals*, Colonial No. 210. (London, H.M.S.O., 1947).
64.   East African (High Commission) Order-in-Council (1948) S.R. and O. 1947 No. 2863.
65.   Lord Hailey, *African Survey* (Rev. ed., 1956), p.189.
66.   Colonial Office, *The Future of East Africa High Commission Services* Cmd. 1433 (London, H.M.S.O., 1961), p.4.
67.   Ibid., p.5.
68.   Y.P. Ghai, and McAuslan, *Public Law and Political Change in Kenya* (London, Oxford University Press, 1970) pp.473-8.

4. The Crisis of Bilateral Integration

Crisis at Home

The crisis of bilateral integration spelt the end of the road for British hegemony in East Africa, and this was as evident in the weakness in its domestic economy as in the Empire as a whole. We have noted this trend already in Chapters Two and Three. The crisis was essentially a crisis of production; Britain's sagging competitiveness in the world market was a consequence of the intense struggle between capital and labour in England. The result was a growth in the cost of production, with the working class increasingly demanding a larger share of the product. But the situation was also an intensification of the crisis inherent in the conditions that had brought about the War, and the stringent curtailment of non-war production. Every resource, including shipping, had been mobilized for the war effort. As we have seen, this also affected the resources that were being produced in East Africa as a region, resources which were put under command of the British army. During the war years 1939-45, production and supply (including prices) were brought under the strict discipline of the marketing boards, bulk supply contracts, and governmental committees: in the 1950s these war-time institutions were inherited by the East African High Commission. Thus the crisis of monopoly capitalism in the late 1920s and 1930s led to war in the 1940s, which led in turn to more centralized control in East African production in the 1950s. Finally this intensified movement toward regional co-ordination by British imperialism led to an equally opposite movement — the intensified strains and stresses in the relations between the peoples under colonial rule.

We have also noted in Volume One how bulk-purchasing arrangements made it easy for large amounts of peasant earnings in Uganda and Tanganyika to be deducted as export taxes and as price stabilization funds ostensibly in order to avoid 'inflation', funds which were either never paid back or only partially; instead they were utilized as 'development funds'. The creation of marketing boards merely continued the same mechanisms for skimming off peasant earnings and diverting them to state activities geared less to the well-being of the people than to helping Britain sort out the balance-of-payments problems her warmongering had brought upon herself. But the struggle of British workers to restore their living conditions to a pre-war level and even to improve them also was putting pressure on British capital.[1] So, too, was the struggle of the peoples of the colonies who were in the early 1950s increasingly pressing for national independence, to remove themselves from the exploitative and oppressive rule of British imperialism. In Uganda a renewed national movement found its feet under the Bataka Party and later the Uganda National Congress; in Kenya the Mau Mau uprising occurred; and in Tanganyika the Tanganyika African National Union manifested the struggle of the workers and peasants particularly in the cotton-growing areas.

All these developments became particularly pronounced at the end of the war and marked a new phase in the struggle of the colonial peoples, particularly with India's realization of its national independence in 1947 and the Chinese Revolution in 1949. All this alerted imperialism to the impending danger to its colonial empire in Africa. The reform measures that it was forced to carry through in the period were merely intended to defuse this growing movement of opposition and turn it into something beneficial to British imperialism and imperialism in general.

Nevertheless Britain's own problems continued to undermine its hegemony in East Africa. The problem of production in Britain and its incapacity to sell abroad and therefore earn enough dollars to pay off its liabilities and discharge its obligations to those countries holding its currency as a result of War needs increasingly compelled her to fall on her knees before U.S. imperialism and beg it to pull it out of its quagmire. The U.S., itself becoming increasingly strong in its production and capital, and therefore in need of markets and outlets for its own capital, now took advantage of this weakness of Britain and the other imperialist powers in Europe and Japan to insist on a redivision of the world under its own leadership on the basis of open-door neo-colonialism. Under this cover, U.S. capital began to impose a new discipline on Britain and the other imperialist powers. Britain had increasingly relied on the U.S. imperialists under the Lend-Lease arrangements, otherwise known as Mutual Military Aid, to wage its war to the finish. Under the terms of these agreements, the U.S. began to spell out its own strategy to the debt-ridden victors and vanquished alike. Under Article VII of the Lend-Lease Agreement with the U.S., Britain was required to adopt a non-discriminatory position in its own trading relationships with the Empire, and to accept the 'Most Favoured Nation' principle. The U.S. demanded that Britain could not expect to get aid from the U.S. while at the same time excluding the U.S. from trade with the Empire.

Britain now negotiated another loan agreement with the U.S.[2] in order to enable her to fulfil her liabilities to other countries which held large sterling reserves and partly to prepare herself to accept the multilateral discipline which was being worked out under U.S. pressure in the various institutions which later came to be known as the Bretton Woods system. It asked the U.S. for a 'grant-in-aid' which was refused. It asked for an interest-free loan of $6 billion which was also refused. In the end she asked for an interest-bearing loan of $3.75 billion which was negotiated and agreed on 6 December 1945, in time to meet the deadline set of 31 December 1945 by which she was required to ratify the Bretton Woods system.

Apart from the fact that the loan agreement specified the manner in which the loan was to be used, it imposed other conditions requiring Britain to set her house in order and undertake her full obligations under the new multilateral system. Article 3 of the Agreement stated:

> The purpose of this line of credit is . . . to help the United Kingdom to maintain adequate reserves of gold and dollars and to assist the Government of the United Kingdom to assume the obligations of multilateral trade, as defined in this and other agreements.[3]

The amount was to be repaid in 50 instalments and bearing an interest rate of 2% per annum. Article 7 stipulated that the U.K. Government was to make arrangements 'as early as practicable' and in any case 'not later than one year after the effective date of this agreement' to ensure that sterling receipts from current transactions of all Sterling Area countries 'will be freely available for current transactions in any currency without any discrimination' arising from 'the so-called Sterling Area dollar pool' which was to be 'entirely removed' with the result that each member of the Sterling Area will have its current sterling and dollar receipts 'at its free disposal for current transactions anywhere'.[4] This was forcing the opening of colonial doors.

The implications of this Agreement cannot be fully appreciated until we grasp the essence of bilateral imperialism, particularly as it operated in the inter-war period and during the Second World War itself. We have already defined this phase of modern imperialism as the highest stage of capitalism: the division of the world by the most powerful imperialist states had been completed and, on the basis of exports of finance capital, each imperialist state had integrated all its colonial, semi-colonial and other states within its own system, using a string of tariffs and other forms of protections against other imperialist states. This phase began in the period 1880-1914, and in the case of Britain took on its specific concrete form with the Safeguarding of Industries Act of 1921. Following the final collapse of the Gold Standard in 1925-31 and the resultant Ottawa preferential arrangement, the British Empire was welded together economically. Although, within this unit, a kind of multilateralism was maintained, it was still centred on London, very much a bilateral imperialism of Britain over the entire colonial network. This contrasted very sharply with the earlier period when Britain, as the 'Workshop of the World', had assured to it a total domination of world resources more or less on the basis of market mechanisms. Now, under the new arrangement in a situation of world war, stringent measures of control were imposed, reinforcing Britain's bilateral control over its Empire in the use of resources.

The Sterling Area as a Device to Exploit the Colonies
It was under these circumstances that the so-called Sterling Area was formed on the basis of a 'gentleman's agreement' between Britain, the Commonwealth

countries (except Canada), the colonies, semi-colonies and other countries 'closely associated with Britain' such as Egypt, Iraq, Transjordan, Iceland and the Belgian Congo. The discipline imposed in the Area was over the control of the exchange of sterling for dollars, limiting drawings of dollars to 'essential needs'. In this way the Gold and Dollar Pool was formed. Into the Pool was paid all the gold, dollars and foreign currencies earned by all the members of the Area (including the colonies and semi-colonies).[5] Unlike the independent Commonwealth countries who were credited their dollars within the Pool, the colonies and semi-colonies were instead credited with sterling in exchange for their dollars which were in turn credited as British reserves. Although the British Government tried to explain away this colonial plunder on the ground that the colonial balances were 'savings' held in London,[6] it is clear the colonies were thereby deprived of tremendous development opportunities (an essential element of colonialism), not to mention actual quantities of currency due to depreciation.

The colonies themselves had no say in deciding whether they should form part of the Sterling Area. It came about simply as a consequence of their status as colonies. The colonial brief argued that the colonial sterling assets were part of the reserves of the 'colonial Governments and peoples', and are an 'insurance against falls in export earnings, as savings for future investment and to maintain the exchange value of their currencies'.[7] But in fact the monopolies over the marketing of the colonial raw materials were merely used as an instrument for denying colonial peoples their badly needed current incomes. The major argument as we have seen, was about inflation. But why inflation? Because Britain did not produce the necessary goods for consumption and development on a sufficient scale in the colonies during these war years. Nor could they obtain them elsewhere precisely because their dollar and sterling earnings were blocked.

Whereas Britain had free access to these balances, the colonies had to postpone their use of them until such a time that Britain was able to produce goods for them.[8] After 1949 in particular, when the British pound sterling was devalued, the colonies' postponment of their imports meant the loss of over one-third of their reserves to the British financial oligarchy.[9] Not only that, the postponement of imports implied a loss of value, due to the inflationary spiral in world prices from 1939 onwards, whereas the colonies would have to some extent 'gained' had they spent their earnings at once while they retained their actual value. Moreover the balances held were paid very low rates of interest – 0.5% up to 1952 and of 2 to 4% after 1952.[10]

The colonial balances were crucial to the maintenance of the British pound during this period, to such an extent that, without these balances, the solvency of the British Empire would have been in jeopardy. The powerlessness of the colonies can be seen in the manner in which the Pool was managed. In 1946, for instance, while Britain doubled her drawings from the Pool, and the independent members of the Commonwealth trebled theirs, as a result, the surplus of the colonies which existed on the books only, went into a deficit.[11] Thus the drawings of Britain and the independent members of the Area were more than matched by the contributions of the colonies and bilateral agreements. East Africa, in particular, experienced a dollar deficit.[12]

Apart from the export earnings which the marketing boards taxed, the reserves of the colonies included colonial government funds of various kinds (including savings bank deposits, sinking funds, etc.), currency board funds, and reserve assets of the commercial banks. All these constituted the sterling balances of the colonies. Over a six-year period, for instance, these reserves expanded considerably. Between 31 December 1950 and 31 December 1956, currency board funds and currency funds held by Crown Agents rose by £182 million to £464 million, and sterling held by colonial banks with U.K. banks by £58 million to £250 million. In the same period the reserve funds of the colonial governments and marketing boards rose by £406 million to £740 million. Over the six years the total colonial holdings rose from £808 million to £1,454 million. The British Government commented:

> The combination of high commodity prices, rising monetary circulation, conservative government finance and the provision of new capital for development mainly from U.K. sources, both governmental and private, has thus resulted in a total of sterling holdings for the colonial group now larger than the Independent Commonwealth group.[13]

The movements in sterling holdings for all the Sterling Area during the six years thus 'offset each other' as shown in Table 4. Despite arguments by the

Table 4
Movements in Sterling Holdings, 1950-56

			£ million
Group A	—	'Non-sterling' countries	− 369
Group B	—	Independent Commonwealth	− 517
Group C	—	Colonial	+ 646
Group D	—	Middle East	+ 267
Net			+ 27

British Government that these reserves were not blocked since they were held for 'convenience',[14] it is clear, as has been argued,[15] that the reserves of the colonial currency authorities were tied up with the sterling earnings, and could not easily be used for imports. They were, therefore, more than a loan to the British Government. This would also apply to colonial government funds like post office savings deposits, pension funds, sinking funds, etc. which were held in British securities.[16] Bell argues also that under the then existing Colonial Sterling Exchange Standard system, 'a large part of the [sterling] balances' could not be used for development purposes because of reserve requirements. This would include balances of currency boards and commercial bank branches as well. He argues that there was a second 'cost' to the Overseas Sterling members in the domestic repercussions from balance-of-payments disturbances 'greater than would have occurred under flexible exchange rates'.[17] He adds:

> Automatic money supply effects of a balance of payments disturbance will normally be less than that experienced by an OSA [Overseas Sterling Area] member from a similar disturbance because of the nature of the monetary mechanisms. The primary money supply effect in the OSA region will normally be equal to the surplus of the deficit; in the United Kingdom it will normally be smaller than the surplus or deficit because of at least part of the shift in sterling balances being reflected in long-term securities. . . . Even if there is never any unemployment, however, serious instability is bound to produce dislocations and losses of productivity, to say nothing of temporary shifts in the distribution of income, with attendant political and social problems, and possibly long-run moral and cultural difficulties as well.[18]

Thus the gain by Britain as banker for the Sterling Area in general, and as a requisitioner of all colonial earnings in difficult situations, helped it to offset its own balance of payments problems and to consume the current goods of others — while postponing the current consumption of others — arresting their development and, in the case of the colonies, using them as the first-resort lenders, with the right to manipulate their earnings with impunity. Whenever the pressure in the colonies gave rise to a revolt, these balances could then be released in 'dribs and drabs'[19] to ease the situation. In East Africa, these exploitative relationships added to the financial problems in the period under discussion, resulting in the stresses and strains in the Common Market, and eventually, with the exit of British imperialism, to its collapse.

Crisis in East Africa

There can be no doubt that the reserves that were built up in Britain from the East African territories contributed to the political problems that Britain experienced in the area. Much of the reserves resulted from the outright exploitation of the peasantry and workers in East Africa both directly and through the high 'anti-inflation' taxation imposed on them. But at the same time the settler agricultural bourgeoisie were paid full prices under the bulk purchasing contracts and even under the marketing board system. The colonial governments tried to justify the low prices being paid to peasants as being 'at levels designed to give the grower a fair return in relation to [his] cost of living'. But the peasants' cost of living was judged to depend on what he produced for his subsistence, and in fact this reflected the level of his wages paid in the form of produce prices. The same could not be said of a white settler employing labour and subsisting on the market. As for the worker, his wage was determined by the market price of his labour power which in turn was determined by his cost of living, this being determined by his access to the subsistence produce of the peasant. It is for this reason that the Royal East African Report pointed out that the 'key' to 'a permanent raising of the supply price of African labour is to foster an increase in the real incomes of the peasants', and this was because the 'governing factor is the real income which can be obtained in alternative occupations',[20] i.e. 'either the production of cash crops or of subsistence.' But it is clear that these occupations tended to have contradictory effects to the extent that the more subsistence production was engaged in, the lower the wages, and the more the cash crop production, the less the subsistence, and hence the higher the wages but the more the subsistence to be obtained from cash sources. But this is merely an abstraction of a process taking place over time. In the historical context of the situation in East Africa where the peasant still predominated, the wages paid to both the worker and the poor peasant would always be minimal prices for their labour power. This fact is crucial to understanding the 'strains and stresses' that manifested themselves in the East African Common Market at this time. Efforts to drag in purely balance-of-payments or budgetary issues as constituting the causes of the problem merely obscure the reality of the situation.

This exploitation manifested itself at two levels: first, by the imperialist monopolist bourgeoisie obtaining a vast amount of surplus value at going world prices as a result of low wages paid to the peasantry; and second, by the colonial state in the form of taxation, whether direct or indirect, over and above the surplus value obtained by the imperialist bourgeoisie, which the state needed for its activities and the provision of the general technical conditions needed for assuring the monopolists' continuing production. The economic situation of the region's economy was undoubtedly worsened in these two ways.

Uneven development *between* the territories also served to worsen the areas of conflict between them. To take Uganda for a start, as we have observed earlier, this was a prize that any financial oligarchy would have fought to preserve. Within ten to fifteen years of its colonization it was already, on the basis of small peasant production, paying its way and to some extent subsidizing the high-cost Kenya settler agriculture and industry. The expenses of running the colony came almost wholly from the peasant for a good part of the colonial period under review. This high level of taxation was achieved by a direct export tax on agricultural commodities, and through Hut and Poll Taxes. Later, with the marketing mechanisms worked out for the war period, a forced deduction from the peasant's earnings was made on the grounds of creating a price stabilization fund, primarily an indirect way of imposing taxation. For instance, out of a surplus of £50.7 million deducted in this way between 1945 and 1960, only £25.8 million was paid as price assistance and the other £24.9 million — almost 50% was utilized by the state in its general budget to finance 'development projects',[21] which otherwise would have come from ordinary taxation. This was in addition to the direct export tax imposed on peasant products. In these circumstances it is even surprising that the Royal Commission found room in their monumental report to shed some crocodile tears for the Uganda peasant when they admitted: 'When this burden is added to the amount of taxation paid by Africans in Uganda, it is clear that the burden of taxation and forced saving upon the African population of Uganda has been extremely heavy.'[22]

The central point is that it was this level of exploitation that was at the very root of the stresses and strains that characterized this period. The mid-1950s, regarded by Professor Raisman as the beginnings of the conflicts, is also the point that this level of taxation became sharpest. As is well known, this also was the period when competition between the industrial monopolies forced down the prices of most raw materials, thus initiating a wave of intensified exploitation of the peasant all down the line. In Uganda this was reflected in a higher level of taxation, in many cases above 50% of earnings. The fluctuations in the prices on the world market (itself a result of monopolistic competition) made the situation worse, as reflected in the territory's budgets. The optimum taxable point of the peasant had been reached. Thus, whereas in the period 1947-51 a vigorous expansion in both government recurrent and capital budgets had been attained at the behest of the Colonial Office, to save Britain dollars, the peak of high prices and high budgets began to recede as world prices fell. From 1954 onwards, as prices fell, private capital saved in Uganda mainly by Asian capitalists, began to flow out at the rate of £5 million a year until the 1960s, thus reducing Uganda's sterling reserves through a reduction of bank balances (erroneously blamed by the World Bank on the inability of non-Africans to obtain land).[23]

This phenomenon of decreasing government revenues as a result of falling prices resulted in budgetary problems at a time when the nationalist movement was putting great pressure on British imperialism, producing a rash of reforms and concessions in order to contain the movement and divert it to the 'more constructive channels'[24] of neo-colonialism. Between 1950 and 1952, Ugandan Government recurrent and non-recurrent expenditures had increased from £8 million to £17.5 million, more than doubling in three years, and that of local authorities more than quadrupling, though the picture was to be very different for the next six years at least.

From the mid-1950s onwards the surplus began to decline on the recurrent budget and by 1957-58 a deficit was recorded. In 1959-60 a 'surplus' was attained only by reducing expenditure (with a slight increase in revenue). Taking recurrent and non-recurrent expenditure budgets together, surpluses were achieved between 1950 and 1954. These were followed by annual deficits up to 1961-62, with the last one reaching £5 million.[25] These deficits reduced the government reserves in London to £1.3 million of the Capital Development Fund. After 1959, therefore, a halt was called to a number of government projects and to the level of government expenditure. It is at this time that the government now considered it necessary to 'increase current revenues by changing the tax structure, since the peasant could not pay any more and to find new ways of financing capital and development programmes', the World Bank Mission observed after a Government Commission — the

Uganda Economy Commission – had reported its findings.

The World Bank Mission recommended the 'overhaul' of the tax system to remove 'both highly inequitable and economically anomalous' aspects. It did not believe that the country was 'overtaxed at the present time', and recommended that an 'international agency' come to look into the tax structure. It recommended a variation in the export tax floor price for coffee to alleviate the somewhat higher tax on cotton.[27] It noted that the present reserve system under the East African Currency Board arrangements and other financial ties to the Sterling Area had 'sheltered' Uganda from experiencing balance-of-payments crises 'in the usual form of a shortage of foreign exchange reserves'. For this reason the Government was forced to reduce expenditure, instead of evading 'the hard facts' by simply printing more currency 'unbacked by real resources'. This World Bank analysis completely obscured the fact that Britain was benefiting from these 'real resources' since they were invested in its securities. But in a thoroughly contradictory manner, the Bank also pointed out that the existing monetary system was 'inadequate . . . in not making available to Uganda the help in economic development that a properly organized banking system in East Africa could contribute.'[28] But this was precisely the point: as the levels of taxation on the peasant were already very high, the situation could only be assisted by recourse to all the possible available reserves which already existed, but, under the existing system, this could not be achieved.

Be that as it may, the problem that the colonial regime in Uganda faced was how to finance its programmes, when its only additional revenue was customs duties. Hence the renewed concern about industrialization in Kenya. Imposing excise duty on Kenyan manufactured goods consumed in Uganda could be justified as a compensation for the fact that it was Kenya which was industrializing and this because of the high external tariff imposed under the Customs Union for the whole region. No one, however, argued that the high level of taxation on the peasantry was itself detrimental to the development of the country because this was the 'natural' order of things. Taxation of one sort or another was the only means colonial officialdom could see to obtain additional revenue for their projects. But this whole question ought to be examined again after we have looked at Tanzania, another area where complaints about Kenya emerged.

The specific problem which created uneasiness in Tanganyika was a little different but equally connected with the high level of exploitation of the people. As we have already noted, after the Germans lost Tanganyika, the British moved in but with very little capital. It was only the very high level of exploitation of African labour on sisal and other settler estates, as well of the peasantry on cash crop production, that kept the colony producing and supplying the needs of the British financial oligarchy. With very little private capital coming into the country, the dominant role of the state in economic activity after independence was almost inevitable. On balance there was a net outflow of private capital, only counter-balanced, even at this early stage by 'increasing doses of official capital',[29] mainly from the Colonial Development and Welfare Funds, which supplied Tanganyika with about £10 million between 1948 and 1958-59. This was quite separate from the £35 million spent on the ill-fated Groundnut Scheme in 1947. Most of the financing came from reserves accumulated from the agricultural production, especially from the 'extra incomes' the peasantry had earned as a result of the high prices following the devaluation of the pound sterling in 1949 and the Korean War boom. The export index had risen by 50% between 1950 and 1951 alone.

This 'excess income' was taxed away, giving the state higher recurrent budget incomes in the year 1954-55. Due to delayed tax collection,[30] the deficit in the Tanganyika budget was postponed until 1956-57. From this year onwards, for at least three years, deficits were experienced. Unlike Uganda, which relied on direct export taxes on cash crops, the major part of Tanganyika's revenue in these years came from import duties, excise duties and income tax. The African population was taxed mainly through the first two taxes and a personal tax which was not very responsive to income. In the period under review, this fall-off in earnings from exports tended to affect government tax income. Since certain expenditures which had been embarked on in the earlier years could not be abandoned,[31] the result was a 'feeling of acute budgetary difficulty'.[32] All the same, the Government was forced to put an embargo on any further staff recruitment. When the capital budget, which had also been financed from surpluses in the earlier period of the boom, now found itself in difficulties, the Government had to borrow, despite the fact that there were still some government reserves in the capital account in London. But with the recurrent budget restricted, the capital budget had also to be limited. The result was a strain in the sources of revenue at this time, and this 'shoe pinch' in the budget is connected with the strains and stresses in the Common Market arrangement.

The East African Common Market
Dissatisfaction with the Common Market was exacerbated by the fact that Kenya had tremendously increased government expenditure, yet still managed to carry out its programmes. The Government was largely financed by earnings from the inter-territory industrial exports within the Common Market arrangement.[33] It was this disparity that sparked off the controversy leading to the appointment of the Raisman Commission. There can be no doubt that British imperialism had intensified unequal development in East Africa. But this uneven development was not between countries alone. The uneven development was based on the exploitation of the peasant to subsidize the more intensive capitalist production in the cities of East Africa and Britain. And capitalist production in turn, was sustained by the exploitation of the working-class labour force. It was this utterly exploited labour force in the countryside and the towns — unable to sustain any more of the state's exactions — that created the 'pinch' in the budgets. The Raisman Commission was required to find a solution to this endemic problem. It failed because such a solution was impossible to find. The Commission, however, did point to what it took to be some of the maladies affecting the High Commission

arrangement, and these observations on the state of uneven development require special attention because they highlight some of the analysis we have made above.

The Report could not comprehend the basic facts and so instead focused on the apparent problems – problems of the Common Market as the 'cause' of the stresses and strains. It observed that in 1959 transfers of internally produced goods between the territories had shown an increase valued at £20 million, some 6 or 8% of the wholesale value of goods for sale. Despite the fact that exports to the outside world were valued at some £120 million, or six times the inter-territorial exchange of goods, the latter had a much steadier rate of growth. Admittedly, dependence on inter-territorial trade was low in relation to the bulk of primary production, but even in this sector it was much higher in regard to certain particular primary products and manufactures. The Commission noted that, whereas inter-territorial trade had increased in every year since the War, this contrasted sharply with the trend in exports to the outside world, which fell by 27% in value between 1952 and 1953, and by some 3% between 1956 and 1957. Thus it could be deduced that there was some tendency for the ratio of inter-territorial to external trade in domestic products to rise over the fifteen year period as a whole.[34]

It further noted that, whereas the region's primary products other than subsistence products were for export, products from the Kenya Highlands where 'quite largely disposed of' in the other two territories – nearly half the wheat and a third of the milk and a seventh of the pig products. Despite this, it was in manufactures that inter-territorial dependence was most marked. Here probably one-quarter of the products of Kenya's manufacturing industry went to the other two territories, and in the case of footwear and cigarettes the proportion was over half. Considering that the combined purchasing power of the other two territories was not much greater than that of the Kenyan home market, the Commission continued, 'this inter-territorial dispersion of Kenya's manufactures products shows a fairly high degree of unity in the East African market for such goods'.[35]

The Raisman Report then went on to examine comparative rates of growth of the three territories. It noted that between 1952-54 and 1957-59 the overall rates of growth were 56% for Kenya, 28% for Tanganyika, and 15% for Uganda. Over the same period, and having regard to the cost of living and population increases in the three territories, the standard of living rose 'very rapidly' (by about 40%) in Kenya, 'rather less than half as much' in Tanganyika, and 'probably [rose] rather than [fell]' in Uganda. It noted that these differences 'in fortune' were attributable partly to differences in the development of production, and partly to differences in the impact of 'world market conditions upon them', particularly in view of the fact that the export trade accounted for 15% of Kenya's total output, 25% of Tanganyika's and 30% of Uganda's.

From all this, the Report added that the volumes of production in the three territories 'were very remarkable indeed'. Kenya's real output rose 3%,

Tanganyika 2½% and Uganda 'some 10%' *more than the real incomes available for consumption and investment in the territories.* In the case of Uganda, the 'terms of trade' had hit harder than in the other two territories because of the fall in her export earnings. These differences could also be traced to other factors like physical output in general and in relation to different branches of production, where incomes received in agriculture rose 20% in Kenya, 16% in Tanganyika, and 'fell slightly' in Uganda; and volumes of exports between 1954 and 1959 which rose 88% for Kenya, 47% for Tanganyika and 54% for Uganda.[36] Non-agricultural incomes rose even more phenomenally for Kenya, mainly due to manufacturing. Incomes in tertiary industries had equally produced higher incomes for Kenya. All these factors indicated a very high dependence of Kenyan economy on the Common Market to the extent of one-third of her production. Despite this, the Report continued, 'the question whether Uganda and Tanganyika have suffered from the development of Kenya within the Common Market by virtue of their trade relations with her is less answered'. The Report then went on to conclude that on their evidence these two territories had still gained rather than lost in real terms and hence that the Common Market should be maintained.

Nevertheless the Report noted the emergence of 'strains' and 'stresses' in the Common Market which since 1952 had 'become more serious'.[37] Earlier the Report had pointed to the reasons for this when it stated (Paragraph 27): 'Changes in the world economy since the mid-fifties appear to have been largely responsible for the emergence, or re-emergence, of the clashes of interest which naturally exist within a common market.' It noted that these differences were over the claim by Uganda and Tanganyika that tariff and industrial licensing favoured Kenya's development and not their own. Would they have faired better without the Common Market? The Report comments:

> There are two ways in which it is possible in principle for Kenya's gain to have been the other territories' loss. First, capital and enterprise might have been attracted which otherwise would have gone to Uganda or Tanganyika. Secondly, the two latter territories might have suffered loss through buying goods from Kenya instead of buying them from the outside world.[38]

Answering the first question, the Report pointed out that the large purchasing power in Kenya attracted industrial development because of the existence of the Common Market. Her purchasing power alone would not have been large enough to attract such development. But, by the same token, the other two territories had far less chance of attracting capital because their purchasing power was even smaller. 'Whatever relative advantage Kenya has over the other two Territories in the attraction for capital and enterprise would have been greater still if they had presented smaller separate markets and Kenya a larger one, instead of all forming part of a single Common Market'.[39] It was unlikely that the absence of a market would have left Uganda and Tanganyika better off. On the second question, it agreed that, to the extent that these territories had bought goods from Kenya at higher prices than from overseas, they *had* suffered a loss. 'This loss, however, is not the end of the story', it added. This was because protected industry in Kenya drew labour into employment in Kenya 'which would otherwise be largely unproductive', and in that way brings in capital from abroad, and generally stimulates activity:

> In so doing it increases total real purchasing power in Kenya, which tends to overflow into increased purchases from the other territories. Since in these territories, also, there are resources capable of being drawn into more productive use by additional demand, extra purchases from them bring about increases in real income which partly offset, and may even more than wholly offset, the loss occasioned by their buying goods from Kenya at prices higher than those ruling in the outside world.[40]

These speculative arguments of the Commission, so highly abstract in themselves, do not tell us much. Indeed they are really intended to obscure the real issues, since they only make sense on the assumption of free trade — and even the Commission itself admitted that did not exist. These arguments ignore the real history of the colonial relationships between the three countries and Britain as outlined by us in Chapters Two and Three. As colonies they had no such choices as those implied above by the Raisman Report. Despite complaints by the Governors, they had no power to work out any policy which contradicted the general interest of British finance capital. How could Tanganyika and Uganda have decided to encourage industrialization in their own territories to compete with the products of British monopolies from Kenya? The Report further ignores the stark fact that in 1935 the Governors of these same two territories had, in a Governors' Conference resolution, decided that they would not encourage industrialization in their own territories. This reflected the real interests of the monopolies; the industrialization that arose in Kenya was at that time considered the sort that would be desirable for the region as a whole. Indeed various efforts by various manufacturers to set up industry in Uganda and Tanganyika were resisted by the monopolies in England. Moreover the Industrial Licensing Law introduced in 1948 was motivated by the fears of unemployment in Britain and the need to bring more discipline in monopolistic competition by means of 'planning'. This law reflected the hegemony of British monopolies in the area where they obtained protection for a number of industries considered necessary for the maintenance of British competition in the region and the world market. It was this policy which determined whether an industry should be licensed to operate or not. Given the laws of capitalist development and given the availability of the Common Market, investment would flow to those areas where external economies of scale existed and where a larger market was expected, and it is not surprising that industrial development went towards Kenya.

These were the real facts that the Report was refusing to face. There was in fact no real question as to whether Uganda and Tanganyika should have more industrial development since, so long as these countries were exploited and dominated, no kind of industrial development would remove the fundamental problems behind these stresses and strains. And indeed the possibility of industrialization was non-existent anyway, as the next phase of development after independence was to show. As for Ndegwa's point[41] in regard to the second question raised by the Report, that it was the East African *consumers* who were being exploited by the protection given to Kenyan industry, though more plausible than Raisman's, this also obscures the fact that essentially it was the actual producers — workers and peasants — who were being exploited by this arrangement. The fact that *consumers*, workers and peasants included, paid more by way of prices for the Kenya produced protected products is not exploitation as such although, to the extent that some of the consumers were also actual producers, it was an aspect of it. More correctly, the consumers at this level were being *cheated* by this arrangement, but then this was the only basis on which British monopolies in this period could deliver these goods. An ideal situation outside this monopolistic situation did not exist anywhere. (Ndegwa's own illusions are soon apparent, however, when he puts his own solutions.[42])

Anyway, the Commission also found difficulty over the issue of the 'loss' of customs duty complained about by the other two territories. The argument was that they 'lost' the potential revenue from customs duty of the protected products they bought from Kenya. They demanded that an excise duty equal to the 'lost' revenue be imposed on the products, and that such duty be paid to the 'losing territory' where the product was consumed. The Commission, following on their earlier arguments as outlined above, pointed out that this would give 'undue benefit' to the territories which were not the producers of the import substitute because 'they would not only suffer no direct loss of revenue because of the decline in customs duty, but they would also receive such increments in their Government revenues as resulted from the spilling-over into them of increased demand from the Territories producing the import substitutes'.[43] It was for this reason that they preferred to give 'a different method of effecting a measure of compensation'. In these circumstances, and having looked at the problem as they did, it is not surprising that their prescription to cure the inequalities in the distribution of the Common Market's 'benefits' should have been no solution at all. They recommended the creation of a Distributive Pool to which would be credited in each financial year 40% of the annual proceeds within the territories of the income tax levied on companies' profits arising from manufacturing and finance, and 6% of the annual revenue collected in the territories by means of customs and excise duties. This pool was then to be distributed by the High Commission equally to each of the territories. By this strategem an independent source of revenue was assured to the High Commission, and it was assumed a redistribution of benefits to the other two territories would take place and the stresses and strains would be removed among the territories at least in the short-term.[44]

This proposal, which resulted in the transfer of about £737,000 from Kenya to the other two territories in 1964, remained the basis of co-operation until the Treaty in 1967.[45] It did not offer nor could it have offered any real medium- or long-term solution.

The Commission further went on to spell out other ways in which the Common Market could continue to operate more effectively. It pointed out that since the War some 'artificial impediments' to the freedom of trans-actions had operated, such as import prohibitions and the concentration of the marketing of certain products in the hands of statutory marketing authorities. Since they were 'in many cases part of the established structure of the East African economy', the Commission argued it would be unjustified to recommend their abandonment. Thus while they stuck to the illusion of the epoch (i.e. the desirability of the *laissez faire* Customs Union), they unconsciously recognized the reality: that what existed in the region were monopolies operating under the super-monopoly of the British trading giants, themselves operating under the multilateral umbrella. All the Commission insisted on was the need to establish 'some discipline and control' in order to bring about 'greater harmony', a kind of 'a regional GATT'.[46] This 'code of agreed principles' for inter-territorial trade and marketing policy should prohibit the imposition of restrictions 'unilaterally', require that goods should not be sold by the boards 'persistently' at higher prices than their f.o.b. export prices 'without the buying territories' agreement', and uniformity of internal marketing policies between territories should not be regarded as 'necessary'. It further recommended that territories should co-ordinate on matters of pricing and trade policy, preferably with the assistance of an Economic Adviser under the High Commission who would have 'no territorial affiliations' and who would head a Department of Economic Co-ordination which should be created for the purpose.

As for industrial licensing, the Report noted that this had been initiated in 1948 with the twofold object of providing an inducement to investment in scheduled industries, and to enable issuance of licences to those enterprises with resources. Since then, it noted, it had become apparent that development was 'proceeding at different rates in different Territories, [with the result that] representatives of the Territories where it was less rapid [especially Tanganyika] became disinclined to agree to the admission of industries to the schedule'. The Report continued that the system had not achieved the object for which it was established, and now served very little useful purpose in relation to the industrial development of East Africa as a whole. Such a system, it pointed out, could not succeed 'without either an overall development plan', or an 'East African view'. The Report therefore recommended its discontinuance after 1963.[47]

These recommendations were then supposed to keep the system going, and we shall see later that in fact some of these broad outlines of policy were incorporated under the Treaty for East African Co-operation, although the Treaty soon produced the same bottlenecks, leading to its collapse. This was inevitable since the very basis of its existence, namely British bilateral imperialism, had weakened to the extent that it could not longer impose a bilateral discipline on the region.

We have already stated our view that the fundamental contradictions that brought about the tensions in the system were caused by the exploitation of the people by imperialism. This exploitation also manifested itself at the level of the market. It alone explains the Ugandan situation consequent upon falling world prices. Falling prices themselves are a manifestation of mono-polistic control and exploitation of the peasant on a world scale and are the very result of monopoly capital's outward push for cheap raw materials. Monopoly capital puts on 'seven league boots' when it exploits the labour of the backward areas of the world because, other conditions being equal, the rate of profit falls or rises inversely to the price of raw materials.[48] The prices will rise or fall because, due to uncontrollable natural conditions, favourable or unfavourable seasons, etc., the same quantity of labour is represented in different quantities of use value, and it is for this reason that a definite quantity of these use values may therefore have different prices.[49] But it is monopolistic competition which fuels these conditions, since investment in the production of raw materials depends on such competition and, all things being equal, prices will fall or rise according to the state of demand and supply which themselves are a product of monopolistic competition.[50]

Thus the deterioration of the terms of trade which was reflected in the falling prices on the world market in this period and which is closely associated with the strains and stresses in the Common Market at this time must be seen in the overall context of the above phenomenon. It is this context alone that can explain the resistance of the people in the entire area to seven league boots exploitation of imperialism, and it is this struggle that explains the strains and stresses. It is for this reason that the Raisman solution failed to address the real cause — namely the question of peasant and worker exploi-tation — and it is because of this that Ndegwa is right at least in pointing out that the operation of this 'device since it was put into effect does not seem to have reduced strains and controversies in the Common Market'.[51] Indeed it was characteristic of the general crisis of bilateral integration that the Commission in its Report pointed to the short-term nature of their 'solution' when it stated that 'our perspective cannot extend further than some three or four years ahead, and we consider that it should be definitely envisaged that a review will be undertaken after such an interval of time'.[52] This was indeed the foggy and ineffective vision of an old and dying imperialism.

The End of Bilateralism

One of the factors that the Raisman Commission cites as contributing to the 'strains and stresses' was the administrative disintegration taking place. It pointed out that, unlike the situation in 1948 when the High Commission was established and the arrangement 'reflected fairly closely the governmental structures of the Territories', that resemblance 'exists no longer'.[53] What had

Table 5
Gross Domestic Product in the Monetary Economy of East Africa, 1957-62

1957	Kenya		Tanganyika		Uganda		East Africa	
	£m.	%	£m.	%	£m.	%	£m.	%
Agriculture[1]	33.5	21.7	40.3	43.4	56.5	51.7	130.3	36.6
Mining & Quarrying	1.3	0.8	5.0	5.4	1.5	1.4	7.8	2.2
Manufacturing[2]	19.8	12.9	5.7	6.1	11.1	10.1	36.6	10.3
Construction	9.6	6.2	5.4	5.8	3.9	3.6	18.9	5.3
Transport, Communications, Electricity & Water	20.7	13.4	10.8	11.7	5.9	5.4	37.4	10.5
Commerce & Finance	37.0	24.0	10.7	11.5	17.2	15.7	64.9	18.2
Government Services	20.2	13.1	10.4	11.2	5.5	5.0	36.1	10.1
Other Services	12.1	7.9	4.5	4.9	7.8	7.1	24.4	6.8
Gross Domestic Product	154.2	100.0	92.8	100.0	109.4	100.0	356.4	100.0
1962								
Agriculture[1]	39.6	22.0	48.5	39.4	46.4	43.0	134.5	32.8
Mining & Quarrying	0.8	0.4	6.8	5.5	2.6	2.2	10.2	2.5
Manufacturing[2]	23.0	12.8	8.5	6.9	9.8	9.1	41.3	10.0
Construction	6.8	3.8	8.0	6.5	3.9	3.7	18.7	4.6
Communications, Electricity & Water	25.2	14.0	15.7	12.7	8.3	7.7	49.2	11.9
Commerce & Finance[3]	42.4	23.5	12.4	10.1	18.1	16.8	72.9	17.7
Government Services	28.0	15.6	17.3	14.0	7.3	6.7	52.6	12.8
Other Services	14.2	7.9	6.0	4.9	11.5	10.8	31.7	7.7
Gross Domestic Product	180.0	100.0	123.2	100.0	107.9	100.0	411.1	100.0

1. Including livestock, forestry, fishing and hunting. Excluding value added
   in processing primary products.
2. Including value added in processing primary products.
3. Including rents.

Source: *Statistical Abstracts* 1963 for Kenya, Uganda and Tanganyika.

happened within a space of hardly seven years? The Commission merely
refers to the 'constitutional progress' that had been made in the Territories:
'As the Territories have progressed, the dissimilarity between their pattern of
government and that of the High Commission has become more and more
marked.'[54]

But these were colonial Governments representing the same imperialist
power. Why was it that this constitutional progress had produced 'different
patterns', and why had 'constitutional progress' been made anyway? The
Commission clearly could not have answered such questions. It only pointed
to the emergence of ministers who were more concerned with the 'interest of

their respective territory' than with the interest of the whole region. What was happening was an important development countering bilateral imperialism, a manifestation of the real forces of liberation pulling apart the whole exploitative edifice. This was the result of the struggles of the people in each of the territories which was ultimately to bring down British colonial rule and hegemony, dismantling all the institutions of bilateral regional integration.

The whole system of exploitation and national oppression upon which the bilateral integrative mechanism depended was under continuing pressure, as we saw in the last Chapter. The policy of 'trusteeship' gave way to the policy of 'partnership' as a way of holding down the forces. These, too, were now being challenged by the people. The first seeds of the struggle had been sown in the 1920s, continued throughout the 1930s, and by the 1940s new violent clashes with the imperialists re-emerged. In 1945 in Uganda a general strike called by the lorry drivers for higher wages throughout the country led to a national uprising in many towns of the country, and produced waves of similar action in Kenya.

The Commission of Enquiry which was appointed to investigate these disturbances noted that all classes of the people supported the strike, including the 'intelligentsia' who according to the Report 'also had grievances'. Although it blamed the uprising upon 'agitators' and politics, it noted that there was an 'economic factor' which appeared to apply 'throughout the country'. This economic factor was the high price of clothing and food, 'since clothing forms a larger part of their annual family budget'. The Report noted that before the war Japanese-dumped cotton piecegoods were selling in Uganda 'at phenomenally low prices and the Africans had reaped the benefit'. The War had eliminated this 'unfair competition' from Japan, and British textiles in the country were more expensive than the former Japanese goods by as much as 250%, representing an increase in the price of cloth from Shs. 4/35 per yard to Shs. 13/35 per yard. Continuing in the usual obscurantist manner of the exploiter, the Report went on:

> Black marketeering undoubtedly exists but the Price Controller informed me that the Shs. 4/35 figure was one which bore no real relation to the economic cost of production and that, fantastic though it may seem, a rise in price of some 250% over the artificially low figure i authorized as being justified by the now existing conditions due to war and cessation of dumping.[55]

These 'existing conditions' under which British monopoly operated and the 'real economic costs' which it bore were the very conditions we have been analysing. The people were now beginning to challenge the system in a violent way.

That is why this strike formed the watershed between the old forms of struggle and the future ones. Four years later, in 1949, the peasants with their own organization, the Bataka Party, joined in the struggle with demands for democratic representation on the basis of free elections, better prices for their produce, release of those deported during the 1945 strikes, and the dismissal of oppressive chiefs. The events of 1949 had themselves been foreshadowed by agitation by the Bataka Party, which was also the leader of the 1949 uprising against the proposals made by the Colonial Office in Papers 191 and 210 of the High Commission. The slogan *Tuwakanya Olupapula Bibiri Mukumi* ('we Oppose Paper 210')[56] became one of the major focus-points of the anti-colonial struggle. Despite various efforts by British imperialism to crush this anti-colonial struggle, political independence was finally granted to the people of Uganda in 1962. The intermediate stages adopted before this date — permitting a measure of African representation in the Uganda Legislative Council from 1945 leading to a virtual majority by 1960 — are precisely what Raisman regrets as creating 'strains and stresses' in the High Commission arrangement.

In Kenya, as well, the flagrantly exploitative and oppressive system, which resulted in the dispossession of the people's lands and their forceable employment on settler lands, attracted its counter-action, namely the violent reaction of the people. Banned as a subversive organization, the Kikuyu Central Association went underground. Its leaders together with those of the Taita and Kamba sister associations were arrested and detained.[57] The formation of the East African Trades Union Congress in Nairobi by Fred Kubai and Makhan Singh (East Africa's dedicated workers' organizer and leader) in 1950, marked a new phase in the struggle of the people against imperialism. The arrest of the two leaders of the E.A.T.U.C. sparked off an 18-day spontaneous general strike in Nairobi, in which demands were made for the release of Makhan Singh, Fred Kubai and Chege Kibachia. Further demands were made for increases in wages, cessation of arrests of workers, abolition of bye-laws oppressing taxi-drivers and 'freedom for all workers and freedom of East African territories'.[58]

Already in 1948 the 'squatters' in the Kenya Highlands had been initiating new forms of struggle against colonialism. As conditions on the farms were becoming harsher and harsher, so also the struggle intensified. New regulations requiring 'squatters' to be permanently resident on the farms and to work solely as labourers led to the consciousness that armed struggle was the only way out. The eviction of 5,000 Soysambu 'squatters' who refused *en bloc* to sign the new contract under the new regulations[59] was a significant factor. The declaring of the state of emergency by the colonial state on 20 October 1952 sparked off the armed struggle. The right of the people of Kenya to self-determination was finally recognized in 1963. Efforts to arrest and deport 183 leading members of the Kenya African Union, and to carry out acts of terror against the population, including turning whole villages into prison camps, did not stop the forces of national independence. In the words of Makhan Singh: 'A new chapter had begun. An imperialist colonial war was now on against the people of Kenya. A new situation had arisen not only for the national movement, but also for the trade union movement.'[60] This new situation led to the collapse of colonialism. So that when Oliver Lyttelton, the British Colonial Secretary, declared in 1953 that 'the day was not far off' when a federation of East Africa would become a reality, he was clearly living in dreamworld, his 'political instincts defective'.[61] British bilateral integration of the region was clearly coming to its end.

Nor was the struggle of the people of Tanganyika and Zanzibar lacking in intensity. Beginning in 1929, elements of the petty bourgeoisie had already taken the initial steps of organizing the people with the formation of the Tanganyika African Association (TAA). The rise of local associations was due to the people's opposition to rural oppression.[62] The colonialists' use of the native authorities through the fraudulent policy of indirect rule under the Native Authorities Ordinance 'for the peace, good order and welfare of the natives' was exposed by these associations, particularly after the Second World War when various 'development schemes' were established under the Colonial Development and Welfare Fund.

The Nationalist Movement

Resistance in this period was put in sharp relief by the famous activities of the Meru people in resisting the acquisition of their lands for European settlement. The Meru Land Case became the rallying point for the nationalists, drawing the attention of the United Nations Trusteeship Council. The real national movement emerged, however, with the Tanganyika African National Union (TANU) in 1954, amalgamating most of the local associations including the TAA.

There thus was established a solid foundation for opposing British imperialist schemes for perpetuating colonial rule. For instance, in a pamphlet written in 1950, Julius Nyerere, then a student at Edinburgh and a prominent leader in the TAA, opposed closer union under the proposals made by the Colonial Office in Colonial Papers 191 and 210, on the ground that this would lead to the domination by Kenya settlers of the three territories.[63] The demand for representation in the territories' Legislative Councils and other bodies was increasingly met as opposition mounted; by 1958 a majority of elected African representatives was possible, thus making it increasingly difficult for the imperialists to continue their oppression of the people of East Africa under the decaying imperialist system of bilateral integration of the regions. The recognition of the right of the people of Tanganyika to political self-determination in 1961 marked the beginning of the collapse of the East African High Commission when, in recognition of Tanganyika's independence a *troika* system was formed for the ministerial running of the new East African Common Services Organization.

Thus, between 1961 and 1963, the three territories with elected governments began to shape the future of East Africa, albeit in a situation involving new forms of exploitation under multilateral imperialism. It is natural, in fact that an imperialist integrationist like Raisman would view such developments with regret, since it implied the breaking down of the very sinews of political control for economic exploitation. Many imperialist economists and even petty-bourgeois elements argued that this 'drift towards disintegration', inherent in the struggle for national independence and the right to self-determination, was 'bad'. For us, the whole movement towards national independence was but *a natural one*. National consciousness among the exploited and oppressed people in each of the territories arose because capitalism had been introduced among the people on the basis of a defined territory and population. Horizontal integration on an East African scale merely reinforced territorial relations as seen concretely at the level of production by each of the social classes struggling against the system. This perspective manifested itself in the struggle for *political control* over each territory. The struggles that arose, therefore, naturally took on a parochial character — and then a national (territorial) character as the maximum expression of such struggle in the national movements UNC, TANU, KANU. The implication of this was that each fought for and won its *national* independence.

This was effectively preparing the way for the development of *national economies* as counterweights to an imperialist economy directed from the metropole. The 'national' bourgeoisie and petty bourgeoisie saw this as the best shell in which to develop commodity production, and this is why Lenin in his *The Right of Nations to Self-determination* emphasized the need for the creation of a national state against a dominant imperialist state:

> For the complete victory of commodity production, the bourgeoisie *must capture the home market* and there must be politically united territories whose population speak a single language . . . . Therefore the tendency of every national movement is toward the formation of *national states,* under which requirements of modern capitalism are best satisfied. . . For the entire civilised world, the national state is *typical* . . . . . Consequently, if we want to grasp the meaning of self-determination of nations, it means the *political separation of these nations from alien bodies, and the formation of an independent national state.* [First and last emphasis added — Author]

Of course, this political transformation created further 'strains' and 'stresses' in the regional politico-legal structures. The achievement of political self-determination by each of the territories was therefore bound to have a disintegrative effect on these structures — particularly given the new forces of transnational corporate integration which took advantage of this transformation to continue the *economic* rule of finance capital. It is this change that the U.S. monopolies took note of and prepared to exploit.

As we have already noted, Britain herself was being brought under the new discipline of multilateral imperialism led by the U.S. By 1958 she was compelled to integrate herself more completely and make sterling fully convertible in dollars under the I.M.F. rules. She now came under the direction of the International Monetary Fund. As the three East African territories began to achieve their independence, Britain took steps to integrate them into the new international monetary arrangement. She set up 'trust funds' under the East African Currency Board to pay for the subscriptions of each of the territories as 'membership fees' in the I.M.F., the World Bank and the African

Development Bank.[64] From now on, the region had to comply with the parity requirements under Article IV of the Fund's Articles, and the convertibility procedures under Articles VII and XIV.

Moreover, under the new order the British Government invited the World Bank to work out development plans for each of the three countries and prepare them for the new multilateral financing that the Bank was to supervise along with the I.M.F. These plans have already been referred to in passing and will be examined in detail in Part Two.[65] They were intended to create a smooth handover from the old to the new system. Under the requirements of another multilateral institution, the British Government also applied for and joined on their behalf the new international trade organization, the General Agreement on Trade and Tariffs (GATT). Under the Articles of GATT, the three countries had to grant the Most-Favoured-Nation treatment to all the member countries of GATT without discrimination, and to regulate their quotas on imports non-discriminatorily and render regional arrangements subject to the rules and supervision of GATT and the I.M.F.

The weakening of British imperialism was also witnessed in East Africa by the diversion of exports to non Sterling Areas in order to earn dollars. From 1950 onwards, British trade with East Africa began to decline in relative terms as the new multilateral rules began to crystallize. The World Bank Report on Kenya noted that 'The fall in the proportion of trade between Kenya and British Commonwealth countries, particularly the United Kingdom has been the most striking development, although these countries remain Kenya's major trading partners.'[66] Despite the fact that under the Congo Basin Treaties, East Africa was a 'free trade area' for the signatories, the various integrative mechanisms we have examined increasingly had put Britain in a hegemonic position in the region. This change in orientation of trade was therefore significant, as the World Bank correctly commented. Trade with West Germany, Italy, Japan, and the socialist bloc increased in all the three territories.[67] This diversion was also true of sources of finance but more pronounced in the multilateral period proper, as we shall see.

The influence of the U.S. in the region had already manifested itself in the 1950s. Dishing out hand-outs in the form of 'foreign aid' was its way of announcing itself in East Africa as a neo-colonial power. Between 1946 and 1961, the U.S. disbursed $12.7 million to the three East African territories as 'aid',[68] so as to prepare the ground for its own entry and that of its transnational monopolies into the region. Kenya was given the bulk of this amount, $7.3 million, while Tanzania took $4.4 million and Uganda $1 million. The new transnational corporate integration now began its process of re-orienting the production activities of each of the new nation-states, thereby integrating them with transnational production strategies worked out on global scale. In Part Two we analyse the pressures thus brought on the existing regional structures and their ultimate collapse.

References

1. A. Shonfield, *British Economic Policy Since the War*, (London, Penguin, 1958), p.15.
2. R.N. Gardner, *Sterling-Dollar Diplomacy* (New York, McGraw-Hill, 1969), pp.199-207.
3. D.W. Nabudere, *The Political Economy of Imperialism* (London, Zed, 1978), p.146.
4. The full text of this agreement appears as an appendix to Gardner, op. cit., pp.387-92.
5. P.W. Bell, *The Sterling Area in the Post-War Period* (Oxford, Clarendon, 1958), pp.51-64.
6. Colonial Office, *Memorandum on the Sterling Assets of the British Colonies*, Colonial No. 298 (London, H.M.S.O., 1953); see also A.R. Conan, *The Rationale of the Sterling Area* (London, Macmillan, 1961).
7. Colonial Office, op. cit., p.1.
8. Bell, op. cit., pp.276-7.
9. C. Cross, *The Fall of the British Empire* (London, Paladin, 1970), p.276.
10. Bell, op. cit., pp.271-2.
11. Ibid., p.271.
12. Ibid., pp.54-5.
13. Quoted in Conan, op. cit., p.65.
14. Colonial Office, op. cit., p.2.
15. A. Hazelwood, 'Sterling Balances and the Colonial Currency System', *Economic Journal,* No. 62,(December 1952).
16. Ibid., p.944.
17. Bell, op. cit., pp.274-6.
18. Ibid., p.277.
19. Cross, op. cit., p.276.
20. Cmd 9475, p.148.
21. L. Schnittger, 'Taxation and Tax Policy in East Africa', in P. Martin, *Financial Aspects of Development in East Africa.*
22. Cmd 9475, p.82.
23. I.B.R.D:, *The Economic Development of Uganda* (Baltimore, Johns Hopkins, 1962), p.30.
24. A. Cohen, *British Policy in Changing Africa* (London, Routledge and Kegan Paul, 1960), p.61.
25. I.B.R.D., op. cit., p.31.
26. Ibid., p.34.
27. Ibid., pp.60-8.
28. Ibid., pp.70-1.
29. M. Yaffey, *Balance of Payments Problems of a Developing Country: Tanzania* (Munich, Welt Forum, 1968). pp.97-8.
30. Ibid., pp.64-5.
31. I.B.R.D., *The Economic Development of Tanganyika* (Baltimore, Johns Hopkins, 1962), p.43.
32. Ibid., p.44.
33. P. Ndegwa, *The Common Market and Development in East Africa* (Nairobi, E.A.P.H., 1965), p.98.
34. East Africa, *Report of the Economic and Fiscal Commission,* Cmd.

1279 (London, H.M.S.O., 1961), p.17.
35. Ibid., p.18.
36. Ibid., p.21.
37. Ibid., p.13.
38. Ibid., p.23.
39. Ibid., p.24.
40. Ibid., pp.24-5.
41. Ndegwa, op. cit., p.107.
42. Ibid., pp.136-50.
43. Ibid., p.26.
44. Ibid., pp.65-70, paras, 203-16.
45. Ndegwa, op. cit., p.105.
46. Cmnd 1279, op. cit., p.30, para. 103.
47. Ibid., p.30, para. 100; p.64, para. 199.
48. K. Marx, *Capital*, (Moscow, Progress Publishers, 1971), Vol. III, p.106.
49. Ibid., pp.117-8.
50. K. Marx, *The Poverty of Philosophy* (Moscow, Progress Publishers, 1955), pp.36-7, 46, 131.
51. Ndegwa, op. cit., p.107.
52. Cmnd 1279, op. cit., p.69 , para. 212.
53. Ibid., p.14.
54. Ibid.
55. U.P., *Report of the Commission of Inquiry into the Disturbances which occured in Uganda during January 1945*, (Entebbe, Government Printer, 1946).
56. This is reference to Colonial No. 210 entitled: *Inter-Territorial Organisation in East Africa; Revised Proposals.* (London, H.M.S.O. 1947). See Chapter Four.
57. D.L. Barnett and Karari Njama, *Mau Mau From Within* (New York, Monthly Review, 1966), p.39.
58. Makhan Singh, *History of Kenya's Trade Union Movement to 1952* (Nairobi, E.A.P.H., 1969), pp.268-87.
59. F. Furedi, 'The Social Composition of the Mau Mau Movement in the White Highlands', in *The Journal of Peasant Studies*, Vol. 1, July 1974, pp.486-505.
60. Makhan Singh, op. cit., p.320.
61. C. Cross, op. cit., p.294.
62. L. Cliffe, 'Nationalism and the reaction to enforced Agricultural Change during the Colonial Period', in Cliffe and Saul, *Socialism in Tanzania* (E.A.P.H., 1972), pp.17-23.
63. J.K. Nyerere, *Freedom and Unity* (Oxford, OUP, 1966) pp.24-5.
64. East African Currency Board, *Annual Reports* for 1965 and 1966, pp.62 and 88 respecitvely.
65. I.B.R.D., *The Economic Development of Tanganyika, The Economic Development of Uganda, The Economic Development of Kenya,* (Baltimore, Johns Hopkins, 1961, 1962, 1963).
66. I.B.R.D., Ibid., p.26.
67. M. Yaffey, op. cit., pp.64-65.
68. V. McKay, 'The African Operations of he United States Government Agencies,' in W. Goldschmidt, *The United States and Africa*, (New York Praeger, 1963), pp.273-98.

Part Two

Integration Under Multilateral Imperialism

5. Multilateralism as a System

The New System of Imperialism

The collapse of bilateral imperialism implied the rise of a new phase of imperialism within the stage of modern imperialism that Lenin analysed.[1] It was distinguishable from the previous phase in many respects. First, the new phase implied the end of direct colonization of territories by particular imperialist powers. This was the result of the anti-colonial struggle which manifested itself in both the strengths and the weaknesses of the main opposing forces, namely imperialism and the people.

The strength of the people lay in utilizing the weaknesses of bilateral imperialism to obtain a unity of all national forces. In this lay the weakness of its dialectical opposite, namely the weakness of bilateral imperialism to withstand this unity and contain the struggle in order for British finance capital to maintain its hegemony. The weakness of the people, on the other hand, lay in the working class being unable at this stage to consolidate the unity in order to sustain the struggle until victory was realized against all forms of imperialism; and in this lay the strength of its dialectical opposite, namely imperialism, which was able as a result to regroup its forces to withstand this struggle and to bring the people within the ambit of continued economic exploitation and domination under multilateral imperialism.

But this strength of imperialism was only obtained at another level and this brings about the second distinguishing attribute of the new phase of imperialism. This was that, in order to withstand the opposition of the people, the imperialist powers had to regroup and 'unite'. But this 'unity' was obtained at the cost of having to accept U.S. hegemony, under whose military and other superstructural umbrellas they were able to operate in the new phase. From super-powers, some of them became second-rate imperialist powers, while the U.S. became the hegemonic super-power.

The U.S. drew its strength from the position its finance capital had achieved by taking advantage of the Second World War. This concentration of capital was further facilitated by the strategies it devised to reconstruct war-torn Europe through the Marshall Plan. The resulting investments that poured into Europe were in fact the entry of U.S. capital. Furthermore, the rise of the former colonies as new nation-states, but without national capital

95

of their own, also gave the U.S. a further point of entry. At first, it brought in military 'assistance' to build up the new neo-colonial armies and later economic 'aid' to soften this nationalism. With the weakening of their national bourgeoisie, a spate of private investments poured in, and so consolidated the phase we have designated 'multilateral imperialism'.

The multilateral character of this new phase of modern imperialism was further concretized in the form of new institutional arrangements. The most important of these were the three international economic institutions which came in to supervise and lay down rules of conduct for international capital. These were the World Bank (IBRD), the I.M.F. and GATT. These institutions, as we already saw briefly at the end of Part One, emphasized non-discrimination in outlets for investments (the World Bank), multilateralism on the basis of the Most-Favoured-Nation principle in all trade arrangements consistent with the level of development of international capital (GATT), and non-discrimination in convertibility of international currencies to maintain the highest level of international production, investment and trade (I.M.F.). In these ways, bilateral structures were rendered obsolete.

The impact of these institutional arrangements on the individual economies of the three East African economies in this phase has been shown at greater length in Volume I.[2] Suffice it to say here, that these institutions further strengthened the penetration of U.S. and other imperialist finance capital in East Africa.[3]

The penetration of U.S. finance capital in Europe, Japan and other capitalist countries, as well as the Third World, led to a restructuring of the capitalist enterprise. Exemplified by the rise and perfection of the transnational corporate monopoly, capital was now concentrated and centralized at very high levels on a world scale, East Africa included. The corporate monopoly had its apex in one or other of the imperialist countries, directed by a President or Chairman and a Board of Directors down through a staff and line management running through all the five continents and countries of the capitalist world, through branches and subsidiaries, joint ventures, licences, distributors and agents. By these means the monopoly was able to export capital and to engage in production, to control markets and have access to sources of raw materials on a world scale from one centre.

The Consequences for East Africa

The implications for any significant economic and political development in East Africa were serious. A new type of vertical integration came into being, but this time at the level of the single transnational firm which tied down entire neo-colonial economies.[4] Since any efforts to consolidate the national economies were thereby ruled out, so too were all attempts to retain and perfect horizontal and regional political and economic structures. Even the form of the monopoly firm itself and its institutions disintegrated in the face of the new global monopoly forms and institutions, and the means of competition they instigated.

The strategies and tactics of this new vertical integration have been explained in Volume I,[5] and here we deal with only their effects on regional economic co-operation. Each monopoly needed to make ever-increasing profits on its investments and responded by minimizing costs. Any barriers — of whatever kind and wherever they were found — were ruthlessly eliminated. The removal of these barriers was very much facilitated by the policies of the neo-colonial states at the level of law, as for instance the duty-free import-ation of capital goods (machinery, intermediate goods and raw materials) and the incentives, protections and guarantees granted to attract money capital for the puchase of capital goods. Equally tax reliefs and control of labour through subservient unions and labour law aided the transnational monopoly firm in its integrative activities and weakened whatever minimal possibilities there were for any national capital to emerge in its own right.

But, however convenient these legal mechanisms, it was the sheer force of the objective economic laws of monopoly capital which promoted the inte-gration of East African economies by these firms. Indeed, the invention of the superstructural legal mechanisms can be attributed to these objective economic laws. Objective laws, which operated to fix wages and prices and rates of profits, as well as the resulting competition, could not be legislated *against,* or even *for,* as such. Through the operation of these economic laws, assisted by the mechanisms of the legal system, the monopolies were able to exploit and siphon off to the metropolitan countries the resources produced in East Africa. This single fact exposed and laid bare the illusion of 'national' economic development of the three countries, as we shall see in the next few chapters.

All these mechanisms continued to impose on East Africa a division of labour for supplying raw materials to the imperialist world and for supplying markets for their products. Attempts to increase the contribution of industry over agriculture were unsuccessful; instead the relation of peasant production to the international bourgeoisie was even more reinforced under the new phase of imperialism. Moreover, the little industrialization that was effected was turned to the advantage of transnational finance capital. Import substi-tution, encouraged by the treaty regime through the 'transfer tax' system and the East African Development Bank, in fact helped monopoly capital to consolidate itself in the region.

Transnational monopolies tend to be located in manufacturing industries,[6] taking the entire world market as the basis for its production strategies. All research and development is carried out on the basis of this world market, and consequently the monopolies take various activities throughout the world as their production points. Thus strategies in East Africa necessarily reflect the dynamic of concentration of capital on a world scale. As technological development in a large number of products is standardized, the pressure to establish foreign production units intensifies backed up by the desire to protect or prolong earlier competitive trading positions based on already established preferential or captive markets or technological leads. As the technological lead is lost through standardization or declonization, a complicated scramble emerges between the newcomers, who think they can take advantage of monopoly 'rights' such as brand name or patents, and the previous market holders.

The net effect is that strategies normally associated with 'economies of scale' are in fact the levers by which a transnational monopoly operating in a number of countries becomes hegemonic. Cost is lessened on the basis of cost claculations on the world scale; the more standardized the product and its technology, the more the need for a captive market to assure monopoly. In this process, the transnational production points become part of the stream and the new vertical integration of economic units takes place. As Vernon and Wells have correctly observed:

> The process of vertical integration often leads to the multinationalization of operations. As enterprises move upstream or downstream to complete their vertical structure, they often reach beyond the national economy in which the integrating process began. Either they need new sources of supply not to be had in their part of the world, or they need markets which do not readily exist at home. In either case, national enterprises commonly become multinational enterprises as they pursue the integration strategy.[7]

The import-substitution industrialization adopted in the neo-colony on the basis of joint ventures, licences or management deals, etc., enables the transnational monopoly to institute this type of production as simply one unit in its global production and marketing activities, whether with state bodies or private individual entrepreneurs. The rise of the nation-state which aims at developoing a national economy, in conditions when the national bourgeoisies are economically weak, in this way actually assists the transnational monopoly to strengthen its hold on this 'national' industry. The drive for capital intensity characteristic of the neo-colonial import-substituted industry is, for the transnational monopoly, the very struggle to sell its standardized products by taking advantage of the law of numbers (economies of scale) on a world rather than a national scale. Any act of 'nationalization' in one country can be offset by expansion elsewhere.[8]

Apart from considerations like size of the country, level of per capita income and the density of population, the issue of transport costs and accessibility of export markets play an important part in deciding the size of the plant and therefore the possibility of import substitution. But the degree of protection and incentives, as well as guarantees granted to an enterprise by the neo-colonial states,[9] are also important. And such protection normally goes to the enterprise with the best all-round resources, which will invariably be the transnational monopoly enterprise. One effect of this is that products which otherwise would be best produced in one large plant will be duplicated in a number of countries or even within one country, after a 'threshold' period. Industries such as cement, beer, nitrogenous fertilizer, and rubber tyres, as well as automobile assembly are cases in point.[10] The automobile industry in Latin America is usually quoted: whereas engineering and economic calculations suggest that vehicle manufacture could be obtained at low unit costs with levels of output as high as 500,000 units a year or more, yet in the whole of Latin America (where regional arrangements existed) in the year 1967 there was a total output of cars and trucks equal to only 651,900 and the number of production points (firms) were as many as 67 in the region as a whole.[11] The average output in each plant was far less than 100,000 units a year – let alone 500,000. Venezuela alone had 13 firms producing 60,300 vehicles, i.e. an average of 4,638. Chile, too, had 19 production points which produced a mere 16,400 vehicles (an average of 863 per firm).[12] Another example, this time of an African country, is Ivory Coast where an assembly plant produced 2,190 vehicles a year (average 6 vehicles a day) and where costs 'were, not surprisingly, higher than in France'.[13]

The East African experience in integration brings to light and confirms much of the above analysis. Rweyemamu has shown how the power normally associated with monopolistic competition manifested itself in Tanzania in a perverse industrialization between 1962 and 1971. Extrapolating from the Nigerian and Tanzanian experience, he argued that in a situation (in this case a colonial situation) where overseas market shares were small and the technical levels low, there was no urgent need for import substitution. As the pressure for markets heightened and there was a threat to the existing market, or where there was a demand to expand by new monopolies into the new market, many companies which had originally imported goods into the market were now prepared (given a level of protection) to vie for the right to set up import substitution plants in the former import market.[14]

Within a few years of these conditions prevailing, Rweyemamu noted a 'clustering' of textile industries in Tanzania,[15] as it now became possible, on the basis of the protection extended to the transnational monopolies competing with one another, to invest in these industries on the basis of joint ventures, or as wholly owned subsidiaries. For the weak bourgeoisies in East Africa, such industrialization was seen as 'national' industry, but for the transnational monopoly it was merely one of its production units, investment outlets, and/or markets for its products – both machinery (including intermediate goods) and raw materials. The importation of intermediate goods under the tariff system of the East African Community was duty free, so that as far as these monopolies were concerned, the markets and capital export outlets were wide open to them despite the common external tariff.

We will see later in the analysis that, as these ties with the transnational firms were strengthened (as evidenced by the increase in the investment of foreign capital and the increase in the imports of machinery, chemicals, intermediate goods as well as raw materials for import substitution), trade links of the member states of the East African Common Market with one another were reduced. This was due to the constraints imposed by foreign exchange shortages which increasingly went to pay the transnational monopolies for their imports, earnings on their investments, as well as charges for insurance, carriage etc. As this problem of foreign exchange shortage intensified, each of the member states imposed exchange and trade controls against the others. With these developments, petty rivalries intensified among the politicians in the region about lack of 'benefits' or 'losses' being incurred through membership of the regional integrative scheme. Yet all this squabbling obscured the real issues of imperialist exploitation and domination of the entire region by transnational monopolies.

Thus East Africa continued, at the level of each of the national economies, to be an appendage of the world imperialist system, supplying the imperialist countries with raw materials and food products. These were being paid for at low wages to the producers — the poor peasants and workers of East Africa — which in turn was reflected as a problem of deterioration in the terms of trade. Meanwhile the monopolies continued to sell freely manufactures and raw materials for the import-substitution industries. In this way, outlets for the export of finance capital which controlled the production and markets of the region were maintained.

Table 6
The Structure of East African Trade, 1972

SITC Section	SITC Sections as % of Total Inter-state Trade Flows	SITC Sections as % of Total Domestic Exports	Total Net Imports
Food and Live Animals	25	58	8
Beverages and Tobacco	4	1	—
Inedible Crude Materials (except fuels)	4	24	2
Mineral Fuels, Lubricants and Related Materials	18	8	9
Animal and Vegetable Oils and Fats	2	—	2
Chemicals	13	2	10
Manufactured Goods	25	6	24
Machinery and Transport Equipment	4	—	35
Miscellaneous Manufactured Articles	6	—	8
Commodities and Transactions not classified according to kind	—	—	1
Total Trade Flows	*100*	*100*	*100*

Source: *Review of Economic Integration Activities Within the East African Community 1973* (Common Market & Economic Affairs Secretariat, East Afr. Literature Bureau, Nairobi, 1973), p.4.

All this is demonstrated in Table 6 which shows that the importation of machinery and transport equipment, manufactured goods, and chemicals constituted about 70% of all the imports of the region; while exports of food and crude materials accounted for 82% of all domestic exports in the year 1972. The inter-state trade, it can be seen, only constituted 25% in manufactures from the import-substitution industries which were dominated by the transnational monopolies. Other items of inter-state trade included the re-exports of imports such as chemicals from the imperialist countries with very little value added to them (13%), mineral lubricants from the refineries (18%), and food products (mainly baby foods and tinned foods) sold and monopolized by the transnational firms under brand names (25% of the inter-state trade in the region). But this trade was only possible through pitched competition battles in the region between the transnational giants, which in turn implied political rivalry between the three territories. This combination of rivalries between the monopolies and between the national forces dominated by these monopolies implied strife at the level of nation-state politics. This explains why the regional structures collapsed, despite the fact that the monopolies were gaining both at the level of the territorial economy and at the regional trade level. We analyse more of these developments in the following chapters.

References

1. V.I. Lenin, *Imperialism, The Highest Stage of Capitalism.*
2. See Volume I, Chapter Six.
3. This is summarized from our *The Political Economy of Imperialism* (London, Zed, 1978). Parts IV and V.
4. See Volume I, Chapter Seven.
5. See Volume I, Chapter Six.
6. R. Vernon and L.T. Wells, *Economic Environment of International Business,* 2nd ed. (New Jersey, Prentice-Hill, 1977), p.4.
7. Ibid., p.14.
8. Ibid.
9. R.B. Sutcliffe, *Industry and Development* (London, Addison Wesley, 1971), p.198.
10. Ibid., pp.216-29.
11. Ibid., pp.226-7.
12. Ibid., p.227.
13. Ibid.
14. J. Rweyemamu, *Underdevelopment and Industrialization in Tanzania,* (Nairobi, Heinemann, 1973), pp.98-105.
15. Ibid.

6. The Politics of East African Federation, 1958–65

The Pan African Ideal

Manifested specifically in the Pan African Movement of the African Continent and the African diaspora, the revolutionary idea that the African people must unite emerges with the development of the anti-imperialist sentiment of the oppressed peoples of Africa. The ideology opposed the enslavement of those Africans who found themselves away from their homelands, exploited and despised. The work of people like Marcus Garvey, Du Bois and others either advocated the return of the former slaves to Africa or the struggle of the Afro-American people for freedom and equality within the United States itself and for unity of the African race with those still in the African homeland.

It was also an ideology for the struggle against colonialism, national oppression and exploitation of the Africans in Africa. Nkrumah and others had, during their student days in Britain, come into contact with the earlier movement in America and a series of conferences, beginning with the Manchester Conference in 1945, began to give more concrete organizational form to the struggle for the independence of Africa from colonialism.[1] The common bonds of race and exploitation forged a unity between the two flanks of the movement to embody the idea of Pan Africanism. As one scholar of the movement has noted:

> European racism heightened by European imperialism gave Africans a new conception of themselves: they began to see themselves no longer in terms of small communities but as people belonging to a despised 'race'. African race consciousness thus generated became one of the early manifestations of Pan African ideology at its inception.[2]

In Africa the grass roots of this ideology lay in the arousing of *national* not *racial* consiousness. The national consciousness was the result of a struggle against alien exploitation going back to the time capitalist production had taken root throughout Africa in the 1920s. As Stalin[3] pointed out long ago, the development of national consciousness in the modern world is associated with the development of capitalism. In Europe it did so against the old forces of feudalism. In Africa, on the other hand, as elsewhere in the Third World, it did so as a revolt against imperialism and foreign domination. This was bound to be so since capitalism did not emerge spontaneously on the African soil through the indigenous confrontation of social and productive forces. On the contrary, it developed as a result of the export of foreign-owned goods and monopoly capital.

It is not surprising, therefore, that Pan Africanism represented at the African end a nationalism against foreign domination and therefore against monopoly capitalism and for national independence. A nationalism that arose on the basis of anti-imperialism in the era of the ascendancy of socialism against capitalism could only lead to socialism in a much shorter span of struggle than in the imperialist world. This is true despite the fact that such a socialism would take longer to build than it would otherwise have done if indigenous capitalism, outside the domination of foreign monopoly capitalism, had developed independently. But such a development to socialism would still be one through stages. The first transitional stage represented by Pan Africanism was the winning of political independence, but this was merely a prelude to the economic struggle. Though the national movement would first combine to achieve political independence, the right to self-determination, such a right did not imply economic independence. On the contrary, the continued exploitation and domination by international finance capital required the second stage. In this, the leadership of the working class over the other classes would have to be assured before any victory for a new democratic state could be achieved.[4]

The Pan Africanist Movement in East Africa

The Pan African movement that emerged in East and Central Africa in the late 1950s reflected the weakness of the first stage. The struggle for political independence without the reality of economic independence equalled neo-colonialism. This reflected the inability of the national bourgeoisie to assert and advance their economic interests over that of international finance capital. Having no such control over production, they could not achieve the Pan African grand dream in which a united Africa would become an economic giant with a large market to withstand the competition of other continents which they desired.

But in the imperialist epoch these were illusions even if countries had had control of their national resources. But, by tracing the origins and politics of the Pan Africanist movement in the region, we shall be able to see why the grand objective of a Pan African federation in East Africa failed to materialize despite the leaders' good intentions and sentiments and the support of the broad masses of the people of the region.

The first public manifestations of the desire for unity in East and Central Africa occurred in 1958 at a meeting on the shores of Lake Victoria at Mwanza in Tanganyika. The initial steps had been taken with the convening of a meeting of African Legislative Council members from Kenya, Uganda and Tanganyika in 1957 which, although it failed to take place, nonetheless was the first step towards Mwanza.[5] In March of 1958, this sentiment was strengthened by the presence of a team of nationalists from East Africa which attended a meeting of heads of independent African states in Accra, Ghana, to observe the proceedings.

It was at this meeting that it was decided to organize the first All African Peoples' Conference in Accra in December 1958. But before this conference, the Mwanza meeting was organized and it was here that the Pan African Freedom Movement for East and Central Africa (PAFMECA) was formed by delegates from Tanganyika, Kenya, Uganda, Zanzibar and Nyasaland. Prominent among these leaders were Julius Nyerere and Tom Mboya. At this conference it was decided to set up a co-ordination freedom committee for the purpose of intensifying the political struggle against colonialism and foreign domination in the region. The objectives of the movement were:

— To foster the spirit of Pan Africanism in order to rid all the East and Central African territories of imperialism, white supremacy, economic exploitation, and social degradation by stepping up nationalist activities to achieve self-government and establish parliamentary democracy.

— To co-ordinate nationalist programmes, tactics, projects, and efforts for the speedy liberation of the said territories.

— To assist in the establishment and organization of united nationalist movements in African territories through political education, periodic conferences, and the encouragement of inter-territorial African contacts in all fields.

— To establish a joint East and Central African Freedom Fund.

— To pursue non-violence in African nationalist struggles for freedom and prosperity.

In the Freedom Charter which they adopted at the same time, they declared that freedom was 'our birthright; self-government our heritage, as sons and daughters of the free men and women' who inherited Africa for the Africans:

> It is therefore not only just but imperative that we restore our birthright for ourselves and our children and our childrens' children . . . .
> We declare that democracy must prevail throughout Africa, from Senegal to Zanzibar and from Cape to Cairo; that colonialism, the so-called partnership, apartheid, multi-racialism and white settlerism are enemies of freedom, and can be eradicated only by African nationalism, virile and unrelenting; that the right of self-determination is God-given and no man or nation is chosen by God to determine the destiny of others; that poverty, ignorance, ill-health and other human miseries cannot be satisfactorily eradicated under imperialism, but only under self-government and international co-operation on the basis of equality and mutual benefication.[6]

This concretization of nationalist sentiment in East and Central Africa enables us to see the immediate problem that confronted the nationalist movements in the region. Tom Mboya recollects that the idea of PAFMECA was 'born' during a conversation between him and Julius Nyerere, 'when he came to my two-roomed house at Ziwani location of Nairobi'. During the discussion on unity and Pan Africanism, they agreed that 'it would be good', ahead of the All Africa Peoples' Conference meeting in Accra, 'to bring together the nationalist movements through Eastern and Central Africa' to discuss the struggle for independence, because 'at that point' they were facing a 'rough period' in the struggle. The objectives they stipulated in the constitution were particularly important, 'for without unity, we were sure we would be victims of the settlers' tactics of dividing and confusing nationalists, in order to delay independence or even to establish a South African type of Government'.[7] It is for this reason, according to Mboya, that it was resolved at Mwanza that the question of East African Federation 'did not arise' at that time. Julius Nyerere also recalled[8] that PAFMECA was formed to give assistance to weaker parties in the area as well as to co-ordinate their activities to some extent.

It comes out clearly that the Pan African movement that arose at this time was concerned essentially with strategies and tactics for winning political independence. As was to become apparent later, this objective in itself tended to mean nationalism through political education, but still a nationalism at the mass level connected with concrete struggles within the boundaries demarcated by imperialism and within which imperialism exploited and oppressed the people of particular countries. What, therefore, PAFMECA was doing was in effect assisting the consolidation of this 'national' nationalism rather than Pan African nationalism. Given the weak material base of the petty bourgeoisie, such balkanization was to be accentuated by monopolistic competition. It is also important to note that at this point PAFMECA, and each of the national movements, emphasized non-violent methods of struggle. In this way, the politics of compromise between the various elements leading the national movement and imperialism placed limitations on the freedom movement in the anti-imperialist struggle and thus helped to maintain the economic domination of the region.

The preoccupation with each colonial territory's *national* independence was also reflected in the Accra Conference in December that year, where the issue of Pan African unity was reduced to the establishment of 'closer unity within five defined regions' within which the nationalist movements would 'work together' to become independent 'and then co-operate in a plan for economic integration and political federation'. Mboya recalls further: 'When these regions had been established, the whole continent could come together to form the United States of Africa. Thus PAFMECA'S plan fell very much in to line with what was later decided in Accra.'[9]

Perhaps it was the fear that this policy of separate independence before federation would in the end frustrate unity that inspired Julius Nyerere in 1960 to offer to delay Tanganyika's independence if this would bring about an East African Federation at the same time. However unrealistic, this offer is nevertheless significant in the politics of the period. In a pamphlet written for the Second Conference of the Independent African States as Addis Ababa in June 1960, Nyerere pointed out that in the struggle against colonialism the fundamental unity of the African people was evident and deeply felt. It was forged against an outside government. But if the triumph in this battle was to be followed by an equal triumph against the forces of neo-imperialism, he forewarned, then this unity must be strengthened and maintained. The feeling of unity which now exists could, however, be whittled away if each country got its independence separately and became open to 'temptations of nationhood' and the intrigues of those who found their strength in the weakness of small nations.[10] There was one way in which this unity of opposition should become a unity of construction, he added, and that was through the combination of the unity and freedom movements to enable the achievement of independence of the East African territories as one unit at the earliest possible moment. This should be done through a decision of the people expressed through their elected representatives at a stage when they have achieved Responsible Government or 'full internal power' which could in Tanzania be reached early in 1961.

He refuted the arguments raised 'by some of our friends' in Uganda who claimed that we must each 'put our separate houses in order first' before we can contemplate federation. Although he 'accepted' this argument to the extent that it would be silly to add chaos to chaos, yet we could all be satisfied that our houses were in order after Responsible Government and not after independence: 'The argument of *bado kidogo* – "you are not ready" – is the same argument the imperialists have always used to delay our independence,' he added.[11] If the advocates of separate independence were consistent, they would, for instance, 'allow the dismemberment of Uganda now and try to put it together later. The suggestion is as illogical in the case of East Africa as in the case of Uganda.'[12] He added:

> I know that the advocates of delay will reply that Uganda is different. It is one country already, whereas East Africa consists of different units. Admitted. But we are adjacent countries, governed by the same colonial power doing many things in common already. The difference is one of degree and not one of kind. [Later still, he added:] Supposing my claim is correct, that separate independence would tend to perpetuate the balkanization of our region, and therefore Tanganyika's separate independence would contribute to this perpetuation of a balkanized East Africa, I, for one, would be prepared to postpone the celebration of Tanganyika's independence for a few months and celebrate East Africa's independence in 1962 rather than take the risk of perpetuating the balkanization of East Africa.[13]

It is quite clear that Nyerere's arguments in this pamphlet were still very much influenced by a rigorous interpretation of the Pan African ideal. The realities of the actual struggles within each of the territories were in fact to compel a different direction to the developments in the region. Although at the Mbale PAFMECA meeting, held early in 1960, the Chairman of the Conference, Tom Mboya, said the time was now ripe to agree and plan a federation of East African states, these real pressures intervened to delay the federation almost *ad infinitum*.

The events that took place at the time of these conferences confounded Nyerere's expectations and in 1963, when he addressed the Conference of Independent States at which the Charter for African Unity was drawn up and adopted as the basic document for the Organization of African Unity, he now modified his views on the speed for achieving African unity, emphasizing that it was 'a process', just as Africa's independence had been a process. He stated:

> There is not going to be a god who will bring about African Unity
> by merely willing unity and saying 'Let there be unity'. It is not in the
> nature of human action that the will and fulfilment of that will be
> simultaneous. That is not in our power, that is only in the power of
> gods. In human action there is an inevitable process between the will
> to do and the fulfilment of the action . . . . None of us is prepared in
> the name of unity to invite Napoleon to come and bring about unity
> by conquest. We are therefore left with one method of bringing about
> African Unity and that method is the method of free government . . .
> Let us accept that Charter as our first step.[14]

Actually it was also not in the power of 'the gods' nor of Napoleon to bring about such unity, for God, if He is to be presumed to be on the side of the downtrodden people of Africa, would have willed that the African people unite. But He didn't and such unity as was achieved was done on the basis of the struggle of the people against a common enemy, as Nyerere himself indeed acknowledged. Nor was unity through conquest by a Napoleon possible, for that would have been imperialistic and would have been resisted just like the federation that was imposed on the people of Central Africa.

But Nyerere's recognition of the lag between human will and action does reveal that, lag or no lag, not all human will can be realized by human action unless material constraints are first recognized and grappled with. These are the constraints which, in this period and later after 1963, explain why East African federation, and indeed African unity, simply could not have been achieved. What were these realities?

The Political Constraints

Before we explore these constraints, it is important to note that there was a disunity in the ranks of the nationalist parties in Zanzibar, Kenya and Uganda which could not be willed away even by the idea of Pan African unity. The situation was different in Tanganyika where a basic unity existed in TANU. Without going into the intricacies of each of the nationalist parties in East Africa, it is possible to pinpoint a few main elements of discord.

Efforts to bring about the unity of the Zanzibar parties to which

107

PAFMECA addressed itself began with a mission led by its first chairman, Francis Khamisi of Mombasa. The three parties were the Zanzibar Nationalist Party (Z.N.P.), the Zanzibar People's Progressive Party (Z.P.P.P.) and the Afro-Shirazi Party (A.S.P.). They represented two distinctive forces that characterized the Zanzibar colonial setting, although their class nature was obscured by all three parties' origins in racially structured political associations: the Indian Association for Hindus, an Arab Association for Arabs, an African Association for Africans and a Shirazi Association for Africans claiming descent from 19th-Century Persian immigrants. The Z.N.P., A.S.P., and Z.P.P.P. found their constituencies in these racial groups, apart from the Indians (mostly traders). This racial form of organization affected the pace of transformation to political independence and the relations, at a political level, between the various classes as they were operative in Zanzibar. The 1957 elections gave a majority to the A.S.P. but in 1961 the result was a 'draw' between the three parties. The Z.N.P., though more radical-looking, in fact failed to find political credibility among the majority of the poor — workers and lower ranks of the petty bourgeoisie — who supported the A.S.P. Since the majority of the poor were Africans, the Z.N.P. was seen as representing the richer Arabs, whose historical image as the enslavers of the Africans thus tended to weigh against it,

During the June 1961 elections, race riots occurred in which at least 68 people were killed. It was alleged that Bibi Titi Mohamed of TANU had stirred up political feelings by campaigning for the A.S.P., and the Z.N.P., was quick to represent her work as interference in the island's politics by mainland TANU. The police declared that half of the rioters were Africans from the mainland. The antagonisms between the PAFMECA comrades-in-arms were reflected in the statement issued by the Z.N.P. and Z.P.P.P. which blamed the riot on 'reactionary elements backed by influential elements in Tanganyika [an obvious reference to TANU leadership] who wanted Zanzibar to support East African Federation.'[15]

Because of the fact that the A.S.P. leadership was less educated and less sophisticated, a fact also reflecting its class character, its leadership was too willing to accept the explanations given by the British colonial state, and this was exploited by the Z.N.P. and Z.P.P.P. as evidence of its subservience to the colonialists. The more radical elements in the Z.N.P., of whom the most outstanding was Babu, tended also to regard TANU as too moderate and a stooge of the British. This attitude on the part of the Z.N.P., added to the racial and historical background, tended to cement the relations and solidarity between TANU and the A.S.P.

It is for this reason that, although the PAFMECA mission led by Francis Khamisi succeeded in narrowing the gap between the two parties, resulting in the formation of a joint Freedom Committee to co-ordinate the struggle for independence, yet this unity was short-lived and the joint committee disintegrated soon afterwards. So that for the most part in 1959, 1960 and 1961, particularly after the riots, relations between the two parties became tense and the possibility of their organizing together to achieve Responsible

Government in 1961 leading to a federation of East Africa was out of the question.

The political developments in Uganda and Kenya were also running contrary to the unification of East Africa on the basis of Responsible Government, if at all, for here too the political parties that emerged were so much at each others' throats that the leading nationalist parties found difficulty consolidating their positions against the others. These difficulties had their immediate roots in the developments of the two colonies' politics in the 1950s.

Party organization in Uganda reflected segmentation of the petty bourgeoisie and rural bourgeoisie even more clearly than in Kenya. The Uganda National Congress (U.N.C.) emerged in 1952 as the first party of the rural bourgeoisie, poor peasants and urban and rural traders as well as elements of the intellectual petty bourgeoisie, but by 1959 it had split into two wings. Since the northern part of the country had become effectively a labour reservoir, the U.N.C., nominally a nationwide party, in fact found the bulk of its political support in the south and to some extent the east.

When in 1954 the U.N.C. coined the slogan 'Self-Government Now' to rally the country behind it, no less a figure than Milton Obote, the future first Prime Minister of independent Uganda, opposed the call on the ground that the U.N.C. was pushing the pace too fast for the north. He demanded instead 'Immediate Local Self-Government in Uganda'.[16]

Obote was later, in 1960, to form the Uganda People's Congress (U.P.C.) from a faction of his own U.N.C. and another small party of Legislative Council members called the Uganda People's Union. In the meantime, in 1954, another party, the Democratic Party (D.P.), had been formed with a strong base in the Catholic areas of Uganda and with the support of the Church. It accused the U.N.C. of 'communist leanings'. In 1955 a split had occurred in the U.N.C. and another small party, the United Congress Party (U.N.P.) had emerged, representing a section of the intellectual petty bourgeoisie with some support in Buganda. At the same time another small party, the Progressive Party (P.P.), also formed by the intellectual petty bourgeoisie, with very little support among the masses but some support from the Anglican Church, also held out opposition to 'communism' as its standpoint.

This conglomeration of political parties marked the whole post-1950s period of Uganda's struggle for national independence. It was in fact a correct reflection of its material basis in the scattered small property relations of these classes, which promoted a proliferation of small parties.

The Wild Committee Report, written after the 1958 elections to chart Uganda's path to Responsible Government, provoked another series of movements and splits resulting in the formation of the Uganda National Movement (U.N.M.) which swallowed up some of the earlier factions including the U.N.C. faction of I.K. Musazi (the former President-General of the U.N.C.) and Mulira's P.P., as well as the United Congress Party. Even then, splits emerged within the U.N.M. itself, and by 1959, after the successful boycott campaign against foreign goods and Asian shops, a faction of the U.N.M. split and called itself the party of *Kabaka Yekka* (K.Y.) – i.e. Kabaka Alone!

Although the U.N.C. was the most progressive and oldest of the national movements, it nevertheless failed to galvanize the whole country behind it. It was tremendously weakened by the small parties that emerged in Buganda and by its own vacillations on the question of the Kabaka. Then, having threatened to declare independence unilaterally in 1960, its failure to do so weakened it even more. In its place, the U.P.C. emerged as the inheritor of the earlier national consciousness, but the D.P. posed a threat to it and particularly the mixing of religious ideology with politics tended to confuse forces that would otherwise have been rallied by it. Moreover in 1958, at the first PAFMECA meeting in Mwanza, it was no other person than Mulira and his small intellectualist P.P. that represented Uganda, since the U.N.C. was bogged down in splits of its own.

Later the U.P.C. was recognized as the leading nationalist party by PAFMECA, but it commanded no overwhelming mass support over the other parties, particularly the D.P. The D.P., for its part, actually dissociated itself from PAFMECA. The relative weakness of the U.P.C. was reflected in its scoring a smaller number of seats than the D.P. in the elections of 1961, albeit with more votes. This anomaly arose because the K.Y. had called for the boycott of these elections in Buganda, so that the D.P., with some support in Buganda which U.P.C. did not have, took the Buganda seats with only 3% of the vote in the region. The D.P. therefore formed the first Responsible Government, with the U.P.C. in opposition.

In his enthusiasm to see East Africa federation emerge in unity, Nyerere did not fully take account of these political dissensions as they existed in each of the three countries — not that sorting out their separate problems first necessarily would have meant unity later. However, ignoring these particular historical problems, deeply based as they were in the economy and superstructure alike, was no way to reach the desired federation. Indeed, there is the failure of Nyerere's own effort on behalf of PAFMECA to unite these parties in Uganda in 1958. It is not surprising that when the time came for Uganda's constitutional talks leading to independence, the various parties were forced to accept a semi-federalist solution for Uganda and this in turn posed problems for the declaration that East Africa should federate by the end of 1963.

In Kenya the problem of regionalism also meant that these earlier sentiments for a single independence and federation were doomed to disappointment. But this problem was very much connected with the land issue. The Swynnerton Plan which had led to the gradual opening up of the Highlands to Africans, did result in a fairly rapid differentiation amongst the peasantry. Around the Highlands in particular, land consolidation and registration resulted in increasing concentration of land in the hands of chiefs and loyalists, as many Kikuyu peasants, and other strata who supported Mau Mau, were rounded up in camps under the Emergency. This has been noted by a number of writers on Kenya.[17]

Conflict over the land question was also heightened by the fact that almost all the fertile land was concentrated in the Kenya Highlands, and became the object of mutual suspicions among the petty bourgeosie about which of them would have a share of it after the departure of the settlers. All the political differences that arose among the African nationalist parties were indirectly connected with this question.[18]

Political differences were worsened by the Emergency manoeuvres of the colonial regime to divide the people. While the settlers themselves also played on these differences. At a time when, elsewhere in East Africa, a whole new political leadership was emerging, in Kenya national parties were banned between 1953 and 1955. Even when the ban was lifted, political party activity was restricted to the district level, and in many cases thus coincided with reinforced ethnic division. Political consciousness was perforce ethnic and local consciousness, a fact that was to stamp the future political development of Kenya.[19] Although in places like Luoland, Odinga made efforts to emphasize national issues, the election of 1957 was fought entirely on local issues.

Thus in 1959 when PAFMECA held its second conference, only a small restricted organization – the Kenya Independent Movement (K.I.M.) – could claim to represent Kenya. Even so, the K.I.M. was only allowed to operate in Kenya on condition that it adhered to multi-racial lines of party organization. The more white-dominated Kenya National Party (K.N.P.), in which Muliro was involved, was rejected by PAFMECA at Moshi on the instigation of the K.I.M. When national parties were finally allowed to operate, the two major African parties, the Kenya African National Union (KANU) and Kenya African Democratic Union (KADU), emerged out of these district organizations and the conflicts that flared up in them naturally reflected this disunity which in turn reflected the dominance of small property in the countryside and urban areas among Africans in particular, worsened by the poverty of the mass of the people. KANU's radicalism lay in its connection with the violent rural struggles led by the Kenya African Union (KAU) banned in 1953. KANU appeared to have inherited this base, along with its informal connection with the trade union movement through Tom Mboya. KADU, on the other hand, found its rural support in areas like the Kalenjin and the Coast, with the new rural bourgeoisie and petty bourgeoisie who feared that their counterparts among the Kikuyu would 'monopolize' the land in the Highlands. With such a constituency, KADU tended to appear reactionary, particularly when the white-dominated New Kenya Party (N.K.P.) on many occasions collaborated with it in demanding a regionalized structure at the constitutional conference in London. This, plus KADU's compromise with the Governor on the issue of Kenyatta's release, resulted in its joining and forming the Responsible Government in 1961, despite the fact that KANU had won the 1961 General Election. Although KADU equally pledged and worked for the return of Kenyatta, when Kenyatta finally was released from his long detention on 16 August 1961, its earlier pledge to join up with KANU to form a single party under his leadership was never pursued. The resulting rivalry and bitterness between the parties soon intensified with KADU demanding federation (*majimbo*) within Kenya as a condition for accepting independence. KADU's own position on East African federation was ambivalent, and it can be seen that even here in Kenya, although KANU was to become the major supporter of the idea of federation, the division and disunity between the two major African parties did not permit the necessary unity for achieving a federation collectively under British supervision.

We have seen, in fact, that the repressive nature of the colonial state, particularly as the struggle for independence intensified, tended to exacerbate the conflicts within the national movements by its divisive tactics. It also blocked efforts to hold PAFMECA conferences in Nairobi and Kampala. It should also be stated here that, in fact, any signs of imminent co-operation between the nationalist parties to achieve federation before independence would have created suspicions and even intensified opposition to it from the more racial parties who condemned federation as a neo-colonial trap. Indeed, the Z.N.P.'s hostility to the idea can be interpreted this way.

Be that as it may, the situation in Tanganyika in the same period differed from that of the other three territories and explains Nyerere's enthusiasm for co-ordinating the various independence dates so as to achieve federation. TANU was in a dominant position as the sole nationalist party, and was, moreover, adequately committed and disciplined to pursue a consistent policy on this issue. The effects of Nyerere's own immense personal dedication to the idea of unity should not be underestimated either. Pratt's account of what he calls the 'critical years'[20] brings this out very clearly. TANU's leading role was established at the electoral level as early as 1958 in the multi-racial elections of that year. Despite efforts by the colonial Government to encourage a United Tanganyika Party (U.T.P.) victory in a number of Asian and European seats, TANU and TANU-backed candidates in fact won a majority of seats. The multi-racial U.T.P. did not make much progress, particularly when TANU had put forward a correct line on the race question which even won the support of many white settlers in the Territory.[21] For this reason, Tanganyika's advance to full self-government was 'remarkably swift'.

Moreover, because of the early roots that TANU had formed through the Tanganyika African Association (T.A.A.), inherited from the earlier district parties, the fairly strong kulak elements around Kilimanjaro, Bukoba and in the Mbeya and Iringa areas did not cohere their forces into a separate party to threaten TANU's leading and uniting role. By 1959 the British Government had decided to transfer full independence 'as fast as was possible'.[22]

There were many reasons for this. Pratt mentions first the strength of TANU, and Nyerere's capacity to win the support of the elected European and Asian members of the Legislative Council. For this reason, the British wanted to establish Tanganyika as a model of 'how the British can transfer powers smoothly and speedily in an African situation'.[23] Pratt adds:

> It is no longer seemed conceivable to continue British rule for a further long period not wise to do so for a brief one . . . . In these added years of British rule, embittered relations between the nationalists and the

British, the final result might well have been significantly less attractive for Britain. The antagonisms and animosities which would have resulted would have destroyed the confidence which the nationalists had in the good will of the British. . . . They recognized the moderation of Nyerere's leadership. They had seen TANU check racialism and overcome opposition to agricultural and other development policies. They had noted the recognition which Nyerere and his colleagues gave to the continuing value of their contribution. They anticipated that independence would involve an alliance of nationalists and British officials with the detailed planning of policies remaining in British hands while its public pronouncements and its local promotion would become the responsibility of the nationalists.[24]

Pratt further notes that, after December 1959, the British strategy rested on the assumption that they were handing over to nationalists who would make few changes to the major economic and social policies of the colonial government. Indeed it has been recognized that the TANU Government, just like the other East African nationalist parties in the first three to four years did tend to follow the policies laid down during the colonial era.

All this should not minimize the fact that TANU's leading role and its swift advance to independence was very much hastened by its anti-colonial struggle. It threatened 'positive action' throughout the country to hasten the country's independence in March 1959. This led to the colonial government's climbdown and its subsequent concession that Tanganyika should move quickly to independence. And TANU certainly had the support to back this up. TANU won the 1960 elections with the loss of only one seat and even this went to an independent in Mbulu who had actually been the TANU candidate until his nomination was cancelled by the party because of accusations of tribalism. The total defeat of Mtemvu of the African National Congress (A.N.C.), who polled less than 1% of the vote, sealed any possibility of the colonial government playing tricks.

It is, therefore, quite clear that Nyerere had no problems as far as Tanganyika was concerned in offering to delay independence. As Pratt shows, it would even have embarrassed the British Government to delay any further. But, given the discrepant position in the other territories, it is not surprising that Nyerere should have, within a few years, recognized the situation as a complicated one. Mboya, too, in 1963 recognized the political difficulties in Kenya and Uganda, and noted that 'the longer we put off its implementation, the more difficult it could be' to unify the region in a federation.[25] Yet he declared that 'one reason' favouring the success of PAFMECA countries in their endeavour was the 'realistic attitude . . . which recognizes that leaders in a particular country know best what is good for that country.'[26]

Tempting as it is to view these constraints as 'internal' and to tack on moralistic assertions about what 'we' should have done to federate East Africa, it is clear that any scientific analysis of the forces at work must take into account all the factors, isolating the dominant forces and relating the secondary factors to them in a dialectical manner. If we do this, we will find behind the apparent ideological unity under Pan Africanism, lay a fundamental lack of unity in the material base as the dominant forces of British bilateral imperialism gave way to a new situation. This was attested to by the lack of success of further efforts to bring about the desired federation. Indeed it is these same forces that compelled the Ugandan U.N.C. to argue that, so long as colonial rule continued, it would not be 'practical politics' to think about a federation.

In 1961 at the Nairobi meeting of PAFMECA, KADU boycotted the discussions about federation, where it was resolved that, after the elections in that year in Zanzibar, Kenya and Uganda, the Prime Ministers should then convene a summit conference to work out the details. But, as we have seen, the elections in all these countries produced unexpected results, with the upshot that no summit was possible. The elections were won by parties which were opposed to or half-hearted about federation.

Tanganyika could not achieve federation alone. With its early independence in 1961, it had to address itself to the economic demands of its own situation when it tried to embark on the 1961-63 Economic Plan. As a result, the East African Common Services Organization (EACSO) was created to deal with the special economic problems of Tanganyika and, as we have noted in Chapter Five, the 'strains and stresses' that had emerged were addressed by the Raisman formula in this special arrangement.

What was in fact happening was that each of the territories was individually becoming more concerned with shifting class demands as determined by the new mechanisms of transnational integration under multilateral imperialism. The creation of EASCO, which was necessary for the day-to-day working of the system, took precedence over the vision of political federation. The economic demands of the monopolies and of the local ruling classes could not be halted even for a day to enable the idea to materialize, and the ideals of Pan Africanism were increasingly put in the background. The continued debates in the Kenya Legislature, and the expansion of PAFMECA into PAFMECSA with the joining of the liberation movements of Southern Africa in 1962 and the declaration by Burundi, Somalia and Ethiopia, all fizzled away in the face of this reality.

The Second Attempt

The idea of a Pan African federation finally died and was buried after further efforts to federate the region failed in 1963, despite the fact that by this date all the three countries, as well as Zanzibar, had each put their separate houses in some kind of order.

On 5 June 1963 in Nairobi the three East African leaders met and made a Declaration:

> We the leaders of the people and governments of East Africa assembled in Nairobi on June 5, 1963, pledge ourselves to the political federation of East Africa. Our meeting today is motivated by the spirit of Pan

Africanism, and not by mere selfish regional interest. . . . There is no
more room for slogans and words. This is our day of action in the cause
of the ideals that we believe in, and in the unity and freedom for which
we have suffered and sacrificed so much.[27]

As events turned out, the Declaration was no more than so many words, not
because the ideals were not desirable, but because they were not matched by
the material conditions at the level of actual daily activity of the forces at
work. These activities, based on competition, tended to divide rather than
unite.

The new classes speaking for the people were in many cases, although
dominated themselves, part of the appropriators on a small scale, and therefore easily amenable to continuing the conditions in which they participated
in the appropriation. This is why even the Declaration itself contained
contradictory statements, condemning the imperialist exploitation and
domination of the people, yet regarding the very mechanisms of that exploitation and domination as a positive basis on which the ideal could be
achieved. It stated:

> For 40 years the imperialists and the local settler minorities tried to
> impose political federation upon us. Our people rightly resisted these
> attempts. Federation at that time would quickly have led to one thing
> — a vast white-dominated dominion. *The East African High Commission
> and its successor, the Common Services Organization, have taught us
> the value of links in the economic field. Indeed, it was the recognition
> of the value of these connections which led the two fully independent
> members to agree to continue participation after they had achieved
> their freedom.* In many practical ways we already are co-operating — in
> scientific research, in communications and in postal services. *An
> important factor in view of our determination to achieve federation is
> the existence of a shared currency; a leading aspect of economic
> working together is the functioning of the East African Common
> Market.* [Emphasis added — Author.] [28]

The ideal of Pan Africanism was being tailored to suit neo-colonialism. What
the East African leaders wanted was to inherit colonial relations of production, its institutions and structures, and to continue, as indeed they did
(without federation), the exploitative and oppressive system based on a multi-
lateralized imperialism. This 'overthrowing' of colonial relations and structures
is brought out in sharper relief by the boasting of an Mboya-led Kenyan
delegation to the E.E.C. Headquarters in Brussels, quoted by Mboya in his
speech to the Kenya House of Representatives on 27 June 1963:

> We in East Africa do not have to be taught about a common market
> by the European nations [sic], *they can learn from us because we have
> had a common market much longer than most countries,* and if

necessary we are ready — this government and the East African governments — to send a missionary to Europe to begin to teach them about the common market.[29]

Indeed Pan Africanism's new role of overseeing the neo-colonial economy on a regional basis was blatant in direct appeals to the monopolists, where what was presented was wider *market* investment opportunities in the region. This comes out clearly in the words of Mr. Kiano, then Kenyan Minister of Commerce and Industry, when he addressed the Conference attended by British monopolists operating in East Africa, organized by the Overseas Development Institute in Nairobi in 1965:

> This morning you discussed East Africa as a unit. I would like to stress that the leaders of East Africa, and particularly the Government Ministers responsible for the economic growth and Pan African aspirations in our respective countries, continue to be dedicated to the maintenance and development of East Africa as one common market [i.e. for the monopolies].[30]

The 'owning' of colonial relations of production and structures is quite different from the 'owning' of the colonial territorial demarcation that later characterizes the neo-colonial nation-state. It might be argued[31] that independence of each of the territories implied the owning of the territory created by imperialism, and the structures built up by it. We have argued that the creation of colonial enclaves as part of the Empire was the only system on which imperialism could exploit and oppress the people on the basis of capitalist relations. But it is a revolt against these relations that enabled the creation of national feeling and consciousness. To the extent that anti-colonialism and anti-imperialism reflected the antagonisms within those territorial boundaries created by these new relations, it was only historical and dialectical logic that the national (territorial) unit was the foundation upon which the struggle against imperialism could be waged, as indeed was the case.

The question of a number of territorial entities uniting in a kind of federation in order to struggle against the enemy (politically desirable as this might be) had no real material basis, since the antagonisms that the new relations created were best combated within individual territorial units. This gave greater unity and determination to all the classes within the unit to identify themselves as an oppressed people and 'nation'.

Indeed it can be said that one of the most useful results of the Nairobi Declaration was that it hastened Kenya's independence, possibly by a year. The Declaration had expressed strong opposition to any attempt to delay the country's achievement of independence, 'since a hold-up in Kenya's advance to independence will hinder the achievement of federation to which we are committed'. It had continued: 'The three governments, having agreed to the establishment of a federation this year, expect the British Government to grant Kenya's independence *immediately.'* Later Obote was reported as saying that in fact the whole purpose of the Nairobi Declaration had been to do exactly that: 'The first objective of the [Nairobi] meeting was to achieve Kenya's independence — regardless of what people today are alleging.'[32]

Since it appeared that the British were keen on federation, (on their terms of course) as this was the wish of the British monopolies operating in the region, according to Morgan's survey[33] Britain did agree to Kenya's independence on 12 December 1963, well ahead of the deadline for federation.

Kenyatta, in a speech at Kisumu on 2 August 1964, actually boasted how he had 'deceived' the British in this matter.[34] Later he corrected this statement, as it implied that the Declaration was a trick and he now stated that what he meant was that the Declaration was an 'ingenuity'[35] and that the Swahili word he had used, *'ujanja',* meant just that.[36] In an earlier speech, his first major one in Parliament as Prime Minister, on 2 July 1963, he had said:

> Mr. Sandys [the Conservative Party Colonial Secretary] assured the Kenya Ministers in London that the British Government, which has long believed in the idea of an East African Federation, supports fully the initiative taken by the East African Governments, and will do all it can to facilitate the early implementation of the aim.[37]

The Reasons for Failure

Various reasons have been advanced to explain why the Nairobi Declaration failed to be implemented.[38] (Many of these have been brought out in Proctor's article in the *Political Quarterly*.)[39] For instance, it has been argued that it was differences over the federal constitution, particularly Uganda's insistence on having a long list of powers reserved for the constituent parts of the federation rather than the federal government. It has also been argued that it was the foreign interference by the imperialists, as alleged by Tanzania, and the interference of Ghana in particular, that tended to create local dissensions in East Africa over the issue after the O.A.U. Conference of 1963, and that this was connected with Nkrumah's grand design for a continental government rather than segmented regional units. The blame has also been placed on 'separatist trends' arising out of Kenya's dominant position in the East African economic arrangements, and the centralization of the Common Market institutions, etc. It was claimed that these separatist trends were also discernible 'internally' in 'tribal' politics and regionalism in Uganda and Kenya. The cause of failure has further been attributed to the three governments' 'divergent policies' on foreign relations, with different interpretations of non-alignment, divergent paths of economic development and political organization and divergent ideologies, particularly the emphasis on the one-party state in Tanzania. Differences in approach between the three countries to trade unions and the training of armies have also been offered as an explanation. Even 'personal interests' of certain leaders have been suggested as factors foredooming the ideal of federation. A Kenyan Minister, Joseph Murumbi, was quoted as suggesting that Obote's reluctance and backpeddling on the issue of federation was caused by his fear (and that of his counterparts) that, if federation was realized, 'they might become nonentities overnight',[40] a fear allegedly shared by junior leaders in the territorial units and party stalwarts. As a result they preferred to remain 'big fish in small ponds'.[41]

All these arguments[42] no doubt have some validity, but they are partial and do not give us an adequate explanation of the real causes of the failure of the Nairobi Declaration to result in a federation. All they do is give us some insights into the secondary, and in some cases minor, contributing factors to the failure. Ali Mazrui, in fact, while emphasizing many of the arguments given above, went as far as blaming Nyerere personally for 'plunging' Tanganyika into a union with Zanzibar:

> The narrower unification of Tanganyika and Zanzibar has harmed the ambition of a broader unification of East Africa as a whole. Nothing would have dramatized more effectively the problems which would attend a prospective East African Federation than the problems already met in relations between Zanzibar and Tanganyika in their modest union.[43]

He even suggested that the throne of the Sultan of Zanzibar had brought 'unification' to East Africa, but that the Sultani's dethronement in 1964, leading to the union between Tanganyika and Zanzibar, had 'destroyed the last hopes so far for a more effective political union in this region.'![44]

These half-baked and ahistorical arguments merely create confusion. The events of 1963 to 1965, do not make sense without a basic grasp of the fact that the failure to realize the Pan African ideal must be traced to the contradictions that imperialism introduced in the region. The yearning for national development by each of these countries was positive and justified but, as we have seen, such development could not be realized given the continuing economic control by imperialism.

It is these exploitative and oppressive relationships that were behind the strains and stresses that became particularly noticeable in the whole period 1958-62.[45] In the most recent phase of modern imperialism we have noted that the forces operating on a world scale, and the new strategies and tactics of transnational corporations operating in separate economies under neo-colonialism, tended to intensify the divisions between states as the huge monopolies battled for capital export outlets, markets and sources of raw materials. This, coupled with local classes yearning for development within each of their own territories, created centrifugal forces working against the regional structures of co-operation which might assist national development. Despite the fact that a larger market was preferable to the monopolies, monopolistic competition at the micro-level of the monopoly firm tended to pull apart such attempts at creating a larger market in the face of the existence of the nation-state.

This development in transnational monopolistic competition was inherent in the so-called national development plans inherited after independence. All the projects worked out in these plans accorded with the needs of international finance capital. In Volume I we have analysed how this arrangement was reflected in the 'old colonial plans'. The immediate task that faced each of the neo-colonial states was to re-examine these programmes in the light of, on the one hand, the democratic pressure of the people to realize the objectives they had fought for in the independence struggle and, on the other, the demand by the monopolies to obtain protection to run these projects, since the 'national' bourgeoisie was too weak to do so.

Tanganyika faced these problems earlier, and was the first to discover that this meant concretely attending to the question of mobilizing resources to implement the programme between 1961 and 1963. Pratt points out that, in these first three or four years, Tanzania addressed itself to the affairs of party organization and economic development on the lines of 'tempered capitalism overseen by a socially responsible Government'.[46] He gives an example of one year, 1963, the year of the Nairobi Declaration, and shows that the only external issue of importance in that year was the East African federation. Otherwise 'development questions were the central focus of Government pre-occupation'.

He cites four main areas of this focus: (1) The village settlement scheme, based on World Bank recommendations, required a lot of external financing, and hence suing for economic aid. This brought Tanzania into direct competition with Uganda and Kenya for such funding. (2) The expansion of secondary schools which, as Pratt points out, 'was largely successful', but which also involved securing 'overseas capital' to support the building of the University of Dar es Salaam. (3) Efforts directed at 'careful economic planning' to bring about 'closer co-ordination of government activities', and a more 'effective mobilization of financial resources for development purposes, and a clear and systematic identification of the priorities as between the different possible major projects'.[47] And (4) Encouragement to the co-operative unions, particularly in the field of crop marketing, as an alternative to existing marketing arrangements and methods of fixing prices.

All these activities, involved not only the allocation of resources, but the use of fiscal and monetary measures which were hampered by the existing arrangements under the East African Currency Board. The associated problem of foreign exchange was also exacerbated by the existing arrangements whereby it tended to leak out of the country.[48] As a result of these pressures, and despite the political will to federate, Tanzania was forced to take measures to break up the East African Currency Board, as we shall see later. In effect, all these activities, covering the whole spectrum of an economy in which the monopolies were active participants in agriculture, industry and the service sector, implied competition between the monopolies and so between the states in the region as well.

These competitions created by the dominant interests of the monopolies can be illustrated by the example, in Tanzania again, of the Dutch company, Philips, and the Japanese monopoly, Matsushita. The former monopoly controlled 90% of the Tanganyika radio market — but all imported. In 1958 the Japanese monopoly joined the competition for the market and by 1964 had moved its market share (also based on importing radios) from 1.4% to 68% with the Philips share correspondingly reduced to only 21%.[49] It was during this period also that the Kampala Agreement was negotiated and agreed but not ratified by Kenya. As we now know, under this Agreement the manufacture of radio sets and components was allocated to Tanzania.

As our theoretical analysis revealed in the previous chapters, transnational corporate strategy seeks to defend existing markets by import substitution, so long as protection can be obtained from the local state to make production worthwhile and profitable. Indeed the neo-colonial strategy which corresponds to such monopolistic competition did provide for such protection. In Tanganyika protective measures had become a regular feature, as Yaffey observes, 'in and after 1961'.[50] In the case of radios, such protection was extended to Philips in 1965 in order to build a plant to import substitute and get rid of the Japanese monopoly. This proves that it was the Philips monopoly which demanded and obtained such protection. As Rweyemamu has argued:

> In view of the fact that the share of Tanzania in the East African market was relatively small, and the short-term interval between the Tanzania Government's initiative to establish the plant and its hasty set-up, there seems to be a *prima facie* case for believing that Philips Industries had already decided to build the plant in order to avert the loss of the market to the Japanese.[51]

Thus the smallness of the market did not operate as a serious constraint for a monopoly in these circumstances where protection was granted, and a monopoly could set up a plant in any market, and still make a super-profit.

Reframing Professor Hirschman's hypothesis based on observations of industrialization particularly in Latin America, Rweyemamu appears to accept the argument that when the market, as mapped out by imports, has reached or is approaching that size which will support a plant at optimum or near optimum efficiency, an investor in search of profitable opportunities will 'come forward', given appropriate publicity and provision of reasonable tariff protection and other fiscal incentives.[52] This is all the more likely to be true if the protection given is more than nominal and allows existing markets to be defended.[53] This means that the motives to 'come forward' are made even stronger for the monopoly.

Rweyemamu's further conclusion is that there is little doubt 'that the import-substitution industrialization which has taken place in Tanzania has been conditional on granting the industrialists adequate tariff protection.' This is confirmed by the account given by officials of the Ministry of Commerce and Industry, 'who deal with these issues', that the initiative to import-substitute 'originates with the potential investors who submit a request for a tariff increase'. This is strengthened further by evidence of the 'simultaneous establishment of industrial projects [i.e. in neighbouring countries and the granting of tariff protection'.[54]

All these pressures in the neo-colonial economy undermined the idea of federation, desirable as it was to the leaders. It is these pressures that were responsible for the impatience exhibited in Tanzania when the Nairobi Declaration was not implemented in 1963 as envisaged. The deadline of six months for federation was itself unrealistic even if federation was achievable. But the haste itself was evidence of the pressures running the other way. This impatience was revealed for the first time when Tanzania insisted that the benefits arising out of the Common Market be 'equalized'. Concentration of industry in Kenya, it was argued, meant that no industrialization could take place in Tanzania and industries (like Philips) could not be supported adequately to import-substitute. In the words of President Nyerere:

> Instead of the secondary effects of investment being felt in the country which has obligation to repay any loan, the increase in the effective market is felt mainly by Tanzania's partners in the Common Market. Because of the common tariff arrangements, and the free inter-East African trade, Tanzania cannot buy in the cheapest market abroad, and equally, she cannot protect her infant industries against competition from long-established and large-scale firms in Kenya, and — to a lesser extent — in Uganda.
>
> This situation did not result from the evil machinations or by the people or Governments of our neighbouring territories. It was a historically determined fact. But as far as Tanzania is concerned, it meant that her own development was hamstrung. Without the establishment of an industrial base Tanzania will never achieve a stable economy or reach the take-off point of economic growth.[55]

Although in terms of our analysis a strategy based on import-substituted industrialization could never lead to a stable economy or to economic take-off, nevertheless the case as argued reveals the pressures for national development that compelled Tanzania to take unilateral actions contrary to the objective of Pan Africanism, and to demand a rearrangement of the existing system. This led to the Kampala Agreement, and on the basis of that Agreement, although not ratified by Kenya, to the 'temporary' imposition of quotas against certain Kenyan products worth £2 million, out of total imports of £9 million.[56]

The need to implement the development plans also required some control over finance, including monetary and fiscal instruments, and it is not surprising that the next step taken by Tanzania and by Uganda was the creation of their own currencies and of central banks for each country. This meant breaking up the East African Currency Board. Nyerere again expressed the bitter reality of the situation which national self-determination and the dominant economic forces implied: 'This change [of the currency] was not decided upon for prestige reasons; the decision was made because it is impossible to plan economic development properly if currency and credit are not within the control of planners – that is the government.'[57] Indeed Tanzania had already taken the lead in calling for the establishment of separate currencies and central banks. According to Bomani, this was because of the 'divergent economic structures and trade relationships' and the 'variations which [had] occurred in respective levels of investment, in overseas borrowing and in rates of economic growth, [as well as in] the marked differences in the quantitative objectives of the three development plans.'[58]

Indeed these divergencies were evident in the 'old plans' and arose from the uneven development of the region. They were also evident in the negotiations to create a central bank of East Africa to deal with this situation had started, according to the official report of the East African Currency Board, as far back as 1961.[59] This had led to the commissioning by Tanganyika of Dr. Erwin Blumenthal, of the West German Central Bank, to examine East Africa's monetary system and advise as to its future. Dr. Blumenthal had recommended a 'two-tier system' under which each state would have its own state bank wholly owned by it, and there would also be an East African Central Bank to co-ordinate the activities of the three state banks of the territories. This was in the hope that an East African federation would eventually take place. In his radio address, Bomani pointed out that, although this prospect had 'receded from the realms of the foreseeable future', Tanzania had nevertheless given priority to setting up a central bank for the region, with devolution of powers to the individual states.

An I.M.F. mission was requested to assist in this task, and it arrived in February 1965 to establish how far common ground existed for the working of an effective central bank issuing a common currency. It found no such common ground. The three states, in the words of the Currency Board Report, disagreed on 'the sharing of sovereignty over a wide range of "bread and butter" matters and in terms of the limitations which this sharing must impose on national economic policies and ambitions'.[60] Of course, a central bank for East Africa could have functioned without a political union.[61] Yet the fact that such a bank was never set up indicated again the strong divergent tendencies in the economies, as implied by monopolistic competition and the desire for national (i.e. territorial) development.

The first move was made by Uganda when it declared through its Minister of Finance, Kalule Settala, two days before the I.M.F. team arrived, that Uganda intended to create a state commercial bank out of an existing bank. At the same time it would set up an Agricultural Credit Corporation and an Industrial Finance Corporation (with capital from various countries including the U.K. and Germany); and to establish the Bank of Uganda to discharge the function of a central bank. Settala declared that the team of experts from the I.M.F. was arriving to draft a constitution 'for the East African Reserve Bank' for which the Bank of Uganda would act as agent.

The discussions of the three governments broke down when Tanzania insisted that a central bank for East Africa could only function properly under a political federation; and when Kenya argued that a central bank responsible for a common currency must be centrally managed by agreement of the three governments together.[62] In the event no agreement was achieved and it was decided to announce separation of the banks. The Currency Board Report concluded: 'Whatever the disappointment felt at the announcements of 10th June, therefore, the decision taken can be welcomed for facing realities and ending a long period of wishful thinking.'[63]

Few economists and political scientists have paid attention to these fundamental facts. Nyerere,[64] exceptionally, did point to the economic forces which threatened the EASCO arrangement but merely referred to the system of industrial licensing and the phenomenon of each country entering into separate trade agreements.

The problems of managing a neo-colonial economy by the use of monetary and fiscal 'incentives', as pointed out by Clark,[65] already implies inter-state conflict in the planning of separate economies. Yet as President Nyerere correctly observed, these economies were 'historically determined'. And if the pace of economic development has to be accelerated by government expenditure playing 'a major leading and energizing role', as Clark states elsewhere[66] (particularly in the cases of Tanzania and Uganda) then, given the uneven development and divergencies in the plans of the three countries involved, it follows that a small-property consciousness on the part of the local bourgeoisie would tend to respond favourably to anti-federalist tendencies.

This is the situation which prevailed. With its atmosphere of pressure, emotionalism, and even petty jealousies, it is not surprising that when the last Working Party appointed after the Nairobi Declaration met in Kampala on 30 May 1964, instead of producing a constitution for a Pan African federation of East Africa, it 'did little but close the books.'[67] This was effectively the end of any idea of a Pan African Unity in East African based on neo-colonialism.

Having thus collapsed the grand idea, each country continued its task of 'attracting foreign investments' in the hope that this would lead to national development. Now it appeared, to Tanzania and Uganda at least, that the Kampala Agreement of 1964 should aim at correcting the imbalances in the region's development by five short-term methods to be applied simultaneously. These five methods were:

(1) Immediate action, with certain inter-territorially connected firms, to increase production in deficit countries and thereby reduce imports from the surplus country;

(2) The need to arrive at an agreement as to the immediate allocation of certain major industries between the three countries;

(3) The application of a system of quotas and suspended quotas whereby exports from surplus countries would be progressively reduced, and local production increased in a deficit country;

(4) The increase of sales of goods from countries in deficit to a country in surplus;

(5) The need to arrive at early agreement within the East African Common Market on a system of inducements and allocations of industry in order to

secure the equitable distribution of industrial development as between the three countries.

It was further stated in the Kampala Agreement that, in the case of four stipulated industries, the Ministers had agreed that 'it was possible to make approaches to each firm' because each of them had productive units in both the surplus and deficit countries. The companies stipulated were: East African Tobacco Co. Ltd. (a B.A.T. monopoly), Bata Shoe Company, East African Breweries, and British Standard Portland Cement (Bamburi) Company.

The Agreement is also instructive in that it reveals that actually all these firms, despite the 'approach' suggested by the Ministers, had themselves in fact already taken steps towards expansion in each territory because of existing competition. The Agreement states that the first three companies had been 'interviewed' by the Ministers in Kenya and Tanganyika. In the case of tobacco, it was revealed that 'the firm had already sent machinery to Dar es Salaam' and had stated that by July 1964 it would be manufacturing in Tanganyika some 90% of the Tanganyikan consumption of cigarettes. The company also indicated that it would 'consider very seriously' any possibility of manufacturing specialist brands.

As regards footwear, it was revealed that Bata Shoe 'which supplies 70% of the East African market' had stated that their policy was also to have specialist plants in different countries, and that they had space at Dar es Salaam for expansion in 'another specialized field' of shoe with leather uppers and rubber soles, 'and that this project would go ahead', expecting the plant to be in production 'by the end of this year'.

In the case of beer, the Agreement stated that the firm already had one plant at Arusha, Tanganyika, and another plant in Dar es Salaam. They had an 'agreed plan' to re-equip the Dar es Salaam Brewery 'and double its output'. They also planned to increase production at Arusha. This plan would take 18 months to complete, 'but the start is delayed by negotiations over a plot of land in Dar es Salaam'.

The Kampala Agreement of 1964 finally stated that, although it had not been possible to interview the cement company, it was understood that that firm too, 'has already spent on the Dar es Salaam plant approximately £300,000 out of a total scheme value of £1½ million', and that they were to make their initial trials early in 1966.

These moves to redistribute industry, which the monopolies were in any case carrying out on their own to forestall any new competition from other monopolies, were presumed to have 'the net effect' of correcting the imbalance between Kenya and Tanganyika to the tune of £1,800,000 and with Uganda to the tune of £650,000. It is in fact interesting to note that the articles on which Tanzania imposed 'temporary quotas' were the very ones — beer, cigarettes, and shoes — in which the relevant monopolies had already decided to expand production in Tanzania. It is also interesting to note that tariff protection had already been extended to shoes in 1961, cigarettes in 1962, cement in 1963 (with beer and radios following in 1965.) Thus, at least in three instances, the state had taken measures to offer inducements to these monopolies as a way of helping them to import-substitute and extend production in Tanganyika.

In addition to the four industries above, it was decided to bring five others under the Industrial Licensing Acts, and to give Exclusive Licences 'to a firm operating in an agreed territory'. It was decided that Tanganyika would have Land-Rover assembly and lorry assembly; radio assembly; and motor vehicle tyres and tubes. Uganda was to have bicycle manufacture, and a nitrogenous fertilizer plant. The bicycle plant was indeed taken up by the British monopoly — Gailey & Roberts, a Unilever subsidiary — which had the market before and was clearly defending its export market. Kenya was given electric light bulbs, with a possibility of a neon and fluorescent tube plant as well.

The Ministers also agreed that 'urgent action was needed in the case of incentives to be offered to industry and that, pending the report of the committee of experts, some incentives should be urgently considered by the Ministers'. There is no doubt that Foreign Investment Protection Acts, rushed through Parliament in Kenya and Uganda in 1964, were the result of this. That very same year Kenya entered into bilateral investment guarantee agreements with Germany and the U.S., and Uganda with the same countries, while Tanzania entered into one with Switzerland.

The allocations in the Kampala Agreement were adjusted the following year when the Agreement was amended at Mbale. Still Kenya failed to ratify the Agreement, and this is what led to the 'temporary quotas' being imposed unilaterally by Tanzania. According to Green and Seidman, this development 'led to a burst of industrial investment in Tanzania, which almost equalled the country's whole previous manufacturing sector for consumer goods'.[68]

With the failure to comply with the Agreement, the lie about the need for a large unified market was exposed. Another U.S. motor tyre monopoly, Firestone, persuaded Kenya to grant it protection to manufacture tyres and tubes for the Kenya market alone and thus compete against another American monopoly, General Tires, which had been promised the whole East African market for its new plant in Tanzania. Once again, it was not the smallness of the market that was the constraint for the transnational corporations — after all they had the whole world market. The crucial factor was the tariff protection and the other incentives lavished on them by the neo-colonial states as they competed amongst themselves.

It is quite possible that the two U.S. monopolies were each bidding for protection before the Kampala Agreement, and that Tanzania's success in obtaining the allocation of the industry for General Tires might have led to Firestone applying pressure on the Kenya Government not to ratify the Agreement so that it too could operate in the market with the promise of providing capital and employment to Kenya. The same could be true of the competition of other monopolies, all thereby creating strains between the three territories. Monopolistic competition of the transnational corporations therefore, underlay inter-state regional rivalries, intensifying the petty competition of the small producers in each country, and further intensifying other minor contradictions among the people of East Africa.

Even more telling was the effect of this new monopolistic competition on the existing institution of EACSO. President Nyerere, in his speech to the Central Legislative Assembly to which we have referred, pointed to the strains which Kenya's granting of landing rights unilaterally to Pan American Airways at Nairobi Airport was having. He pointed out that the Kenyan decision went against two unanimous decisions of the East African Authority:

> But clearly, Kenya felt in the end that she could not afford to lose the advantages she expected from such a decision, despite our common fears about the effect of such landing rights on the prosperity of our jointly-owned East African Airways.[69]

The editorial in the *Nationalist* (20 July 1965) had gone at some lengths to bring out the background to this conflict. It pointed out that Kenya's action had broken the Agreement between the three states. It noted that, as far back as 1962, the three governments had decided to restrict any new landing rights to Entebbe (Uganda) and/or Dar es Salaam (Tanganyika) in order to enable East African Airways — 'our own airline — room to pick up the profitable side of the business at Nairobi Airport'. This decision, it added, was rescinded in 1964 when Lufthansa was granted landing rights in Nairobi The number of foreign airlines increased to nine and this resulted in a revenue loss of £1 million pounds to East African Airways. It was the realization of this error that had led the three governments to restrict any further landing rights. Kenya's decision unilaterally to grant rights to Pan Am was an act of 'bad faith' for 'how can any sovereign country command respect if it goes on tearing into shreds agreements solemnly entered into just for the sake of getting a casino here and a hotel there for Big Business?'[70] (The reference to the casino and hotel was part of the deal made between Kenya and Pan Am.)

It can be seen here that the rivalry and bitterness that this one decision created among the East African leaders was actually the result of the pressure of this U.S. monopoly airline to gain a competitive advantage in the region by promising Kenya landing fees, a casino and a hotel as part of a deal which must have been considered by Kenya as being vital to the country's tourist industry. And this is explained by President Nyerere again in the following words:

> The trouble is, of course, that each difficulty of this kind uses up our stock of emotional unity. Kenya clearly feels extremely bitter about Tanzania's pressure to restrict the freedom of entry into the Tanzania market. Tanzania, on her side, feels that if East Africa does not federate there must be some effort to accept the inevitable consequence of such failure. Similarly, Tanzania feels let down by what she regards as a weakening of the airline, which the three countries own jointly, while Kenya feels that we have failed to appreciate her needs in relation to this Pan American proposal.[71]

With the failure of the Kampala Agreement, but with the transnational mono-polies operating all the same, it was felt by the three leaders at a meeting in Mombasa in 1965 that they should take some further action. So they formed a Commission on East African Co-operation, to be presided over by Kjeld Philip, a former Finance Minister of Denmark but now working for the United Nations. His task was to 'examine existing arrangements in East Africa for co-operation between Kenya, Tanzania and Uganda on matters of mutual interest, and having regard to the views of the respective governments, to make agreed recommendations on [the matters considered]. With these developments, any hopes of federation were finally sealed and the task reduced to trying to sort out the problems of economic co-operation in the Common Market and Common Services. Even this was to collapse later for the same reasons. Yet the integration of the East African economies through the transnational corporate monopolies and other new institutional forms continued.

References

1. For a history of the Pan African movement see C. Legum, *Pan Africanism* (London, Pall Mall); V.B. Thompson *Africa and Unity: The Evolution of Pan-Africanism* (London, Longman, 1969).
2. Thompson, op. cit., p.16.
3. J.V. Stalin *Marxism and the National Question*, 1913.
4. K. Nkrumah *Neo-Colonialism: The Last Stage of Imperialism* (London, Nelson, 1965).
5. A.J. Hughes, *East Africa; Kenya, Tanzania, Uganda* (London, Penguin, 1963) from which most of this information is obtained.
6. Quoted in T. Mboya, *Freedom and After* (London, Andre Deutsch, 1963), p.208.
7. Ibid., pp.206-8.
8. J. Nyerere, *Freedom and Unity* (London/Nairobi, O.U.P., 1966), p.5.
9. Mboya, op. cit., p.210.
10. Nyerere, op. cit., p.85.
11. Ibid., p.89.
12. Ibid., p.93.
13. Ibid., pp.93, 96.
14. Ibid., p.216, see also C. Hoskyns, 'Africa's Foreign Policy: the Case of Tanzania', *International Affairs*, Vol. 44, No. 3, July 1968.
15. Quoted in Hughes, op. cit., p.204.
16. *Uganda Herald*, 24 April 1952.
17. See for instance J.M. Lonsdale, *A Political History of Western Kenya 1883-1958* and K. Sorrenson, *Land Reform in Kikuyu Country* (Oxford, Clarendon, 1960).
18. Cherry Gertzel, *The Politics of Independent Kenya* (London, Heinemann, 1970).

19. Hughes, op. cit., pp.117-9.
20. C. Pratt, *The Critical Phase in Tanzania 1945-68; Nyerere and the Emergence of a Socialist Strategy* (Cambridge, Cambridge University Press, 1976).
21. Ibid., p.41.
22. Ibid., p.55.
23. Ibid., pp.56-7.
24. Ibid., p.58.
25. Mboya, op. cit., p.214.
26. Ibid., p.211.
27. A Declaration of Federation of East Africa by the Governments of East Africa, as reproduced in D. Rothchild, (ed.) *Politics of Integration* pp.76-8;
28. Ibid.
29. House of Representatives Debates (Kenya), *Official Report,* First Session, Vol. 1 (27 June 1963) cols. 403-430.
30. Quoted in D.J. Morgan, *British Private Investment in East Africa* (London, O.D.I., 1965), p.49.
31. C. Leys and P. Robson, *Federation in East Africa: Opportunities and Problems* (London, Oxford University Press, 1965), for discussion of O.D.I. Conference. See Volume I p.183, where they argue that the concept 'East Africa' was no less real to a peasant than the concept 'Uganda' or 'Tangankyika.'
32. *Uganda Argus,* 11 May and 27 June 1964.
33. See Volume I, Chapter
34. J.H. Proctor Jr., 'The Effort to Federate East Africa: A Postmortem', *Political Quarterly,* Vol. 7, No. 1, January-March, 1966, p.68.
35. *Daily Nation,* 5 August 1964.
36. *East African Standard,* 3 August 1964.
37. J. Kenyatta, *Harambee! The Prime Minister of Kenya's Speeches 1963-1964* (London, O.U.P., 1964), p.28.
38. See Leys and Robson, op. cit., and Proctor, op. cit.
39. See Proctor, op. cit.
40. *East African Standard,* 25 October 1963.
41. Well brought out in Proctor's article, op. cit. See also Leys & Robson an *Uganda Argus,* 17 June 1965.
42. Leys and Robson, op. cit., particularly introduction and conclusion.
43. A. Mazrui, 'Tanzania versus East Africa', *Journal of Commonwealth Political Studies,* Vol. III, No. 3, November 1965, pp.220-5.
44. Ibid.
45. P.G. Clark, *Development Planning in East Africa* (Nairobi, E.A.P.H., 1965), pp.17-26 see also P. Ndegwa, *The Common Market and Development in East Africa* (Nairobi, E.A.P.H., 1965).
46. Pratt, op. cit., pp.172-8.
47. Ibid., p.178.
48. See Volume I, Chapter
49. See J. Rweyemamu, *Underdevelopment and Industrialization in Tanzania* (Nairobi, Heinemann, 1973), p.75.
50. M. Yaffey, *Balance of Payments Problems in a Developing Country: Tanzania* (Munich, Welt Forum 1965), p.75.

51. Rweyemamu, op. cit., p.125.
52. Ibid., p.98; see also A.O. Hirschman, *The Strategy of Economic Development* (New Haven, Yale University Press, 1957), pp.61-90;
53. See Volume I, Chaper
54. Rweyemamu, Table 4.4, p.131.
55. J. Nyerere, *Freedom and Socialism* (Oxford, Clarendon, 1968), p.64. This is his speech to Central Legislative Assembly in Dar es Salaam on 10 August 1965.
56. Ibid., pp.60-5. For a good account of these strains, see R. Green and A. Seidman, *Unity or Poverty: The Economics of Pan-Africanism* (London, Penguin, 1968), pp.142-5.
57. Speech in the National Assembly, 13 June 1966, *Nationalist* 14 June 1966, p.7.
58. P. Bomani, Radio Address as Minister of Finance of Tanzania, reproduced in H.E. Smith (ed.), *Readings on Economic Development and Administration in Tanzania* (Institute of Public Administration, University College of Dar es Salaam, Tanzania, 1966), p.121.
59. East Africa Currency Board, *Report for the Year Ended 1965*, (Nairobi) pp.1-22.
60. Ibid.
61. Ibid.
62. Ibid.
63. Ibid.
64. J. Nyerere, 'The Extent and Viability of East African Co-operation' in Leys and Robson, op. cit., pp.43-4. See also C. Rosberg and A. Segal (eds.), *East African Federation,* Int. Conciliation, Vol. 3.
65. P.G. Clark, *The Role of a Central Bank in Accelerating Economic Development in Problems of Economic Development in East Africa* (Nairobi, E.A.I.S.R./E.A.P.H., 1965), pp.83-92.
66. Clark, *Development Planning,* op. cit., p.55.
67. T.M. Franck, *East African Unity through Law* (New Haven, Yale University Press 1964), p.163.
68. Green and Seidman, op. cit., p.145.
69. Nyerere, op. cit., p.66.
70. *The Nationalist* (Dar es Salaam), 20 July 1965, p.4.
71. Nyerere, op. cit., pp.66-7.

7. The Structure of Regional Economic Integration

The Philip Commission

The political transformation of the three countries of East Africa into three separate nation-states was the result of the struggles of the people in each of the three countries for national independence. All classes agreed that it was only on the basis of national independence that their societies could be further transformed into developed democratic societies. In a word, national independence was to be a precondition for the economic and social development of the people and a basis for future struggles.

The new slogan was the development of the national economy and the consolidation of political independence against imperialist attempts to reinstate the *status quo*. Although we know that the consolidation of the national economies was impossible because of their continued domination by transnational finance capital, yet the political achievements that the people had won and the further aspirations to its consolidation were important political developments and the potential groundwork for future struggles.

The nation-state constituted in reality the very basis on which the region's future transformations would have to be made. This reality had now gripped the minds of the leaders in the three territories. Having failed in their effort to create a Pan African political federation of East Africa, each territory now decided that any future co-operation in the region would have to be on an economic basis alone. It is to this that the three leaders now agreed when, at their meeting in Mombasa at the end of August 1965, they agreed to Kenya's call made in June for the review of the EACSO Agreement.

The Philip Commission addressed itself to the problems arising out of this new situation. Taking these developments as the starting point, they tried to find the best ways of continuing some kind of economic co-operation between the three states. It was Philip himself who pointed to the continuing need, however, for some kind of political binding force, even if short of a political union:

> We cannot expect the Common Market to function as long as there is no common political power to take decisions. Not to have a political power in this field would only be possible provided all three countries

were following the principles of 19th century liberalism. As all the three countries are practising economic planning and all three wish to intererefe in the economic development, it is necessary that there exists a responsible political body to govern the Common Market. As modifications would have to be introduced in the Common Market, and as a machinery will have to be established, it is necessary to make a Treaty concerning the Common Market between the three countries, Economic life is, however, developing so fast that a Treaty of this kind should contain, mainly, general principles and the provisions necessary to establish the machinery. This meachinery should have three levels, namely, political, official, and a tribunal to solve disputes.[1]

It will be seen later that, despite the Commission's acknowledgement of the changes in capitalism, their own economic logic was still rooted in the theories of 19th-Century free trade capitalism. It is not that the three countries had a 'wish to interfere' in economic development — this had long been necessary even in the most developed capitalist countries — the issue was rather what were the overriding economic forces under which the three countries' economies were operating. Seeing that the dominant forces in the three economies had a strong tendency towards competition at the level of the individual enterprise, this tended to pull apart any moves towards economic co-operation, despite the political institutions that might emerge to give direction to regional co-operation. It is these forces which had been mainly responsible for the failure of political federation and it is these same forces that were ultimately to bring about the disintegration of the political structures worked out by Philip and his colleagues.

These regional structures were designed as an alternative to a direct integration of the economic activities of the three nation-states into the trans-national monopoly forms. Such an integration was seen by the three countries as a possible consequence of the economic weakness of the 'national' bourgeoisies there. Nonetheless the parameters were dictated by the international institutions which spelt out the basic logic of finance capital based on the transnational monopoly firm. In their re-arrangement of the Common Market, the Philip Commission had to pay attention to these multilateral disciplines.

For example, one of the Working Papers of the Commission discussed whether the existing Customs Union could be maintained, although it had existed before GATT came into being. New elements were likely to be introduced in the new GATT treaty, but these were not likely to be substantial: the restrictions the treaty imposed on intra Customs Union trade would probably cover only a moderate fraction of say 20% of reciprocal trade flows. Thus, the Commission argued, it would probably be possible to apply to GATT for a waiver under Article XXIV of their rules, so long as these restrictions were of a temporary character. This was because the GATT rules required that a customs union must cover 'substantially all the trade' in such union. As is well known, this GATT Article is based on the free trade logic that a customs union will be beneficial if on the whole it is 'trade creating' and harmful if it is 'trade diverting'. In the first case, the removal of tariffs on 'substantially all the [intra-union] trade will tend to increase trade between the countries comprising the customs union in that production will be diverted to the most efficient producers in the union, and in this way benefit also the world market. It would have been trade creating.' It was with these arguments in mind that the Commission, despite their acknowledgement of the fact of a new situation, set out to provide answers to the question of East African economic co-operation.

On the issue of the Common Market, its basic objectives were to work out structures that would foster more rapid economic growth in all three countries, in order to remove inbalances in their development and avoid any one of them lagging behind the others. The future of such growth would lie in industrial expansion on the basis of a large integrated East African Common Market. It acknowledged that for some time such industrialization would depend on import-substitution based on the home market rather than on exports. Such integrated development, the Commission argued, would provide for efficient and full utilization of productive resources through economies of scale, including specialization in respect of final products and the production of components for assembly industries etc. The resulting increase in competition for the market was seen as a further spur to increase efficiency. This would then increase the applicability of various instruments, such as co-ordinated and guaranteed protection, and increase the availability of financial resources, while generating activities in infrastructure, small-scale and service industries etc.

But such development, it was further argued by the Commission, would have to be within the context of a balanced development between the three countries. Given the current industrial imbalance in East Africa and the fact that this could be corrected only gradually, it followed that, for a time, the balance of advantage in respect of industrial preferences would be in favour of the more industrialized of the three countries, i.e. Kenya. The machinery they recommended to achieve a balanced development was the creation of a Common Market Council, a Secretariat for an Industrial Development Board, a Tax Board, and a Trade and Agricultural Board, as well a Common Market Tribunal.

The desired equalizing and balancing effects in future industrial development, it was further recommended, could be achieved primarily through a surcharge on goods being exported from a surplus country to a deficit country. Also a development bank would direct most of the investment capital available to the less developed countries in terms of industry. And there would be maintained the protection afforded by the common external tariff and the co-ordination of other investment incentives such as duty refunds and rebates, tax allowances, as well as special railway rates in support of industrial and mining development.

The allocation of industries would be carried out by the Industrial Licensir Board on the basis of existing legislation, with the additional industrial location criterion of a balanced spread of development throughout the whole area. This would supposedly enable the development of 'East African industries' serving the whole market. The new surcharge system should not apply to such industries.

As regards agricultural products, the Commission noted that the impediment to free flow in the Common Market was the monopsonistic and monopolistic decisions taken at the national level, and was not the effect of the workings of 'impersonal and competitive forces'. Under such conditions it would be idle to propose a total free trade in these products and two different sets of arrangements would have to be devised: free trade mechanisms for most agricultural products and special marketing arrangements for the rest. It would also be necessary to create gradually mechanisms for co-ordination of future agricultural policies.

In the field of co-ordination of economic policy and planning, the Commission noted that the three national plans had been prepared with very little contact between the three countries' planning units, without consultation about planning methods, assumptions, production structures and techniques, potential markets, etc. The best starting point for future co-operation, the Commission believed, would be provided by a thorough common analysis of each country's national plan, leading up to 'a confrontation of the plans', both of the overall structure and of the many sectors of which they are composed, enabling differences in method, assumptions, facts and statistics to be reconciled. This would help to identify inconsistencies or clashes in the implications or results of the separate national development plans and policies, thus enabling adjustments to be made, resulting possibly in a comprehensive development plan for East Africa.

As to the East African Common Services and in accordance with their terms of reference, the Commission recommended that, in the interests of efficiency and economy, each of these services should be maintained as a 'joint endeavour', but that there should be a considerable measure of reorganization and/or decentralization of management and operations. These common services were those which were being run as 'self-contained services' under EACSO as well as what were known as general fund services.

As regards services like Railways and Harbours, the Commission was careful to note that whatever recommendations they made for reorganization and/or decentralization would have to take into account the fact that the World Bank would have to agree to such changes since, under the Loan Agreement signed the previous year by the three governments, no major changes should be made in the constitution and organization of the E.A.R. & H. without the 'prior approval of the Bank'.

There was also the question of research services and taxation. Here the Commission recommended that the research services run by EACSO, except industrial and marketing research, should be continued. For industrial and marketing research, new proposals were made to accord with the recommendations made at the Lusaka Economic Commission for Africa conference to bring the services into a wider regional arrangement encompassing more than just East Africa. It was emphasized that all these services should now move away from 'British thinking' to reflect East African conditions. The income tax services were also to be retained at the regional level involving collection and disbursements to the partner states; also the customs services.[2] It was on the basis of some of these observations that the Treaty for East African Co-operation was finally drafted.

The Treaty for East African Co-operation

The Treaty[3] merely formalized the existing arrangements for regional co-operation while, at the same time, introducing new institutions and procedures to maintain, strengthen and modify certain imbalances in trade and industrial growth. The principal aim of the Community was declared in Article 2 of the Treaty; it was to strengthen and regulate the industrial, commercial, and other relationships, so as to achieve an accelerated, harmonious, balanced, sustained development of the economies of the three countries. It was also declared to be a long-term aim of the parties to establish a common agricultural policy. Article 3 stipulated the institutions of the Community. The Preamble stated:

> *Whereas* the United Republic of Tanzania, the Sovereign state of Uganda and the Republic of Kenya have enjoyed close commercial, industrial and other ties for many years:
> *And whereas* provision was made by the East Africa (High Commission) Order-in-Council 1947 to 1961 for the control and administration of certain matters and services of common interest to the said countries, and for that purpose the East African High Commission and the Central Legislative Assembly were thereby established:
> *And whereas* the East African Common Services Organization has, since its establishment, performed on behalf of the said countries common services in accordance with the wishes of the said countries and its Constitution:
> *And whereas* the said countries, while aware that they have reached different stages of industrial development and resolved to reduce existing industrial imbalances, are resolved and determined to foster and encourage the accelerated and sustained industrial development of all the said countries:
> *'Agreed'* to the Treaty for East African Co-operation creating the East African Community.

It established an East African Common Market (EACM) as an integral part of the East African Community (EAC), and provided for the continuation of common services and the harmonization of monetary, balance of payments, fiscal, and economic planning policies (although in the case of the latter these were only stated to be aims). There was to be an Authority comprising the three Presidents as the highest political organ of the Community. There were also Councils of Ministers and officials of the Community, as well as Corporations running the institutions and implementing policies. A Secretariat headed by a Secretary-General was to act as the executive to the Community, and an East African Legislative Assembly to legislate on EAC matters. There were to be four Corporations running the common services of Airways, Harbours, Railways and Posts and Telecommunications, on commercial lines. Other institutions were to include an East African Court of Appeal, the East African Industrial Court to settle labour disputes, an East African Tax Board as an advisory body to keep under reveiw the administration of the East African Income Tax Department and the Customs and Excise Department, to study the correlation of tax systems and to assist in taxation planning. There was also to be an East African Common Market Tribunal to supervise the operation of the Common Market.

A Common Market

The main provision about the Common Market was the continuation of a common customs tariff in respect of all goods imported into the partner states from foreign sources (Article 5). The customs duty collected was to be paid to the consuming state (Article 10). It was further provided that no internal tariff or any quantitative restrictions were to be imposed on East African goods. A new element consistent with the needs of 'balanced' industrial development in the region as a whole was the basis of an exception to the above general rule, in that the Treaty provided for the imposition of what the Philip Commission had called 'a surcharge' in the form of a transfer tax (Article 20), as well as the setting up of an East African Development Bank (Article 21), as levers to promote 'balanced' industrial development.

The Transfer Tax System

The Treaty provided that an industrially less developed parter state could impose a transfer tax on manufactures from an industrially more developed partner state in order to protect its own industry that either was in existence or was likely to come into existence within three months of the imposition of such a tax. This tax could, however, be imposed only by a country which at the same time was in deficit so far as intra-regional trade in manufactured goods was concerned. Moreover, such tax could only be imposed on imports from the country with which it had a deficit. Furthermore, the tax could only be applied to those types of goods which the tax-imposing country had the capacity to produce on a significant scale (15% of the domestic consumption of goods in the year before the imposition of the tax or a value of £100,000). The tax was not to exceed the deficit recorded.

The rate of tax was not to exceed 50% of the external tariff on that product. The tax was seen as a temporary device which was to expire eight years after imposition and the whole system was to be reviewed after five years (Article 20) and to come to an end after fifteen years. Annex IV to the Treaty spelt out the products that would be subject to the transfer tax. These included, besides the usual factory products, such items as bacon, ham, tinned milk, cheese, butter, ghee, flour, roasted coffee and other processed foods, petroleum products, cigarettes, textiles, tobacco, sugar, chemicals etc. In this way it was argued that the less developed partner states would become more attractive for industrial investment in the same products, but to do this, as Hazelwood has pointed out, the inter-state trade balance in manufactures was used as a 'proxy' measure for such industrial development.[4]

The rationale behind the system was given by the Philip Commission: briefly, it was that the tax would help the import-substitution of certain products which were 'viable' within the national markets, while ruling out the establishment of the larger industries which could only be viable on an East African basis. This would therefore also permit such 'East African industries' to be established in any of the three territories on the basis of licensing, thus establishing complementarity in the regional economies.

But even in the case of an 'East African industry', if subsequently there was room for two such industries to be established in the region, a transfer tax could be used for a second factory to be built in another state, thus giving such industry a degree of tariff protection. But such a factory could only be built by a monopoly other than the one which had a plant in the first territory, for in such a case the threat of the tax would probably make it preferable to expand production in the first than invest in an entirely new one.[5] This was because the first plant might export more cheaply to the tax-imposing state, even taking into account the transfer tax, rather than produce with a new plant in that state. Yaffey has given the following example in support of this hypothesis: supposing there are two producers, one in Uganda and one in Kenya, and a transfer tax of 10% is applied against the latter, the external tariff being 20%; and supposing that the 20% tariff gives just sufficient protection to enable the Ugandan industry to compete against overseas imports but that the Kenyan industry requires only 5% protection. Then the Kenyan producer (paying, let us suppose, only 4% for transport costs to Uganda) can still undercut the Ugandan producer in Uganda as well as in Kenya and Tanzania. Yaffey qualifies this by emphasizing that this would be the case only where the external tariff is very high, and where the hypothetical Ugandan producer is very inefficient.[6] This example of Yaffey's is an important one. Although it is based on the concept of free competition, it reveals possibilities of new competition in the region even under conditions of tax regulation.

But the hypothesis is equally applicable in the reverse case, and this is the crucial point. Where the initial Kenyan investor prefers to expand in Kenya given the tax, it would still be possible for an 'efficient' monopoly to establish itself in the Ugandan market. But since this 'efficiency' will in fact depend on the other monopoly privileges it would obtain in Uganda such as short write-off periods and other tax remissions, it would be possible for such a monopoly to move in to Uganda and establish a second plant there, thus removing any complementarity in the region's overall industrial development. And indeed this was to be a real feature of East Africa's industrialization even in those areas where 'East African industries' were supposed to develop, as we shall see in the next section. Thus the transfer tax system tended to reinforce parallel industrial development in the region overall, re-emphasizing the new nation-state as a firm basis on which monopolies could base their competition.

Indeed President Nyerere was to point to this fact when he indicated the complexity of the new situation posed by monopolistic competition:

> Each of the Partner States goes ahead on its own, trying to interest foreign firms or foreign governments in such a project. And the foreign firms do sometimes agree. After all, their main concern is to sell their machinery to us, either for purposes of extending their competition to East Africa, or simply as a means of making immediate profit for themselves. In either case, the cost of the necessary subsidy will have to be borne by us. So we have the absurd position where both Kenya and Tanzania, in partnership with competing foriegn firms, set up a tyre factory — each of which requires the whole East African market to be economic.[7]

Such a situation, Hazelwood has argued, would result from the fact that the foreign investor would not view the high costs of producing in a small market as 'a decisive concern' for him, since these would be offset, as we have noted, by provision of favourable terms by the states,[8] more often than not as a result of pressure by the monopoly.

The East African Development Bank

The second instrument that was supposed to play a role in removing the imbalance in the industrial development of the region was the East African Development Bank. The Treaty, in Articles 21 and 22, established the Bank and provided for a charter for its operations in Annex VI. The charter enjoined the Bank to provide financial and technical assistance to promote the industrial development of the partner states. It was to give priority to industrial development, according to stipulated principles, to the relatively less industrially developed partner states and to finance 'where possible' projects designed to make the economies of the partner states increasingly complementary in the industrial field. Furthermore, it was required to supplement the activities of the national development agencies by jointly financing projects and to co-operate with other institutions.and organizations, private or public, national or international, which were 'interested' in the industrial development of the partner states; and to undertake such activities and provide such other services as might advance the objectives of the Bank.

The initial capital of the Bank was limited to Shs. 600 million of which Shs. 120 million was to be paid-up capital and the rest made up of loans. The charter prescribed the territorial distribution of its investment in given percentages in order to help remove the imbalance in industrial development. It required the Bank to invest 38½% of its funds in both Tanzania and Uganda and 22½% in Kenya, or as near as possible to these percentages, over a five-year period. Since the partner states contributed equal shares of capital to the Bank, these investment ratios were supposed to have the effect of redistributing investments away from Kenya in favour of the other two states in the Bank's operations, as a means of removing the imbalance in their industrial development.

The Bank's charter was, however, silent as to how the Bank could achieve complementarity in its operations. No guidelines whatever were given. This left the discretion to the Bank, although it didn't amount to very much. Any such complementarity that the Bank could have helped create was militated against by the fact that there were other major sources of industrial invest-ment funds. Thus, even if the investment distribution formula was applied rigorously, the imbalance could and indeed did remain because Kenya raised funds from external sources for its industrial development in order to supple-ment the Bank's funds.[9] And since the Bank's investments were being made in an atmosphere dominated by this type of competition, it was very easy for the Bank's strategy to be thrown out of gear. Moreover the Bank itself was a competitor with each of the partner states in the world money markets for some of its projects.

The forces against complementarity were also inherent in the stipulations as to what types of investment activities the Bank should get involved in. The charter stipulated that the Bank should only invest in manufacturing, assembly and processing industries. It could not therefore invest in agriculture, buildings, transport, tourism or commerce. Due to the overriding reality that the East African states produced what they did not consume and consumed what they did not produce, this restriction had an important bearing on the industrial development that the Bank could help bring about.

First, most of the existing import-substitution industries imported much of their raw materials. Second, most of the agricultural plantations exported their agricultural products in a semi-processed or unprocessed condition; so that even in sectors like vegetable and fruit canning, meat packing, poultry processing, bacon, vegetable oil extraction, oil-seed processing etc., expansion was hampered by non-availability of raw materials and agricultural products since these were being produced for export 'to earn foreign exchange'.

Thus the Bank in its prescribed investment policy, tailored as it was to the neo-colonial character of the three countries' economies, could not finance the production of raw materials necessary to enable their processing to be undertaken, particularly in those industries based on local natural resources.[10] For this reason it appeared, at this stage at least, that the Bank's solution was not much of a solution to the problem of removing uneven development in the region.

Industrial Licensing
To compound the problem of industrial development, the Treaty in Article 23 pointed out that the partner states had agreed that the present industrial licensing system should continue for 20 years after the commencement of the relevant legislation. Since these statutes had been applied on an East African basis from 1953, this meant the system was to continue until 1973. It was

agreed that no additions were to be made to the allocation schedules of industrial products in the Acts. There was to be a replacement of these laws by a new law when agreed, which was to be a Community law. An Industrial Licensing Board was to continue and an Appeal Tribunal 'on matters of law only' was to be set up. This meant that, until the new law was passed, no new industries could be established enjoying protection over the whole of the East African market. This encouraged competititve import-substitution between the territories and so worked against complementarity. Indeed as our hypothetical case of duplication of 'East African industries' shows, the possibility that a monopoly, given certain privileges, could 'efficiently' build a second plant in another partner state, introduced a new element in the region's industrialization which went some way to making nonsense of this part of the Treaty provisions.

To confirm the neo-colonial nature of each of the economies of the three countries, the Treaty in Article 13 provided that, with the exception of a few products, the partner states shall 'have the right' to introduce quantitative restrictions against the importation of the other partner states' agricultural products when these are basic staple foods or major export crops. It was further declared that it was to be the long-term aim of the states to establish and maintain a common market in agricultural products accompanied by co-operation and consultation in the field of agricultural policy, particularly in trade arrangements between national agencies and marketing boards, within a single system of prices and marketing services and facilities. Annex III listed the products to which the Article applied. They included all the major staple foods like maize and maize flour, wheat, rice, beans, meat, milk, eggs, fruit, groundnuts, millet and simsim. The major cash crops for export were coffee, pyrethrum flowers, cotton, cotton seed, sisal etc. Thus the three countries guaranteed raw materials and agricultural products to the industrialized imperialist countries for their industries, but none to themselves for their own local industrial development, while also restricting the movement of food products within the region.

Other Provisions

The other provisions concerned currency and banking matters. It was stipulated that the three currencies would be exchanged at par without paying exchange commission. Payments for current transactions were to be guaranteed but transfers on capital account could be restricted to the extent necessary to further the economic development of the restricting states. Inter-state settlements were to be made by the central banks in open accounts. The member states also agreed to pursue an economic policy aimed at ensuring an equilibrium in balance of payments — an impossible task since they did not have any control over their economies — and a harmonization of monetary policies to the extent required for the 'proper functioning of the Common Market' and the fulfilment of the aims of the Community. For this reason, the Governors of the central banks were to meet four times a year to consult, co-ordinate and review their monetary and balance-of-payments policies (Articles 24-27). Article 28 provided for reciprocal credits in case of balance-of-payments difficulties. The support was to come from the surplus state towards the one in deficit. We shall see in the next section that these provisions did not have much substance.

The Common Services
The Treaty also addressed itself to the existing common services built up by British imperialism to serve the entire region. The new Community was, on behalf of the partner states, to take over and administer these services for the needs of the region. These were listed in an Annex and included such services as civil aviation, meteorological services, customs and excise collection, income tax collection, audit and a number of scientific research services. These were to be paid for out of a general fund and special funds in a distributable pool of revenue from income and customs collections.

In addition, the Treaty provided for the continuation of the 'self-contained' services which were to be restructured as corporations. It was provided that these corporations shall, on behalf of the partner states, administer the railways, harbours, posts and telecommunications as well as the airways hitherto run by the East African Common Services Organization (Article 13). They were to conduct their business 'according to commercial principles' and to ensure that, 'taking one year with another', their revenues were not less than sufficient to meet their outgoings. The outgoings — which were to become very heavy and create problems in the future — were to include depreciation of capital assets, pension liabilities, interest on loans, and the repayment of the loans themselves, as well as the operating costs. The corporations were to distribute their non-physical investments so as to ensure an 'equitable' contribution to the foreign exchange resources of each of the partner states, taking into account the scale of thier operations. They were also required to arrange their purchases in such a way as to ensure an equitable distribution of the benefits (Articles 71 and 72).

A number of other institutions, including an Industrial Court to settle workers' disputes with the Community and a Court of Appeal for the three states, were also provided for.

But perhaps one of the major provisions of the Treaty was the one which took account of the desire of each of the states to strengthen its national economies, the provisions relating to the *decentralization* of services and institutions. In many ways these provisions marked a stage on the path towards the further dismantling of colonial regional structures and therefore reinforced the yearning for national independence and the dominant forces of transnational monopolistic competition — interests which converged in this respect. Article 86 and Annex XIV of the Treaty provided measures for the decentralization of services administered by the Community to each partner state in respect of customs and excise, income tax, meteorological departments and the directorate of civil aviation. They also provided for the decentralization of railways, posts and telecommunications, and airways corporations. As far as the services provided by the Community were concerned, the decentralization measures envisaged the appointment of commissioners or directors in each of the services to exercise some control in each of the states. The decentralization measures envisaged the establishment of 'strong and functionally comparable' railway and posts and telecommunications regional headquarters and of ensuring that future development in the airways should, so far as was possible, be sited in Uganda and Tanzania, as well as the giving of special consideration to the development of harbours in Tanzania.

All these measures involved a lot of bargaining and their implementation or non-implementation, as we shall see later, was one of the elements in the problems that faced the Community in the period of crisis after 1971.

References

1.   K. Philip, 'The Future of the East African Economic Activities' Working Paper of the Commission on East African Cooperation.
2.   For a brief discussion of these arguments see A. Hazelwood, *Economic Integration: The East African Experience* (London, Heinemann, 1975).
3.   E.A.C., *Treaty for East African Co-operation*, (Nairobi, E.A. Community Printer, Revised Edition 1972). Most of the summary that follows is from this edition.
4.   Hazelwood, op. cit., p.73.
5.   M.J.H. Yaffey, 'The Treaty for East African Cooperation' in P.A. Thomas, *Private Enterprise and the East African Company*, (Dar es Salaam, T.P.H., 1967), p.274.
6.   Ibid., p.275.
7.   J.K. Nyerere, *The Standard* (Dar es Salaam), 9 February 1972, p.76.
     F. Ojow, 'East African Industrial Bank and the Industrial Development of East Africa', Mimeo, 1972, Social Sciences Conference of the East African Universities 1972, Kampala'.
9.   Ibid., p.3.
10. Ibid., pp.4-5.

8. The Economics of Co-operation

The economic developments that took place henceforth in the region and particularly in the area of economic co-operation and integration were very much determined by the dominant forces of a new monopolistic competition. The structures and institutions for regional co-operation introduced under the Treaty of Co-operation merely went to strengthen these forces. This comes out very clearly in the type of industrialization that took place as soon as the Treaty was accepted.

As we have seen in the previous chapter, it was envisaged that 'industrial imbalance' would be corrected if the relatively undeveloped territories were given instruments of protection which could guarantee them a level of industrial development. This was to be based on an import-substitution strategy, with certain 'infant industries' for 'mass products' dependent on the home market. The development and further enhancement of co-operation would then be assured by the industrial licensing system under the existing legislation which provided for a number of 'East African industries' in which economies of scale were presumed to be vital. Predictably, what in fact happened was that a state of parallel industrialization began to emerge within each territory.

Import-Substitution Industrialization

This period saw three types of development in industrialization. The first was the decay of the old protected industries which had produced for the entire East African market before 1963-64, i.e. industries — usually based in Kenya — and protected under the structures of British monopoly. This corresponded to the rise of similar industries but now based on the transfer tax system. These industries covered sectors like beverages and tobacco, footwear and clothing and non-metallic products (especially cement). Within a few years, industrialization in these sectors, in Tanzania and to a lesser extent in Uganda, was intensified with the result that trade between the partner states in those products began to decline.

The second type of industrialization took place in those sectors in which there was a relative growth of gross industrial output but involving negligible growth in exports to the other partner states. Some of these industries arose after 1964, although others had existed before. They included industries like leather and rubber, textiles, food and metal products. They were based almost entirely on the home market for their growth and further fuelled the parallel industrial development within the region, thus contributing greatly to non-complementarity.

The third category were those post-1964 industries based on the East African market as a whole and whose growth depended therefore on inter-state trade. These products were in the chemical, petroleum, electrical machinery, and wood (pulp, furniture and paper) industries. Most of these were not protected in any way under industrial licensing and were based in Kenya. Petroleum and chemicals, for instance, accounted for 25% of the gross industrial output of Kenya in 1970 while inter-state trade in these same products accounted for 36% of Kenya's trade with the other two partner states. But as the crisis in the neo-colonial economies intensified after 1971, efforts were made to import-substitute in these categories as well, particularly in Tanzania.

It will be noted that the allocation of the 'East African industries' reco-mmended under the Kampala/Mbale Agreement of 1964-65 did not become operative nor were they licensed. Two years after the Treaty, efforts by the Community to introduce 'multinational industries' in the iron and steel, automobile, chemical and fertilizer sectors failed. Since each country was engaged in a strategy of import-substitution and, given the competition of international finance capital seeking a foothold in each of the territories, there was no serious urge on the part of any of the states to push for a rational allocation of any of these industries using the existing legislation.

1973 was the expiry date for the colonial industrial licensing legislation which had been retained under the Treaty. Because of the economic crisis which had gripped the region since 1971, no efforts were made to produce a new East Africa Community legal provision for licensing as required by the Treaty. The result was that competitive import-substitution also entered this category of industrialization, thus leading these 'East African industries' to under-capacity situations.[1]

Thus, overall, we see a pattern in which consumer goods were predomin-antly national market industries while certain intermediate products to some extent catered for the East African regional market. But despite this there was very little complementarity or linkages between the production units in the region. Inhibited already by the dominant international linkages of which East Africa formed a part, complementarity was also limited by the regional structures created under the Treaty, such as the transfer tax and the Devel-opment Bank.

Under the new arrangements it was no longer possible to maintain even the pre-1966 linkages, such as Madhvani group of companies in Uganda which imported certain raw materials from Tanzania and Kenya to manufacture vegetable oils and soaps, glassware, sweets etc. for the whole market.

The linkages which had been established by Bandora Steel Mills in Kenya to take another example; using iron and steel billets from Uganda and scrap collected from the whole of East Africa, came to a halt.[2] This occurred despite the fact that a (very low) pattern of specialization had begun to emerge with Kenya's main role in East African production being in chemicals and petroleum products, Uganda's specializing in iron and steel as well as some kinds of textiles and Tanzania in another kind of textiles as well as metal products, especially aluminium.

Although Kenya's production was more diversified than Uganda's and Tanzania's, it too did not have any internal or intra-state linkages. Even though Kenya therefore had a trade surplus compared with the other two states, such surplus was siphoned out of the country because of her own economic weakness, and this deficit also tended to lead to a reduction in intra-state trade. For this reason, Kenya's ability to tap increased incomes in the other two countries was not redounding to her advantage.

Tanzanian and Ugandan duplication of Kenyan industries under the import-substitution strategy was not leading to any short-term or even long-term benefits. Already high-cost for the benefit of the same monopolies, more importantly no real integrated economic development was in fact taking place.

This dependence of the three countries on imperialist monopolies was not merely structural but organic since it was based on exploitation and domination established during the colonial era, and is properly to be understood at the level of production. We argued in Chapter Five that the fundamental cause of the strains and stresses in the East African High Commission arrangement of the mid-1950s was the increased rate of exploitation of peasant and semi-proletarian labour in the region. Now this over-exploitation showed up as a structural problem of the terms of trade in international trade relationships, specifically in the low prices of primary commodities.

International and Inter-State Trade

East African studies in this period showed that, whilst the prices of manufactured goods increased, those of primary export commodities produced by the peasantry and semi-proletarian labour fell considerably. Taking 1954 as the base year, the terms of trade in East Africa declined by 67% by 1971 over the very limited range of agricultural exports produced by the peasantry. It can be seen why the value of imports rose very sharply while those of exports declined in the same way. Taking 1964 as equalling 100, the growth in the value of Kenya's imports increased to 240 by 1971, while the value of her domestic exports rose only to 157. In the case of Tanzania and Uganda, taking the same base as for Kenya, the growth in the value imports went up to 257 and 208 respectively in 1971, while the increase in the index of their domestic exports went up only to 121 and 130 respectively. The overall picture is a relative decline in export earnings vis-a-vis the imports index in all three countries.

These developments, neo-colonial as they were, would not permit fundamental changes in the trade pattern of the region. Due to these countries' true character as complementary units for the transnational corporate monopolies operating there, they could not divert trade away from the imperialist countries to which they were tied by innumerable threads of exploitation and domination. The result was that they could not sell much to each other while the transnational monopolies increased their imports. All three continued to produce virtually the same main primary products, which could not be the subject of inter-state trade but had to be exported to the same monopolies to fulfil their industrial needs. From these exports of raw materials, the monopolies supplied most of the imports of the region as well as raw materials for the import substitution industries.

A comparative analysis[3] of East African trade structures carried out by the Common Market Secretariat revealed that imports from third countries (mainly imperialist countries) grew faster than trade transfers between the states in the region. The reason given was that the structure of regional production had not evolved in line with the structure of regional demand. For this reason it was concluded that the performance of the Common Market had been 'disappointing' relative to the hopes the partner states had entertained when they signed the Treaty. It was now asserted that the assumptions on which the Treaty had been based were either wrong or that the states had behaved in ways that frustrated its potential benefits. Moreover, it was also stated that the underlying assumption of the Treaty, that trade 'was a substantial engine of growth' capable of causing expansion of the region's economy and creating incomes so as to lead to balanced and more efficient location patterns of East Africa's industry, had been shown not to be correct after five years of operation of the Treaty.

The study went on at length to show some of what it considered to be the fundamental problems inherent in this type of integration. First, it was pointed out that the existence of an important asymmetrical relationship between the structure of production and consumption led to a situation where the region produced 'what it did not consume' and consumed 'what it did not produce': 'This yields a narrow base on which to liberalize trade, and a correspondingly narrow scope for potential benefits from trade liberalization.' Such asymmetrical relationships might occur not only at the level of final demand, but also at the level of demand for intermediate inputs if much of the manufacturing activity depended upon imported inputs from non-East African sources. In that case, *expansion* of production and trade actually *disintegrated* the Common Market, 'because it calls forth a structural dependence on non-East African inputs'. Expansion and integration were not the same thing. If demand was weighted to favour exports, expansion in each depended on outside forces.

Second, the trade expansion approach to integration may not change the structure of the system because it does not direct investment towards the areas that are most essential to the process of structural change. The trade expansion approach tends to widen the market precisely for those goods already being imported, thus inducing an import substitution of similar products having the same design and similar input specifications, technology etc., as the former imports. The tariff merely went to reinforce this strategy by high rates of effective protection to final output:

> The rationale is the apparent ease with which manufacturing develops in the regional market, because the goods retain immediate marketability characteristics, and there is no need to develop designs, processes or inputs prior to final or semi-final assembly. It also maintains lucrative business connections with metropolitan firms supplying the inputs, the technology and even the management.[4]

These important (but structuralist) observations of the study in the end fall to grasp the fundamental problem — which was the imperialist control still being exercised in the region. Instead it advocated a co-ordinated, planned industrialization in the region as a whole, forgetting entirely the dominant forces at work, which it referred to rather as 'constraints'. Nevertheless the study gives us enough material to understand these dominant forces. Table 7 gives us some of the data to confirm these observations and thus to further confirm our thesis.

Table 7
East African Volume of Trade, 1962-71 (Shs. million)

Year	Inter-State Trade	External Trade	Inter-State + External Trade	Inter-State as % of Total Trade
1962	1,070.60	5,503.83	6,574.43	16.3
1963	1,258.18	6,312.86	7,522.03	16.6
1964	1,626.34	6,985.69	8,522.03	19.1
1965	1,802.72	7,200.40	9,003.12	20.0
1966	1,808.32	8,672.61	10,480.93	17.3
1967	1,712.52	8,343.50	10,061.02	17.0
1968	1,662.40	8,915.68	10,578.08	15.7
1969	1,740.32	9,138.52	10,878.84	16.0
1970	2,034.73	10,651.77	12,686.50	16.0
1971	2,102.60	12,498.00	14,600.60	14.4
Annual Growth Rate	7.7%	9.5%	9.2%	Average 16.8%

Source: E.A. Customs & Excise, *Annual Report, 1962-71.*

Thus, there was an annual growth rate of 7.7% for inter-state trade within the region and an annual growth rate of 9.5% for external imports, which implied no change in the relative importance of inter-state trade. Indeed 1970 and 1971 saw a decline in inter-state trade which continued throughout until the collapse of the arrangement. With the exception of one year in the case of Uganda in which imports declined absolutely, the gap between inter-state trade and external imports increased in the period 1968 to 1972 from 1:9 to 1:13 for Kenya, while that of Tanzania increased from 1:5 to 1:8. Uganda's, on the other hand, hovered around 1:2 to 1:3.

In the case of East African trade, Kenya's traditional position remained unchallenged. There was a noticeable decline in the dependence of Kenya and Tanzania on partner states' supplies, while that of Uganda increased, then decreased and then again increased. In the case of Kenya and Tanzania the growth of external imports in 1972 was very high (54.7% and 69.6% respectively), while that of Uganda (untypically) declined somewhat (−7.2%). Its transfers from the other partner states increased (possibly due to being land-locked) but in reduced quantities. The intra-East African trade had greater impact on transfers between Kenya and Uganda, and on Tanzania's transfers from Kenya. Tanzania's performance seems to have been more dynamic but only on a very narrow range of goods. By 1973 Uganda's transfers to Tanzania had almost fully ceased, even before the collapse of the Community in 1976.

Perhaps it is important to note the products in which there was an increase in imports from external sources. For Kenya, the largest increase in external imports was in chemicals, capital goods and miscellaneous manufactures including foodstuffs. Uganda imported more foodstuffs and petroleum and, since these could easily be obtained through Kenya, her reliance on external imports was somewhat reduced. Tanzania imported from external sources more foodstuffs, petroleum, chemicals and, like Kenya, intermediate goods and capital goods. In all three cases, most of the producer and intermediate goods went to import-substitution industries and, to a lesser extent, to construction and agriculture. Table 8 shows the evolution of this trade by end-use between 1968 and 1971.

Thus capital goods, intermediate goods and food and drink accounted for a large share of imports in all three states and, for this reason, went to show how imports were bound to increase as import-substitution proceeded in the region, since none of the partner states, with the slight exception of Kenya could satisfy this pattern of demand. But even Kenya's capacity to supply some of these goods depended on her imports from external sources with very little value-added, and this is why Kenya's imports from external sources are greater than that of the other two.

Siphoning Off of Resources

This type of investment activity and trade pattern must lead to a great siphoning off of resources to external sources of capital and commercial suppliers. Once this is added to the super-profits earned by the monopolies on the capital export account (which is also siphoned off), as reflected

Table 8
Evolution of Imports by End-Use, 1968 and 1971

	Kenya		Tanzania		Uganda	
% shares	*1968*	*1971*	*1968*	*1971*	*1968*	*1971*
Food and Drink	4.1	5.6	7.2	3.9	3.9	4.4
Spares and Accessories	6.7	6.7	5.8	6.4	5.6	5.5
Consumer Goods	20.1	18.4	25.5	13.2	27.2	23.8
Total Consumption	*30.9*	*30.7*	*38.5*	*24.8*	*36.7*	*33.8*
Producer's Materials	40.4	39.7	29.1	36.8	29.7	31.1
Producer Capital Goods	27.5	28.8	30.5	37.9	30.2	35.0
Total Production Goods	*67.9*	*68.5*	*59.6*	*74.7*	*59.9*	*66.1*

Note: Producer Goods plus Consumer Goods do not add up to 100% due to rounding off as well as the exclusion of the 'Miscellaneous' category.

Source: U.S.A.I.D., *The Industrialization of Tanganyika,* pp.53-5.

in the balance-of-payments deficit the result is catastrophic, as demonstrated in another study by the Common Market Secretariat.[5] This study pointed to the 'openness' of the economies of the region to international pressures and their 'dependency relationship' with the developed countries. It pointed out that with the regional gross domestic product at factor cost of Shs. 25,889 million, and external imports and exports standing at Shs. 12,329 million — a ratio of foreign trade to regional G.D.P. of 1:0.47, that is nearly half of the regional economy — the dependency relationship is almost total.

In these circumstances it followed, as the study pointed out, that the balance-of-payments position of the partner states would be affected by the ownership, management, and marketing of industry, commerce and agriculture. Equally the balance-of-payments constraints would arise out of inter-state and international transactions in a combination of various current and capital accounts. Taking the current account, which includes merchandise, freight and insurance, transportation, international investment income, travel and education as well as government inter-state and external transactions, there was a net outflow of funds overall.[6]

The negative impact in outflows was very noticeable in 1970 and 1971, for it is in these two years that the largest negative balances on the current account of these three countries were recorded. Kenya recorded a negative balance of Shs. 1,028 million, Tanzania of Shs. 559 million and Uganda of Shs. 618 million. This big growth in outflows in these two years indicated a sharply accelerated rate of foreign exchange outflow. With these developments, Kenya's deficit increased ten-fold, Tanzania five-fold and Uganda five-fold between 1966 and 1971. Kenya's 1971 deficit was thus twice that

Table 9
Partner States Fund Flows, 1968-71: Kenya (Shs. Million)

1968	Inter-State	International	Total
Inflows	989.9	1,267.3	2,264.2
Outflows	316.3	2,725.9	3,042.2
Net	+670.6	-1,458.6	-778.0
1969			
Inflows	872.2	1,566.0	2,413.2
Outflows	357.9	2,921.4	3,279.3
Net	+489.3	-1,355.4	-866.1
1970			
Inflows	930.8	1,763.8	2,693.8
Outflows	463.2	3,440.3	3,903.5
Net	+467.6	-1,707.3	-1,239.7
1971			
Inflows	991.6	1,724.7	2,716.3
Outflows	496.8	4,076.9	4,573.7
Net	+494.8	-2,352.4	-1,857.2

Table 10
Partner States Fund Flows, 1968-71: Uganda (Shs. Million)

1968	Inter-State	International	Total
Inflows	232.5	1,353.0	1,585.5
Outflows	452.9	985.8	1,438.7
Net	-220.4	+367.2	+146.8
1969			
Inflows	226.6	1,424.4	1,651.0
Outflows	532.0	1,689.5	2,221.5
Net	-305.3	-165.1	-570.5
1970			
Inflows	296.4	1,756.9	2,053.3
Outflows	522.2	962.4	1,484.6
Net	-225.8	+794.5	+568.7
1971			
Inflows	283.5	1,677.6	1,961.1
Outflows	566.7	1,484.1	2,050.8
Net	-283.3	+193.5	-89.7

Table 11
Partner States Fund Flows, 1968-71: Tanzania (Shs. Million)

	Inter-State	International	Total
1968			
Inflows	143.0	1,667.4	1,810.4
Outflows	593.2	1,665.2	2,258.4
Net	- 450.2	+ 2.2	- 448
1969			
Inflows	191.4	1,720.1	1,911.1
Outflows	375.3	1,555.7	1,931.0
Net	- 183.9	+164.4	+19.9
1970			
Inflows	238.0	1,752.2	1,990.2
Outflows	479,8	2,100.6	2,580.4
Net	- 241.8	- 348.4	- 590.2
1971			
Inflows	290.0	1,830.4	2,120.4
Outflows	501.6	2,561.8	3,063.4
Net	-211.5	-730.4	- 943

Note on Tables: Although inter-state flows of funds included in these tables cover about 90% of the total inter-state flows, the international flows shown here do *not* cover all balance-of-payments transactions, because flows on account of transportation, foreign travel, transfers and central government etc. are excluded.

Source: Ibid.

of Tanzania and Uganda.

But this dramatic increase in outflows was mainly due to the international merchandise account. The overall growth in earnings from inter-state trade as well as foreign exchange outflows due to external imports, for the years 1966-74 are shown in Table 12.

Table 12
Foreign Exchange Consequences of Trade, 1966-74 (%)

	Increase in Net Earnings from Inter-State Trade	Increase in Foreign Exchange Costs of External Imports
Kenya	20%	70%
Tanzania	16	56
Uganda	16	43

Here, too, 1970 and 1971 were the critical years in the negative balances. In 1971, Kenya recorded a deficit on this account of Shs. 1,780 million, Tanzania of Shs. 865 million, while Uganda recorded one of Shs. 295 million. In the case of Uganda, this deficit was the first in six years. It is thus important to note that the merchandise account was responsible for the greater part of the balance-of-payments problems.

In the single year, 1971, this deficit accounted for Kenya's deficit of 160% of the total current account deficit, 155% for Tanzania and 55% for Uganda, showing that for the three countries the trade imbalance with the rest of the world greatly contributed to the stresses in inter-state relations. But Kenya's position, it should be emphasized, was in fact the worst of the three. Her imbalance also existed on the international investment income account. While she had an overall deficit of over 150%, greater than that of Tanzania and Uganda combined. Thus Kenya's outflows to the outside world were greater than the other two countries put together.

The study attributed these difficulties to infrastructural investment with high import content and little export potential. Second, it pointed out that the 'directly productive investment' had been of the import-substituting variety with a high import content of intermediate goods, and producing a product consumed locally instead of being exported. Third, it noted the already mentioned declining export earnings from the agricultural sector. Finally, inflation, imported from the developed capitalist world and its currency revaluations, had a devaluing impact on local East African purchasing power.

The cumulative effect was a situation in which the index of imports (by volume) had increased by 20% between 1966 and 1971, while the corresponding export index had increased by only 10% and the unit value index had risen by only 13% in the same period. This inflationary process had been made worse by over-invoicing of imports, according to the study 'a very difficult matter to control' on the scale required to reduce the trade gap significantly (for it only required a very low percentage of over-invoicing (say 1 or 2%) to create an addition to the import bill that was large relative to the trade deficit).

When it is realized that over-invoicing in Tanzania was estimated at 10 to 20% and in Kenya at 20 to 30%,[7] and when we add to this the under-invoicing of exports by some of the monopolies and small firms producing agricultural and raw materials in East Africa, we can see the colossal exploitation of the region. No wonder regional integration proved impossible.

The siphoning off of super-profits via trade was also supplemented by movements on the international investment account (concerned with movements in the payment of interest, dividends, profits of foreign companies and their local branches, commercial bank interest, rents etc.), both directly with the monopolies and also inter-territorially. Proceeds and payments on this account were highest in Kenya because the inflows from the other two states were transfers to the transnational monopolies operating from Kenya. There were also movements back to these two countries on this account with

the exception of central bank incomes from overseas investments, while the
inflows from these sources increased considerably between 1966 and 1970
(see Table 13). Thus, what is sometimes alluded to as Kenya's 'gain' from the

Table 13
Investment Flows, 1966-71 (Shs. million)

	Kenya			Tanzania			Uganda		
	In	Out	Net	In	Out	Net	In	Out	Net
1966	125	374	-249	54	192	-138	44	169	-125
1967	118	400	-282	39	159	-120	32	167	-135
1968	168	452	-284	64	96	- 32	22	141	-119
1969	248	438	-190	76	96	- 20	26	151	-125
1970	338	568	-230	76	101	- 25	21	128	-107
1971	276	562	-286	67	188	-121	22	183	-161

other two states, is not correct. Her outflows were greater than her inflows or
'gains', as indeed we saw in Volume One.[8] The other categories of foreign-
exchange movements included freight and insurance payments on merchandise, other transportation, travel, and transfers on account of grants, gifts,
pensions, etc. Most of them showed a net outflow to Kenya from the other
two countries and a net outflow out from Kenya to the West. As we have
noted, these outflows occurred on account of monopoly investments in
Kenya, and partly through Kenya from the other two territories. But payments
by governments and the East African corporations also contributed to this
outflow, as we shall see below. But in the case of Kenya, one-fifth of the
outflows were an imputed portion of the undistributed or retained profits
accruing to private investment. The study nevertheless points out that, even
if this imputed outflow was not included, the outflow on this account would
still 'exceed her inflows and the marginal growth rates would probably still
show no consistent trend over the period'.

In addition, there were outflows connected with the operations of the
corporations. This is one of the areas in which there was a lot of wrangling
between the partner states, particularly after 1971. Under the Treaty the
function of the East African Railways and Harbours Corporation was to
facilitate the movement of exports and imports at the cheapest possible cost
to the transporters. But to do this a lot of equipment in the form of rails,
rolling stock, cranes, ships and maintenance materials had to be imported by
means of loans from the World Bank and other agencies and banks. This was
a way of exporting capital to East Africa and earning super-profits on it.

So also with postal and telecommunications equipment and installations,
as well as aircraft and aircraft hangars, to say nothing of personnel. The
monopolies who supplied these infrastructural and production goods engaged
in vigorous competition for the lucrative markets and this competition not
only resulted in corruption of top officials of the corporations and leading

politicians but also went to create pressures on the whole arrangement. In 1970 for instance a Shs. 100 million order for locomotives from British Electric was held up by the Authority on allegations of corruption. It was also alleged that the British Aircraft Corporation had corrupted leading East African Airways Corporation officials to sell five VC-10 and Super VC-10 aircraft to the Corporation when these aircraft were too expensive to operate. It has recently also been revealed that the U.S. aircraft monoply, McDonnell Douglas, paid officials of the East African Airways Corporation bribes in order to push their DC9s which the Corporation bought in 1969 and 1970.[9] Of course, these large bribes were added to the prices of the equipment — all of which went to add to the debt burdens of the corporations.

The loan burden of the four East African corporations was therefore very considerable, particularly since none of them (with the possible exception of East African Airways) earned any significant foreign exchange to pay back the loans and the interest on them. The partner states had to pay up in some kind of three-way proportion, and this is where again the tension rose when it came to the balance of payments. Inter-state quarrels intensified as a result, mainly due to the fact that overall the flow of the corporations' funds between states placed Kenya in a more 'favourable' position. Actually, this again obscured the fact that Kenya remitted considerable funds overseas to pay the corporations' debts, particularly in 1967 and 1968. In Uganda and Tanzania, too, the inter-state balances on this account were particularly negative, and this was worsened by their own remittances overseas between 1968 and 1972. By that year, the Post Office and Harbours headquarters had moved to their respective countries and remittances had to be made from the headquarters of these corporations. Between these two dates the interaction of negative balances and heavy overseas remittances had the combined impact of increasing the net outflows, particularly in the period 1970-71.[10] The largest drainer of funds overseas was the Railways Corporation whose total fixed assets were almost wholly financed by loans. By 1976 the debts of the corporations had increased considerably, as many of the loans had matured for repayment, as Table 14 shows for a single month for a single creditor. — the I.B.R.D.

This big outflow of funds from the region was only assisted, from the balance-of-payments standpoint, by inflows on the long-term foreign capital account and the short-term capital movements to the region. These inflows were able to reduce the deficit for Kenya to a net deficit of Shs. 164 million for 1969, Shs. 110 million in 1969, Shs. 66 million in 1970 and Shs. 34 million in 1971. For Uganda it decreased too, but widened again due to outflows in 1969, 1970, and 1971; while for Tanzania it was reduced, went into surplus and then decreased, but only as a result of stringent controls by the Bank of Tanzania.

Despite these 'surpluses', the Community study emphasized that this did not necessarily mean that more and more capital inflows of foreign exchange would continue to come in to 'compensate' for the current account deficit:

Table 14
East African Community Corporations Schedule of I.B.R.D. Debt Service Payments due 15 June 1976 (based on fixed assets ratios)

Borrower	Loan	*Percentage and Amount (£ Sterling)* Kenya	Tanzania	Uganda	Total
E.A.R.C.	674 EA	(48%) £387,424	(37%) £298,640	(15%) £121,070	(100%) £807,134
E.A.H.C.	638 EA	(51%) £399,030	(49%) £383,382	—	(100%) £783,412
E.A.P. & T.	657 EA	(47%)	(28%)	(25%)	(100%)
Total Amount		£902,488	£751,149	£182,790	£1,836,427

Source: Computed from a number of sources.

A large proportion of long-term capital inflows are in the form of capital goods for which foreign exchange equivalent is imputed as a capital inflow. As a result, there is an increasing dependence on those countries which supply the capital goods and credit. This is not a long-run solution to the problem of huge foreign exchange outflows on the current account because much of this credit must be repaid in the future, and it need not be assumed that invested capital will generate enough exports to finance these repayments. In fact, it may generate increasing outflows of investment income to foreign principals.[11]

This siphoning off by the monopolies of value created in East Africa naturally led to stringent exchange controls first in Uganda, then Tanzania and lastly in Kenya against the movement of currencies within the region and against inter-state trade. In Uganda, although external imports were subject to exchange controls, it was more the inter-state trade, particularly with Tanzania, that was affected under the exchange controls imposed by it in May 1970. This naturally contributed to the disintegration of trade relations between Uganda and Tanzania (and the lessening of trade between Tanzania and Kenya). The trade between Uganda and Tanzania ceased altogether in 1973. This was also brought about by Tanzania's own exchange controls and import restrictions which were imposed in March 1971 in order to 'correct its increasing net deficit with the other two partner states'. The imposition of these controls by Tanzania helped to reduce the deficit by more than 50% over 1970. The deficit did not abate permanently, however, because in 1973 there was a hike in the prices of imported oil and food imports. As a result there was a new spate of exchange controls in 1973, which could partly explain why the trade with Uganda ceased entirely that year. Although provision had been made in Article 28 of the Treaty for the states to extend facilities to each other to assist with the balance-of-payments problems, this proved impossible due to the fact that the foreign exchange shortages were faced by all three states at the same time and for the same reasons. A Report of the East African Community had this to say:

> This handicap originates from the fact that similar factors affect the balance of payments of the three states because they have the same items as major export earners and have similar needs for development imports. They have reached the stage of development whereby demand for capital and intermediate goods is rising sharply as each country implements its industrial growth objectives. For the same reasons capital investment is being attracted from third countries and repatriation of profits and other foreign investment income may be expected to increase. Furthermore, the desire on the part of some communities to export capital funds out of East Africa is not likely to cease.[12]

This state of affairs, the Report continued, was likely to increase. This meant a 'heavy strain on the scarce foreign source earnings' and hence the need for continuous stringent balance-of-payments management. It is for this reason that all the partner states became susceptible to severe balance-of-payments pressures 'more or less at the same time'. The Report further noted that, until 1970, all three states enjoyed 'a fairly comfortable position' in their foreign exchange reserves:

> But as early as the first quarter of 1970 signs of stresses on the balance of payments of the Partner States were beginning to appear. And in subsequent months all of them had to tighten up their import controls and certain exchange control measures were extended to the Partner States.[13]

It was for this reason that Uganda imposed controls in May 1970, Tanzania in March 1971 and in the same year Kenya imposed a total ban on the export of each other's currencies. In addition to the long-term capital inflows that 'helped' balance the accounts, Uganda resorted to Special Drawing Rights from the I.M.F., while Kenya leaned heavily on reserve drawings of the I.M.F. Tanzania too had to rely heavily on SDRs in the period 1970-72. It can thus be seen how the exploitation of the region by the transnational monopolies was very much behind the tensions that were being generated in the region.

It is true that the 'economic war' in Uganda also contributed to these strains, as did the disturbance in her international trade links. This explains why Uganda now increasingly relied on Kenya not only for her inter-state trade but also for her external imports as well. Thus it was the external link here which seemed to consolidate trade links with Kenya. Later, as foreign exchange shortages hit Uganda as a result of the military regime's mess up of the economy, smuggling became the semi-official means of conducting inter-state trade. Nevertheless the main cause of the strains remained the exploitation of the region by imperialism.

The disruption of inter-state trade did not affect external trade with the monopolies. All the foreign exchange was earned and 'saved' for imports and for the import-substitution industrialization. Agricultural exports were sent out to earn foreign exchange to pay for the imports, and when these earnings fell short, as they invariably did, foreign investment — both long-term and short-term — was sought 'to fill the gap' — the profits on which were paid for out of the next foreign exchange allocations, and so on *ad infinitum*. Thus foreign exchange earnings became the real issue, and the very basis for the existence of the neo-colonial states, all in the interest of the monopolies

Before 1971, and in accordance with the Treaty, there was a free movement of funds, including capital, between the partner states. The balance-of-payments strains put a stop to these movements in 1971 as well. East African currency was also restricted in its movement in the region, while the doors were wide open for foreign capital from any other source. With these restrictions, it became increasingly harder to carry on 'legitimate trade'. But at the same time the black market began to thrive. There was an increase in the smuggling of goods and currency, including sophisticated techniques to export foreign exchange. What is more, the smuggling was a game in which the top bureaucracy and top politicians engaged as part of their *matunda ya Uhuru*, while the workers and poor peasantry were left on their own with the 'grapes of wrath'.

Restrictions on inter-state trade and flows of capital produced insecurity among small businesses, and this led to an increase in the illegal export of capital and funds out of the 'insecure' areas to the liberal atmosphere prevailing in Kenya. From there it was smuggled out to Europe and elsewhere in an even more sophisticated way by the bigger sharks for, as the Community study on exchange controls of the partner states pointed out:

> If funds flow to one or other [of the partner states] for subsequent extra-regional expatriation, it is mainly because the black market in certain kinds of transactions is better developed in those places, and not because the regulations are very different. [14]

As the black market replaced the Common Market and as currency and foreign exchange evasions resulted in commodity shortages, so the flows out of the region to the monopolies increased, with the result that, by 30 June 1976, Kenya was ready to have the Common Market closed down for all practical purposes. As Tanzania closed its borders against the black market in Kenya, and as the black market between Uganda and Kenya also gained ascendancy, particularly over Ugandan coffee, the colonially structured and neo-colonially restructured regional arrangement crumbled under the weight of its antagonisms, while transnational corporate integration of the region continued at the level of production with the market of each of the territories assured to them.

Thus we come to the conclusion that the dominant forces that brought down the Common Market were the forces of international monopolistic competition which were stronger than the forces struggling for a national economy. Vacillating and outmanoeuvred, the national forces could only compete for the remains left by the monopolies, and had no conception of a consistent struggle against the economic exploitation.

The Politics of Co-operation

It is for this reason that we are unable to agree with those who have hitherto concentrated all their analysis on the so-called 'gains' and 'losses' as factors in the disintegration of the East African Community. Consider, for example, a recent paper by Mbogoro and Ngila Mwase.[15] In their review of the literature on this issue, they came to the conclusion that there were 'difficulties involved in trying to gauge the gains and losses of an integration scheme' as presented by Robson, Ghai, Raisman, Brown, Newlyn, Hazelwood and Elkan and, while they had 'no intention to invent a new approach', they later in their own analysis conclude, albeit inconclusively, that 'a good number of indicators . . . show that benefits were really flowing to the already advanced Partner in the Community', the implication being Kenya. They go further to exclude the element of imperialist exploitation by transnational monopolies as a factor contributing to this 'demise' of the Community. To quote them:

> What about the influence of the MNCs? It has been argued (without substantiation though) that they had a hand in the EAC demise; just as there were arguments a decade ago to the effect that they gave birth to the Community. Be that as it may, East African state economies individually or even collectively are not critical to the global strategy of finance capital and the EAC presence could for a majority of firms simplify their operations than if the states operated individually.[16]

Yet, after all this, these authors quickly accuse Kenya of having opened up 'the market for greater MNC penetration' while Tanzania is praised for not having been 'inclinced towards reducing the influence of the MNCs'.[17] All this suggests that these authors have very little understanding of the workings of international monopolies, if indeed they are inclined to think that trans- national monopolies did not see the region as 'critical' to them. They also implied wrongly that the MNCs were less of a problem in Tanzania. It should be clear to all that the spate of import-substitution encouraged in Tanzania after 1961 was only possible, despite the nationalizations of 1967, given the dominant participation of transnational monopolies who continue up to this time to reap very high returns on their joint investments with the Tanzanian state. Tanzania and Kenya are as dependent on these monopolies as any Third World countries. This is confirmed by the data we have produced above.

Moreover, the authors of this paper imply that the transnational mono- polies would have 'preferred' a larger East African market to the three separate markets. The implication is that they did not already have the entire market! Actually the monopolies do not prefer one alternative to another. They operat on the basis of what is available and on competition, and this competition leads to rivalry which tends to disintegrate markets at the national level. With high tariff protection in each nation-state, the monopolies are able to reap super-profits in any market whether this be national, regional, or whatever. This was the case and continues to be the case in East Africa. The collapse of the Common Market has indeed created even more markets for many other monopolies now supplying three management systems for each of the three countries' separate airways, railways, harbours etc.

Further arguments have been advanced that the Idi Amin coup in Uganda led to the break-up of the Community, or that it was due to ideological differences.[18] There is no doubt that the changes in Uganda created problems in continuing discussions about harmonization of fiscal and monetary policies but it should be noted that the balance-of-payments crisis intensified precisely in that year in all three countries. It is very doubtful that mere discussions wo have solved the problem created by these developments since earlier discussio had not resulted in any meaningful solution. On the contrary, the record from 1961 onwards shows a trend towards consolidation of national institutions at the expense of East African ones. Indeed the Treaty was a compromise, on the one hand, preserving the Common Market and common services but on the basis of internal surcharges (transfer tax, etc.) to strengthen national development; on the other decentralizing common services as a means of preserving them.

As President Nyerere said ten years after the Arusha Declaration:

> In the fight for economic independence, co-operation with other Third World countries has increased since February 1967, although difficulties have not been absent. The signing of the East African Treaty of Co-operation was a matter of rejoicing, in Tanzania and elsewhere in Africa; it seemed to take African unity a stage further forward. Unfortunately, political developments in Uganda, and a number of unilateral transgressions of the Treaty by Kenya, have put the Community in jeopardy. The Government is working to overcome the current difficulties and to get agreement on Treaty revisions which will enable all partner states to work together. . . . But I must confess, with great sadness, that the hope of reviving the East African Community is now a very slight one. We tried; but it appears that we shall be defeated. Our colleagues neither had, nor have, the desire for real co-operation. There is a long way to travel before Africa is liberated.[19]

It is interesting, too, that Uganda blamed both Kenya and Tanzania for breaking up the Community, while Kenya blamed Tanzania. Correct as specific charges may be, it is not adequate in our view to leave matters at that level. Our location of the general problem and the 1971 crisis that led to the eventual breakup of the Community is connected with the heightening of the exploitation by imperialism of the people of East Africa. That is the dominant factor. Most of the problems in the politics of the three countries, including the Uganda coup itself,[20] are connected with this fundamental event.

A former Tanzanian Minister of Finance in the East African Community has also pointed to this date as the culmination of other forces that had been at work.

> Ever since 1971 the Community has gone through a most difficult period, although disagreements on some aspects of the Treaty began earlier. The environment in which we have had to operate has been one where bilateral relations between partner states have been seriously strained, while damaging developments were taking place within the Community itself. As such, much restraint had to be exercised by those in positions of responsibility to ensure the very survival of the Community. Within the Community's operations we encountered complex problems which needed to be sorted out and these included among

the first the financing of the East African Airways. Then came the need for the orderly passing over of the responsibility for the operations of the Income Tax Department to the partner states, an extremely difficult and tricky question of evolving a new, albeit interim, formula for financing of the General Fund Services, since the provisions of Article 65 became unacceptable. The financial affairs of the Community Corporations also became more and more intricate and exacting as time passed. There were many other developments, too, that needed careful handling. They were not and are not easy times and one had to exercise extreme caution in coping with the situation as best as one could in the circumstances.[21]

Most of these problems were connected with the balance-of-payments strains we analysed earlier in this chapter. Divergent income tax rates in 1971, problems about transfer of funds between partner states, the financing of the General Fund Services, etc. in one way or another were connected with foreign exchange, which never recovered. Even for Kenya, the I.L.O. Report pointed out that, while the early 1960s had been a period of 'easy growth', this was shattered in 1971 when imports rose sharply and the rise of export earnings 'petered out' while the inflow of capital decreased. 'Foreign exchange reserves sank. . . The Government started to take a series of measures to stop the loss of foreign exchange . . . . It has suddenly become clear that the boom had been a kind that caused stresses in the balance of payments.'[22] The I.L.O. called for revision of priorities. This kind of thing was happening in the region as a whole and no doubt provided the very ground for the difficult days that the Minister referred to as beginning in that year.

By 1976 the situation was irreversible despite the appointment of the Treaty Revision Commission, headed by William Dem of the Caribbean Central Bank. It failed to get the partners to agree on anything. The future of the East African Community were clearly sealed, never to be revived again. It is paradoxical that when Kenya announced withdrawal, refusing to pay its Shs. 800 million contribution to the General Fund Services, it was Tanzania and Uganda who announced they would continue the servies of the Community and that their Ministers were going to meet to discuss the funding of the General Fund Services. This too failed and Uganda also pulled out. Meanwhile transnational corporate integration of the three countries continued unabated while new institutional forms of integration of East Africa with Europe were worked out and intensified. The breaking up of the East African regional arrangement was, however, not negative but positive in the sense that it helped to focus on the nation-state as the most concrete organization in continuing the struggle against imperialism. There was never any real basis for a positive regional integration under neo-colonialism. Further, the struggle by the people of East Africa for real national independence is the only meaningful way in which they can each address themselves to their economic development. Until imperialist domination is removed regional economic integration will not have positive results for the people.

References

1. A. Hazelwood, *East African Production, Investment and Inter-State Trade since the Treaty,* 1971, Report for the E.A.C. (unpublished), pp.41-3.
2. E.A.C., *A Report of the Working Party on the Possibilities for Closer Harmonization of Monetary/Fiscal and Payments Policies within the East African Community,* Paper on Industry, pp.421-48 from which most of this data is derived.
3. E.A.C., 'A Comparative Analysis of E.A. Trade Structure' in E.A.C., op. cit.
4. See *Imperialism in East Africa,* Vol. I., *Imperialism and Exploitation*

5. 'An Overview of Partner States International Balance of Payments 1966-1971', in J.K. Nyerere, *The Arusha Declaration Ten Years After* (United Republic of Tanzania, Government Printer, Dar es Salaam 1977), from which most of the material that follows is drawn.
6. J. Rweyemamu. *Underdevelopment and Industrialization in Tanzania,* (London/Nairobi, Oxford University Press, 1973).
7. *ILO Report on Kenya,* p.454.
8. See Volume I, Chapter Nine.
9. *Sunday News,* 17 December 1978, p.1.
10. 'Fund Flows of the East African Community Corporations' in Nyerere, op. cit.
11. 'An Overview', op. cit., and E.A.C., op. cit.
12. E.A.C., op. cit.
13. 'An Overview', op. cit.
14. Ibid.
15. Mbogoro and Ngila Mwase, 'The East African Community: An economic analysis of the East African Integration Scheme', mimeo, ERB.
16. Ibid., p.11.
17. Ibid., pp.35-6.
18. A.P. Mahiga, 'Pitfalls and Promises of Regional Integration in East Africa', *UTAFITI,* Vol. II, No.1, 1977, pp.25-44.
19. Nyerere, op. cit.
20. For a discussion of the forces at work which brought about the coup d'etat in Uganda, see my book *Imperialism and Revolution in Uganda,* Ch. XIII, Section 3-4, Ch. XIV.
21. Al Noor Kassum, 'The Future of the East African Community', *UTAFITI,* Vol. II, No. 1, 1977, pp.9-10.
22. *ILO Report on Kenya,* pp.98-9.

9. New Forms of Integration with Imperialism

We have already noted in Chapter Seven the new institutional and corporate forms of integration with imperialism that were behind most of the developments in the neo-colonial economies of East Africa, and the role they played in the regional economic arrangement that finally gave way in the face of these forces. Here we shall continue to look at other supplementary forms of integration that were being worked out as one aspect of the monopolistic competition between a number of countries involved in the exploitation of the region.

One of these institutional forms was the attempt by some of the former colonial powers of Europe to retain links with their former colonies through the European Economic Community's associate arrangements with a number of African countries.

Other forms of institutions were those encouraged by the United Nations, and particularly by the United States, with a view to cutting down the former colonies' old links with the European powers by establishing what on the surface looked like regional arrangements but were actually structures for the continued exploitation of the region under new guises of 'co-operation'. Some of these links, such as those encouraged by the United Nations Economic Commission for Africa, have encouraged a more multilaterized form of vertical integration with imperialism, rather than the horizontal integration more typical of neo-colonial links in the chain of exploitation and domination.

Integration with Europe

When most of the African territories under French colonialism gained their political independence, France decided to encourage new forms of neo-colonial linkages with these territories, adapted to the changed conditions. France was now a member of the European Common Market and any links between her and her former colonies had to be within this framework. In fact former colonies of Belgium and Italy were also involved.

Thus the Strasbourg Plan of 1952 sought to integrate the former colonies of members of the Council of Europe into an arrangement whereby these imperialist powers would continue to have the full benefit of their resources on promise of 'aid' and trade. The Plan called for increases in the purchase of these countries' products on the basis of a new kind of preference system.

France was particularly insistent on this new link and indeed made it a precondition for her becoming a member of the European Economic Community. It was due to this pressure that Part IV was added to the Treaty of Rome entitled 'Association of Overseas Countries and Territories'. Under Article 238 of the Treaty, it was provided that the Community could enter into an agreement with a third state or states, a union of states, or an international organization, involving 'reciprocal' rights and obligations, common action and special procedures in their relationships with Europe.

Under these arrangements a number of former colonies of France, Belgium and Italy were accorded special 'associate' status in the European market under the so-called Yaounde Convention, and it was because of this link that the neo-colonial states in East Africa felt themselves threatened by the preference given to the 18 Association of Afro-Malagasy States (AAMS) and decided to establish their own link with the E.E.C.

The Arusha Agreement

Under these arrangements the three East African states entered into negotiations to establish a neo-colonial link with the E.E.C. Such a link was 'better' than the colonial links only in the sense that East Africa was demonstrating its political independence from the domination of Britain. That this bid for autonomy somehow led back to the same old exploiters was a most important and educative demonstration to the East African people of the serious limitations of the political gains made under the first phase of the struggle.

The negotiations to enter into a new link with Europe soon led to the agreement between the E.E.C. and the three East African states of an Associate relationship on the lines of a trade agreement. The three states rejected the full Associate relationship under which they would have been entitled to financial assistance like their AASM counterparts only because they were still proud of their independence, for they correctly labelled such a link 'neo-colonial' The Nigerian Attorney-General, Dr. Elias, put the position clearly when he stated:

> This choice was dictated by Nigeria's desire to avoid being accused by certain radical elements at home and abroad of becoming assimilated to the position of the eighteen African and Malagasy associated states which were then popularly regarded as economic satellites of France and, therefore, of the European Economic Community.[1]

The Arusha Agreement was neo-colonial all the same. It came into force in 1971 and under it a number of 'reciprocal' rights and obligations were entered into between the E.E.C. and the three East African states. Under it

163

East Africa granted the E.E.C. countries tariff concessions on 59 industrial products out of some 200 items demanded by the E.E.C. The concessions ranged between 2 and 9%. The E.E.C. for its part granted East Africa duty free entry to goods 'originating' in East Africa providing the treatment would not be more favourable than that enjoyed by the E.E.C. members among themselves.

This proviso had the effect of reducing any such duty free entry to only three agricultural commodities considered 'sensitive' in the E.E.C. because of the Common Agricultural Policy. Even then the three items were subjected to a quota system so that unroasted coffee could enter 'duty free' to the extent of 56,000 tonnes only, while cloves and tinned pineapple (canned by Del Monte) could each also only gain entry for limited amounts. Any amount in excess of these quotas was to be subject to full duty.

These reverse preferences, as they were called, were later queried by the U.S. and Japan as being contrary to GATT since they discriminated against third parties. This was in 1972 at a GATT working party. As a result, the subsequent Lome Convention was amended to remove the objectionable discrimination clause, thus according the arrangement a multilateral character consistent in some measure with the U.S. and Japanese demands.

The trade carried on under this agreement was of the typical colonial type of raw materials production most desired by the European monopolies. The main commodities admitted duty free — most welcome to these monopolies and consumers within Europe — were coffee, cordage, rope and twine made of sisal, pineapples (fresh and tinned), pyrethrum extracts, pyrethrum flowers, cloves, canned beef, meat extract, oilseeds, cotton and tea — the latter two entering duty free from all sources.

In the case of the 59 E.E.C. produced items which received tariff concessions from the East African countries, these constituted 15% of East Africa's imports from the E.E.C. and were calculated as involving a loss in terms of customs revenue to the extent of Shs. 5 million. The concessions made to the E.E.C. were given in order to retain to some extent Britain's own traditional Commonwealth treatment which still remained at this time.

Thus it can be seen that East Africa's exports to the E.E.C. countries (six at that time) were dominated by a small number of raw material and food commodities which the three countries were relegated to produce under the international division of labour imposed on them by colonialism. To the extent that any of these commodities were semi-processed or processed, this was done by either European or U.S. or Japanese firms in joint ventures with the government or on their own in East Africa. In this way the monopolies were in a way participating in the exports of these raw materials. Indeed some of the products like tea, coffee, sisal, pyrethrum and beef were products of plantations and/or large European estates such as those Beckford has analysed so well in his book on plantation economies.[2]

A further characteristic of this trade under the Arusha Agreement was something which we have already noted as contributing to the strains and stresses that led to the collapse of the East African Community. This was the rapid growth in imports to East Africa from the E.E.C. over the eight-year period before and after the Agreement. Imports from the E.E.C. almost trebled in value between 1964 and 1971, the rise being particularly marked in the year the Agreement was signed.

It should also be noted that the increase was most noticeable in the imports of chemicals, a major item of expenditure in the merchandise account. As Table 15 shows, this item alone accounted for almost one-quarter of all East African E.E.C. imports in 1971. East Africa's exports to the E.E.C., on the other hand, declined in value by Shs. 100 million between 1964 and 1971. In that year the E.E.C. took only 14% of East Africa's products as compared to 21% in 1964.

The sharpest decline was in the mid-1960s, compared to which 1970 and 1971 represented a slight rise. The decline in exports was sharpest for Tanzania and Uganda, but less so for Kenya. Kenya exported one-fifth of her products to the E.E.C., while Tanzania and Uganda remained more dependent on the U.K. market for their exports. In fact, only two to three products accounted for the bulk of East Africa's exports to the E.E.C. These were coffee (just under one-half), cotton and sisal. Unlike the E.E.C. manufactures, the prices of these products fluctuated very widely, thus contributing to the crisis in the East African Community.

The Lome Convention

The entry of U.K. into the European Economic Community in 1972 created new conditions for widening the exploitative relationship with East Africa. The remnants of bilateral integration were modified within the European Associate system. Like France, Britain pressed for and obtained special protocol inserted into its Treaty of Accession to the Rome Treaty providing for the special status of association enjoyed by the AASM to be extended to its former colonies, now members of the Commonwealth.

Under this protocol (Ab. 22) it was stipulated that the E.E.C. shall offer the independent Commonwealth countries the option of ordering their relationships with the European Community in the spirit of the Declaration of Intent adopted by the European Council in 1963, which had been made applicable to the A.A.S.M.-E.E.C. relations. The protocol gave these new countries the option of joining either the Second Yaounde Convention by entering into their own Convention under Article 238 of the Rome Treaty, or of concluding a trade agreement with the E.E.C. under which they would enjoy certain preferences in the European market.

The offer was to be accepted as soon as possible after Britain became a member of the E.E.C., and for this reason the E.E.C. fixed a specific date — 1 August 1973 — for negotiation with these new countries. Countries which chose to join the Yaounde Convention were encouraged to do so since these were also about to negotiate a new Convention.

These were the beginnings of the Lome Convention in which East Africa

Table 15
Structure of East African Trade with the E.E.C., 1970-71 (Shs. millions)

	Total Domestic Exports				Domestic Exports to E.E.C.(6)				Total Net Imports				Net Imports from the E.E.C. (6)			
	1970		1971		1970		1971		1970		1971		1970		1971	
	Value	%	Value	%	Value	%	Value	%	Value	%	Value	%	Value	%	Value	%
Food and Live Animals	2,796	57	2,674	54	377	58	422	63	245	3	400	6	46	4	59	4
Beverages and Tobacco	56	1	59	1	5	1	4	1	37	1	40	1	16	1	14	1
Inedible Crude Materials	1,149	23	1,131	23	255	40	186	28	103	2	151	2	26	2	35	2
Mineral Fuel, Lubricants, etc.	280	5	356	7	–	–	–	–	471	8	559	8	24	2	28	2
Animal and Vegetable Oils and Fats	27	1	15	–	1	–	–	–	70	1	116	2	16	1	23	1
Chemicals	84	2	95	2	–	–	2	–	576	10	672	10	253	20	291	19
Manufactures classified by material	434	9	500	10	5	1	58	9	1,518	27	1,985	27	268	21	320	21
Machinery and Transport Equipment	4	–	6	–	–	–	–	–	2,051	37	2,818	38	526	43	697	45
Miscellaneous Manufactures	24	–	31	1	–	–	–	–	439	8	633	9	58	5	90	6
Commodities and Transactions not classified according to kind	7	–	5	–	1	–	1	–	134	2	37	–	–	–	1	–
Total	4,861	100	4,871	100	647	100	676	100	5,645	100	7,411	100	1,233	100	1,558	100

found itself together with the Yaounde Group and 43 other African, Caribbean and Pacific neo-colonial states (the so-called A.C.P. states) entering into a new association with the E.E.C., a link that was further to consolidate the vertical link between East Africa and the E.E.C. to the detriment of East Africa.[3]

The forces of vertical integration were here operating in unison with the forces of transnational corporate integration, dealing a death blow to local regional integration. Both took advantage of the economic weaknesses of the region to link the production activities of the three East African countries to the production activities and markets of the transnational monopolies. In this way the new Lome Convention gave maximum strength to the vertical integrative forces.

To begin with, the Convention which came into force on 1 January 1975 spelt out the basis upon which trade links, financial assistance, industrial co-operation and the stabilization of the export earnings of the A.C.P. states would be achieved within the context of integration with Western Europe and not in the context of local regional arrangements. It was stipulated that the purpose of the arrangement would be to promote trade between the parties, 'taking account of their respective levels of development' in order to secure 'additional benefits' for the A.C.P., and to help accelerate the rate of growth of this trade by improving conditions of access for their products to the European market.

But since these products were the primary products which Europe most required for her own development, growth in this trade involved a growth of the European economies, but an increase in the amount of time required by the East African peasantry for the production of these raw materials and food products. And since, further, the income from this one-sided trade was constantly falling in relative terms, the Convention also tried to assure the A.C.P. neo-colonial states of the possibility of 'stabilizing' these effects through a special fund (Stabex).

The Stabex fund was to 'remedy the harmful effects of the instability of export earnings' without eliminating the causes of the earnings instability. Thus the further promise that this mechanism would help 'achieve stability, profitability and sustained growth of the [A.C.P.] economies' was just so much empty talk on the part of the E.E.C. since such a development was impossible. Furthermore, since the stabilization funds were after five years to be 'reconstituted' (a process to be paid for by the recipient A.C.P. states) it turned out that there was no net gain on the part of the borrowers save a certain breathing space.

The improvement in the earnings of the A.C.P. states as a result of this Fund was in any case to be whittled away through unequal trade between the A.C.P. states and the E.E.C. in the other direction, since the rise in prices of European manufactured goods was not tied to the earnings of the A.C.P. states. The E.E.C. exports to these markets gained under the Convention went a long way to channelling back the trade earnings of the A.C.P. states by means of the super-profits made by the E.E.C. on these exports. The result

167

was that these countries, very much harassed by balance-of-payments crises, found it even more necessary to borrow again to 'fill the gap'.

For this reason the Convention also provided for 'financial assistance' to the A.C.P. In East Africa the fear of 'radical elements' who had long ago been silenced by the neo-colonial states, was no longer an issue. It was now possible to go in for financial assistance without any fear of being accused of neo-colonialism. Under the Convention this financial and technical assistance was to be given to 'correct the structural imbalance in the various sectors' of the A.C.P. economies. The assistance and co-operation was to relate to the execution of programmes which contributed essentially to the economic and social development of the states.

That the execution of such projects and programmes would fall to the ever-present European monopolies was assured, for the Convention also gave these monopolies 'rights of establishment' within the A.C.P. states. The A.C.P. states accepted this insofar as they guaranteed to 'treat the nationals and companies or firms of [European] Member States and the firms of the A.C.P. states respectively on a non-discriminatory basis', in matters connected with the establishment and provision of services.

Furthermore, with regard to capital movements linked with the European investments and the super-profits arising therefrom as well as payments for current transactions, the A.C.P. states were 'expected' to refrain from taking action in the field of foreign exchange transactions which would be incompatible with their obligations under this Convention. These obligations arose from other provisions relating to trade in goods, services, and industrial co-operation.

These measures in the Lome Convention, to which East Africa was party, went a long way to consolidate the position of the European monopolies in the region, while weakening further the national economies. As foreign exchange problems increased, whatever foreign exchange was earned by the three countries first went to meet payments on investments by the monopolies, then on current account to pay for goods and services provided by the same monopolies. What little foreign exchange was left was then given to finance trade within the region, so that, when the exchange controls and trade restrictions are analysed, the restrictions fell with greater force on regional trade than on trade with the E.E.C. and other imperialist states, whose interests were thus more organically protected than the local structures of regional integration. Thus, either way, regional integration was increasingly hounded by vertical integrative mechanisms such as the Lome Convention, and Commodity Agreements like the International Coffee Agreement, and transnational corporate monopolies that were reaping the super-profits.

All these forces relied on the East African national productive forces for their survival and found it easy to run down any regional arrangements. In their weakness, the national forces offered little resistance and for this reason national forces of production and the international forces of appropriators were more exposed for all to see than at any time.

Trade since the Convention has been expanding in all directions. Unlike regional trade in East Africa, which excluded agricultural products and increasingly limited trade in manufactured goods, the trade with the E.E.C. countries increased in both primary commodity exports and imports of manufactured products. With the exception of 1975 when recession in Europe reduced imports from the A.C.P. states, trade relations remained brisk throughout. As the first Lome Convention was coming to an end, all parties appeared well satisfied with the deal. A special correspondent of the Tanzania *Daily News* was able to report: 'The special and preferential relationship between the nine-nation E.E.C. and the 53-nation A.C.P. countries is here to stay.'[4]

A New Regional Arrangement?

Marx and Engels once remarked that what distinguished the capitalist mode of production from all previous modes was its capacity to change structures and never to leave a situation to ossify.[5] But this did not imply that the bourgeoisie would manage to outsmart history by manipulating structures and institutions indefinitely. Rather, the need to change structrues was part of its ongoing struggle to contain the gigantic contradictions that it generated, but even then, each such manoeuvre diminished the chances of containing future contradictions. The collapse of the East African Community signalled such a restructuring. If June 1976 may be taken as the date on which this collapse finally took place then, within months of its dissolution, the U.N. Economic Commission for Africa (E.C.A.) was already proposing another regional arrangement encompassing ten countries in Eastern and Southern Africa.[6]

To be sure, such a proposal was not the first of its kind. In October 1965, as the proposed East African Federation failed to take off, as we have seen in Chapter Seven, the same E.C.A. had been quick to propose the formation of an alternative arrangement — an Economic Community for Eastern Africa. The three East African countries in EACSO plus Zambia were to form the core of this arrangement. Ethiopia and Burundi also appeared to be committed to the formation of the Community, while Somalia, Malawi and Rwanda were also mooted as possible members.[7]

The 1965 idea was to form an economic union in which there would be joint allocation and development of industries, co-ordination and linking of transport and communication systems, and the creation of multilateral and 'balanced' trade patterns as well as co-ordination and standardization in other fields and services.[8]

The proposal was eventually initialled in a draft form by ministers at Addis Ababa in May 1966 and a provisional council was set up to work out the details, but nothing followed despite an initial agreement on the allocation of industries.[9] There had been no serious thought given to the whole thing and in the meantime the monopolies in these countries were busy making offers of import-substitution industrialization to each of them. In the meantime the Treaty for East African Co-operation was being negotiated as well so that, although there was a further meeting in Addis Ababa in 1967 in connection with the larger union, the East African Community was already being set up. A negotiating team was appointed to examine how these countries could enter the Community but nothing came out of it.

It was the collapse of the East African Community that now seems to have signalled the new effort. A paper prepared by the E.C.A. went through the usual economistic arguments about the need to create a regional grouping. It pointed out that 'historically' the countries of the proposed region had their agriculture 'geared' to the export markets of the former colonial powers. It then pointed out the obvious by stating that today only 6% of the agricultural exports of these countries were exported within the region. It blamed this continuing phenomenon, however, on the 'lack of specialization' and random production 'without reference to the studies of comparative advantage'!

The study then went on further to confirm what was but an inevitable trend in neo-colonial economies in the field of industrialization. It pointed out that intra-regional exports in manufactures had declined. This was due first to the lack of export markets and a lack of critical inputs such as skilled manpower, and the small markets. It then regretted that 'for various reasons' each of these countries had 'in recent years' placed more emphasis on import-substitution industries than on 'export-oriented industries'. Then, as if all this was to be cured by the proposed new institution, it noted that the utilization of industrial capacity had been low, ranging from 30 to 60%, and that the costs of production were high as a result, also quality requirements could not be met.[10]

It was further suggested by the study that, since the area under consideration was still very reliant on external transport facilities, it was essential to correct this by removing the causes of such a situation by bringing about a standardization in rail systems, building of feeder roads, removing of customs barriers and in that way co-ordinate transport development by setting up an institutional framework which could bring about the required standardization and harmonization of policy in the transport sector. There was also need to make provision for clearing and payments arrangements, and for this reason it was argued that it would be better 'to settle for a multilateral payments arrangement'.[11]

All these lame analyses by the E.C.A. can of course be understood in the context of its role as one of the institutions intended to maintain neo-colonial discipline in Africa for multilateral imperialism and the transnational monopolies. Its articulation of the need for regional integration is perfectly consistent with this objective requirement. In the foreword to an earlier document drawn up by the Commission on multinational corporations in Africa, the Secretary-General, Robert K. Gardiner, had pointed out that industrialization in Africa was being promoted in an economic atmosphere that had no historical parallel: He stated:

The growing power and looming influence of the multinational corporation is giving rise to a new economic system and international structures in which the capacity of the nation state to influence events is becoming increasingly limited. In the face of this dynamic development, traditional instruments of economic policy appear inadequate.[12]

He warned that at a time when Africa was attempting to achieve 'a measure of economic independence' the multinational corporation was 'threatening to invade the sovereignty of individual nations'. The purpose of the E.C.A., he said, was to draw attention to this phenomenon, and to point out that, whereas the multinational was an instrument for investment and transfer of technology for production and marketing on a global basis, its activities also raised vital issues concerned with ownership, monopolistic bargaining power, etc.

It was the view of the E.C.A., according to Gardiner, that these and other issues would have to be explored systematically 'if satisfactory mechanisms and arrangements are to be evolved that would minimize the areas of conflict and exploit to advantage the areas of harmony in the relationships between the multinational corporation and the host government'. Thus the E.C.A.'s policy was essentially to avoid conflict by 'harmonizing' the strategies of the monopolies and the neo-colonial states of the region. On regional co-operation, the Commission pointed out that one of the most interesting features of the multinational corporation was in the development of specialization and international exchange of components between affiliates of the same enterprise. In the case of Latin America, the E.C.A. pointed out that this type of arrangement and strategy had helped overcome the 'diseconomies' of small-scale production for automobiles in the region, 'characterized by a proliferation of many makes and models'.

A proposal had been put forward for this to be done in Africa, it pointed out, although no concrete action has thus far been taken. But Latin America had, before this arrangement, gone through a process of import-substitution based on small-scale, high-cost production for local markets. In this respect, the E.C.A. pointed out, Africa was 'happier than Latin America' since this had not happened to any great extent! Africa could very happily start with large-scale vertical integration on a regional basis. Pushing hard the case for transnational corporate integration of the region under multilateral imperialism, the E.C.A. argued for an end to this 'costly round of uneconomic import substitution' and the high cost of production of intermediate goods, not in order to advance national development but to bring in multinationals on a larger scale. It added:

> With further development of manufacturing in Africa toward complex durable consumer goods and intermediate products, it can be anticipated that the multinational corporation may play a significant role particularly in relation to regional co-operation. The need of such firms for a large market in order to enjoy economies of scale will tend to exert pressure for regional co-operation.[13]

It pointed out that multinationals which were smaller, less innovating, financially weak, more dependent on cheap labour and less involved in Africa's economy as a whole would be more likely to oppose regional integration:

> It is worth underlining that the firms who have the most to offer Africa in capital, technical expertise, managerial ability, greater efficiency of operation and pioneering of new lines of economic activity are those which will tend to benefit from, and be encouraged to expand or initiate African-based operations by economic integration.[14]

This generalization in fact ignores monopolistic competition as an important element in determining the whole necessity for regional arrangements. It is this competition, as we have seen in the East African experience, which breaks up the existing groupings characteristic of an earlier bilateral imperialism. But this point is absolutely vital for it is the basis upon which the E.C.A. recommended regional arrangements for monopolies in particular industries, like pulp and paper, where it would be 'in the firms' interest, as well as in the interest of the countries concerned, for a plant in one country to specialize in one type of paper products and a plant in the neighbouring country in another, *provided there is agreement to reciprocal access to the two markets'*. It added:

> Still tighter integration on regional basis may be needed in the case of an industry like the automobile industry, involving not merely co-operation in the production of components and assembly operations but also import of some components from the parent company overseas.[15]

What the Commission was putting forward here was not its own wisdom, but the strategy that the transnational monopolies have worked out and which they have been implementing with or without regional arrangements. The transnational monopolies are well versed in the political and institutional environment of the world economy and have always taken the nation-state, however small, as a reality to be dealt with. Monopolistic competition, and the political environment, forces this course of action which tends to militate against effective regional co-operation. The ideology of the E.C.A. was no more than a cover-up for the small-capitalist fears of backward countries dominated by monopolies about sizes of markets which the huge transnational monopolies saw as no barrier at all.

Thus although, on 5 February 1979, the 17 countries in the Lusaka-based Multinational Programming and Co-operation Centre (MULPOC) brought together by the E.C.A. agreed to set up a Preferential Trade Area by 1981, it appeared that such arrangement could not be expected to succeed, let alone take off.[16] Nevertheless, we ought to examine carefully this latest in the now long series of proposals to secure some form of regional economic integration in East Africa.

The first steps to this end had been taken at the Third Conference of the Multinational Programming and Co-operation Centre (MULPOC) Council of Ministers held at Lusaka, Zambia in November 1977. At this meeting the Ministers entrusted to an extraordinary meeting of Ministers of Trade, Finance and Planning the formulation of the principles for the establishment of a Preferential Trade Area (P.T.A.) and clearing and payments system for the Eastern and Southern African states.

At the First Extraorindary Conference of Ministers held in Lusaka on 30-31 March 1978, the Ministers signed a Lusaka Declaration of Intent and Commitment to the Establishment of a P.T.A. and a Clearing and Payments System for Eastern and Southern States under which a body to be known as the 'Inter-Governmental Negotiating Team' (I.N.T.) was created to handle the detailed negotiations. It spelt out the terms of reference and a timetable. The proposed P.T.A. was to include seventeen countries: Angola, Botswana, Comoro, Djibouti, Ethiopia, Kenya, Lesotho, Malawi, Malagasy, Mauritius, Mozambique, Seychelles, Somalia, Swaziland, Uganda, Tanzania and Zambia. The timetable envisaged the holding of the Second Extraordinary Meeting of Ministers by April 1979 at which the report of the I.N.T./ P.T.A. would be received and a date fixed for the signing of the Treaty that year.

The Ministers further undertook to direct and execute their economic activities in such a manner as to create conditions favourable to the achievement of these purposes. It was further agreed that the Treaty to be signed would be under constant review so that, within a period of ten years, consideration could be given to 'upgrading' the co-operation to a sub-regional Common Market with a view to the eventual creation of an Economic Community for Eastern and Southern African States.

Among the principles agreed to be included in the Treaty were the reduction and elimination of customs duties; the relaxation and abolition of quantitative and administrative restrictions; the 'fair and equitable' distribution of benefits; the giving of compensation, adjustment and development assistance to member states who may suffer as a result of the arrangement; the gradual evolution of a common commercial policy and the gradual harmonization of policies in the financial, monetary and fiscal fields. A number of Protocols to achieve these aims were authorized to be drawn up.

Despite the early optimism, the Treaty had not been agreed by the end of 1979. At the fifth meeting of the Inter-Governmental Negotiating Team, held at Addis Ababa, Ethiopia, in October 1979, it was decided that 'because of the complexity of the negotiations', it was necessary to have a further meeting in January 1980 'to review the progress' of the negotiations. At the Addis Ababa meeting, it was forewarned that the Inter-Governmental Team might not have completed its task by the January meeting, and that the extraordinary meeting of the Council of Ministers which was expected to consider the Treaty might have to do so in June 1980. At the January meeting held at Gaberone, Botswana, the Ministers agreed to hold the June meeting in May 1980, and to hold a further meeting of Ministers of MULPOC in

August or September 1980.

This I.N.T./P.T.A. meeting held in Addis Ababa in October 1979 was attended by twelve countries only (Angola, Botswana, Djibouti, Ethiopia, Kenya, Lesotho, Mauritius, Mozambique, Swaziland, Tanzania, Uganda and Zambia), and it appeared to have encountered the usual problems created by international monopolistic competition.

One of the issues that became a stumbling block was over the Protocol dealing with 'rules of origin'. These rules define the type of goods originating from each of the member states that would be entitled to preferential treatment in the markets of the member states. The provisions of the rules are intended to exclude goods manufactured substantially outside the region. To ensure that goods manufactured outside the P.T.A. do not enjoy benefits within the area, it is normally provided that a company manufacturing goods for export within the P.T.A. should have a certain minimum level of its equity held by nationals. It is also sometimes spelt out what quantity of 'value added' must be produced within the member state if such goods are to enjoy the privileges.

It turned out at this meeting of the I.N.T./P.T.A. that the fixing of equity to be held by nationals or governments of member states at 60% was 'too high' for some countries. It was agreed to reduce this to 51% — but, even then, it appeared that this too was 'so high' for at least two countries that 'most of their commodities might not qualify for P.T.A. purposes.' Instead these two countries proposed a 30% equity holding instead. They also urged that the requirement that such companies be under indigenous management might have a 'negative effect' on production in their countries.

Such problems arose because of the continuing foreign economic domination by transnational monopolies in these countries. The rule about 'value added' was also modified to allow a low minimum of 25% to be allowed. This meant that many of the enterprises in these P.T.A. countries would merely be used as unpacking and repacking points for transnational goods substantially produced by the monopolies in the imperialist states.

Regarding the Protocol on Co-ordination of Agricultural Policies, many delegates objected to the use of the phrase 'harmonization and co-ordination' which had been agreed by the Ministers on the grounds that this 'implies a degree of commitment, and might impinge on national sovereignty when it comes to formulating such policies'. Instead they prefered the word 'co-operation'. Although other delegations insisted that, if the ultimate goal of the arrangement was to form an economic community or common market, a certain level of 'commitment' was necessary, such divergence of views at such early stages of negotiation clearly testified to the dominating pressures inherent in the economies of these countries as well as the yearning for a national development which was quite unachievable under those conditions.

These 'new' patterns in regional integration which were initiated, according to the Declaration of Intent, because of the low level of and even deterioration in trade among the countries of this area during the 'last five years' (i.e. from 1971), and the adverse terms of trade affecting the countries of the area, clearly go to show the vicious circle in which these countries find themselves. We have observed earlier that it was the same forces mentioned by the Declaration of Intent which eventually led to the collapse of the East African Community, yet the Declaration cites these same ills as the basis for a new regional arrangement continuing the same exploitative arrangements.

Should it surprise us that these new efforts are already encountering the same forces of disruption that characterized earlier moves? Does it not prove, if proof was required, that so long as the economies of these countries continue to be subjected to the exploitative hand of transnational finance capital, any effort to create unity amongst a number of countries to resist their stranglehold will fail?

These developments must awaken us to the fact that *the struggle at the national level against foreign economic exploitation and political blackmail and arm twisting has to be handled by strengthening the class struggle of national forces based on a broad democratic front in which the working class plays a leading role. Without such a political front at national level no resistance to the strangling hand of transnational finance capital is possible, nor is any meaningful economic co-operation between nations* (whether regional or international) possible. In encouraging Third World countries to create institutions to co-ordinate their economies, it must be fully realized that such efforts, unless preceded by political struggles to complete our democratic revolutions, will increasingly be frustrated by the activities of the transnational monopolies which go to hinder the economic development of our countries and the unity of the peoples of the world.

References

1. T.O. Elias, 'Association Agreement between EEC and Federal Republic of Nigeria', *Journal of World Trade Law,* 1968, p.190; see also D.W. Nabudere, 'The Arusha Agreement with the EEC', *East African Law Review,* Vol. 6, No. 2, 1973.
2. G.L. Beckford, *Persistent Poverty* (London, Oxford, 1972).
3. D.W. Nabudere, 'Lome Convention and the Consolidation of Neo-colonialism' in *The Theory and Practice of Imperialism,* (London/ Dar es Salaam, Onyx Press/TPH, 1980).
4. *Daily News* (Dar es Salaam) 17 August 1978.
5. K. Marx and F. Engels, *The Communist Manifesto.*
6. *Daily News* (Dar es Salaam) 27 October 1978.
7. R. Green and A. Seidman, *Unity or Poverty: The Economics of Pan-Africanism* (London, Penguin, 1968), p.149.
8. Ibid.
9. A. Hazelwood, *Economic Integration: The East African Experience* (London, Heinemann, 1975), Ch.10.
10. As reported in *Daily News* 27 October 1978.
11. Ibid.

12. E.C.A., *The Multinational Corporations in Africa* (London, Rex Collings, 1972).
13. Ibid., p.16.
14. Ibid. — quote from R.H. Green, and K.G.V. Krishna, *Economic Co-operation in Africa*, (Nairobi, 1967), pp.81-82.
15. Ibid., p.16.
16. *Daily News* (Dar es Salaam) 6 February, 1979.

10. The Nation State and Integration

The Central Argument in Brief

We have seen that East African integration in the world capitalist economy originated in the need for European imperialism to expand. This outward push by Europe was itself a reflection of Europe's economic needs and can be further broken down into the specific demands of each period of outward expansion, as we have seen. The specific needs that led to the scramble for the remainder of the uncolonized world in the period 1880-1914 was thus directly connected with the competitive requirements of capitalism busy reproducing itself in Europe.

But this capitalism had, by this period, transformed itself out of the contradictions of its own development into monopoly capitalism — a capitalism that was parasitic and moribund, no longer regenerative but, on the contrary, a fetter on the further development of the productive forces not only in Europe itself but in the new lands that were being brought under the colonial control of the European metropolitan powers.

Thus production in these countries of Africa and Asia was tailored to meet the specific requirements of the monopolies that lay behind the European states' tendency towards expansionism. It is in this context that we identified the rivalry between European powers which led to the colonial division of the world on the basis of bilateral imperialism. This phase established exploitative and oppressive bilateral relationships between the metropolitan powers and their colonies, and it was in this context that the colonization of East Africa by Britain and Germany was undertaken.

This oppressive system was naturally opposed by the people and this is what led to its disintegration. The system of regional-horizontal integration that Britain designed to meet its imperialist needs itself soon had to confront the consequences of this exploitative relationship. The administrative structures began to feel the strain and tried to contain the forces now pressuring for *national* independence by restructuring the arrangement in the form of the East African Common Services Organization (EACSO). But these structures increasingly came under pressure from the forces of national liberation.

It has also been seen that these forces of national independence were weak in terms of their class composition. Because the 'national' bourgeoisie that had led the struggle for national independence had been a dominated class, they were flabby and spineless. They did not own and control the *national* means of production, exchange and distribution. This new class was basically a petty bourgeoisie owning *very small* property in land and commerce, with no control over industry at all. National independence had historically been associated with the rise of the national bourgeoisie in Europe, which played a progressive and revolutionary role in fighting against feudalism; they had built a national capital and market which they owned and controlled. The political rule of the earlier European bourgeoisie had been established on the basis of the nation state, and economic power transformed into political power.

In the case of East Africa, however, its flabby and dominated bourgeoisie, *nay* petty bourgeoisie, could not rally the economic resources necessary as a basis for its *national political power*. Economically weak, it was also politically weak, and found itself easy prey to the dominant new economic forces in the world. Relegated to the role of wielding political power without economic power, its political power was now used to exploit the national resources on behalf of those economic interests that still dominated the world market.

These dominant interests were the same old economic forces which had exploited these countries in the past but which had now reorganized themselves to take advantage of the weakness of the neo-colonial nation state. What they wanted, however, remained the same: to be able to exploit the resources of these countries, in particular their cheap labour. It was the cheapness of this labour power that made the raw materials and food products that the monopolies required cheap too.

With this reoganization of imperialist strategy, there went the restructuring of the monopoly capitalist firm. Earlier bilateral exploitation had operated with national monopolies; now transnational monopolies were able to cope with the existence of nation states of all kinds in their exploitative activities under a system of multilateral exploitation. This transnational monopoly system was thus partly a reaction to the new phase of national liberation movements which, within a decade, meant that neo-colonies now *outnumbered* the European nations. But the system was also a reflection of the gigantic concentration of capital in the U.S. as a result of the world wars. So much for the predictions by bourgeois scholars that the nation state would soon be dead. Indeed such a notion was shown up for the reactionary ideology it was. It opposed the idea of the right of nations to self-determination. An imperialist ideologue and empire seeker, Chamberlain, had in 1902 declared: 'The day of small nations has long passed away; the day of empires has come.'

The U.S. imperialists were, however, quick to take advantage of the idea of the right of nations to self-determination in order to prepare the ground for the penetration of U.S. finance capital into countries where the 'national' bourgeoisies were not in control of their economies.

This was a new phase within the stage of modern imperialism now led by the United States. As it advanced in its march towards hegemony, as it built up its military might, it began to be recognized by the peoples of the Third World as an imperialist power in an open way, thanks to proletarian politics. Armed to the teeth to 'contain communism', commanding the skies of the imperialist world and the Third World, its intellectuals also began to advance an ideology to undermine the nation state. With this imperialist military might behind them, they declared that the atomic bomb had blown the roof off the sovereignty of the nation state.

The Myth of the End of the Nation State

One such ideologue of U.S. imperialism declared that the 'territorial state' concept had been historically valid only to the extent that the state unit was a physical, corporeal entity, an expanse of territory encircled for its identification and its defence by a 'hard shell'. This concept implied the 'impermeability' or the 'impenetrability and hence the territoriality' of the modern state: 'The fact that it was surrounded by a hard shell rendered it to some extent secure from foreign penetration, and thus made it an ultimate unit of protection for those within its boundaries.'[1]

But, the argument then continued, beginning in the 19th Century, certain trends had become visible which tended to endanger the functioning of the classical system. The trend towards war threatened this historical hard shell. The rise of economic, psychological, air and now nuclear warfare had lifted the roof off the territorial state: 'What remained of the impermeability of states seems to have gone for good.'[2] What remained was the reality of destruction, which threatened 'everybody'. In the circumstances national interests were receding behind the common interest of all mankind in 'survival', in a new 'universalism' through which 'a rational approach to world problems would at last become possible'.[3] This was a pacificism, an imperialist pacificism, based on a balance of power between the superpowers that wielded their instruments of destruction over the peoples – an imperialist blackmail.

It was in these circumstances that Chairman Mao Tse-tung's declaration that the atom bomb was a paper tiger made a lot of revolutionary sense. U.S. imperialism, Ho Chi Minh argued, can be defeated despite its nuclear weaponry. As the people of Indo-China did just this in 1975, 'the roof' over the imperialist ideology of the anti-nation was itself 'blown off'. The imperialist bourgeoisies and their ideologues who had argued for submission to weapons began to rethink.

Hans Moargenthau[4] had argued that imperialism meant force which wanted to distrub existing relations and he argued that therefore the revolutionary forces of the world were also imperialistic. Now he was discredited, likewise, those who had argued that the concept of the nation state was 'only an abstraction', a 'figment of human imagination',[5] now found their arguments at variance with reality too. The struggle of the world's exploited peoples to form nation states as part of their revolutionary struggles against imperialism the world over made its mark, as the imperialist ideologues had to acknowledge:

> But if [national] sovereignty is 'obsolete' in Western Europe, it is coming into its own in Asia, the Middle East, and Africa. While the Atlantic Community is moving toward cohesion, these other areas are veering toward fragmentation. In fact, more sovereign states have been born in our generation than in the preceding 300 year history of the nation-state system. As a result of the triumph of sovereignty of the non-white peoples of the earth, the membership of the United Nations, has, since 1945, more than doubled. Hence, we would seem to live in one of those rare and fascinating transitional periods in history in which mankind is at the same time looking both forward and backward. When we consider the Western world and see sovereignty beginning to be replaced by new forms of regionalism, we see signs of the future. When we turn to the new nationalism in Asia, the Middle East, and Africa, we witness what is in effect a rekindling of the past. Until, therefore, the world has internationally evolved somewhat further, sovereignty is bound to remain an integral part of our lives.[6]

The above quotation is full of half-truths and mystifications. It is not true that sovereignty is 'obsolete' in Western Europe, for European integration has not done away with national sovereignty, nor can it do so as long as modern imperialism, based on monopoly capital, with all its inherent contradictions at the national level, still exists. Similarly, the 'veering' towards 'fragmentation' is not a creation of the Asians, Arabs, Africans and Latin Americans, but the result of the anti-imperialist struggles of these countries against the scramble by Europe that chopped them up into fragmented colonies. Nor can the struggle of these countries for national independence and sovereignty be described as looking backwards, since nationality is still the dominant relation in international affairs. It is 'backward-looking' in only one sense, that, unlike Europe which established the nation state as the basis of building capitalism, the countries of Asia, Africa and Latin America are establishing their nation states as the basis of struggle against modern imperialism which is monopoly capitalism. For, as Mao Tse-tung said, the struggle for 'new democracy' is both a struggle against imperialism and at the same time a struggle for socialism, since such national struggle forms part of the international proletarian struggle, regardless of what the individuals involved in those struggles think of it.[7]

Moreover the world will be able to evolve a little more only when imperialism is crushed and uneven development substantially removed. But such uneven development cannot be removed without national independence and national sovereignty for backward peoples, for it is only the peoples' control over their productive forces on the basis of *national* and international *class struggle* that can ensure such control, and so development.

It follows that national sovereignty is neither an abstraction nor just a figment of the human mind. It is a reflection of the reality of class forces at work on a world scale. So long as conditions for exploitation and oppression persist, the demand for national independence is a demand by all the classes in a given territory for control over their productive forces and enhancement of their permanent sovereignty over that territory. It is for this reason that such a demand is national *and* democratic, for it is based on a general consensus of all national forces for progress. Thus national independence confronts us as a reality and an important reality at a time when a majority of the people of the nations of the world are still dominated and oppressed nationally.

What does all this imply for the present analysis? It implies one thing, namely that the nation state is today the most revolutionary instrument in the majority of the countries of the world — with the exception of the superpowers — for redressing the uneven development that has been exacerbated by imperialism.

But whence arises the idea that small nations are not 'viable' economic entities for such development? Under modern conditions, brought about by the development of capitalism, the pressure for the establishment of nation states in Europe brought about the notion of the national entity being 'progressive' in economic advancement and progress. As Hobsbawm has pointed out:

> The champions of the 'nation state' assumed not only that it must be national but also that it must be 'progressive', i.e. capable of developing a viable economy, technology, state organization and military force, i.e. that it must be at least moderately large. It was to be, in fact, the 'natural' unit of the development of the modern, liberal, progressive and *de facto* bourgeois society.[8]

The rationale for this ideological position was the law of accumulation of capital in its youth. It appeared reasonable to assert, at the time, that economic development would occur more rapidly if capital could be reproduced on an ever-increasing scale. This implied capitalist production on the basis of a national market that was sufficiently large to enable the capitalists to 'break even', at a given level of technological development, and then to make more profits to enable them to accumulate further and compete not only in the home market but in the world market.

This argument took on strength with the rise of small nations in Europe in the early 20th Century. In fact it never actually applied to 'small' nations like Britain which were first in the world market and which developed the home market and then expanded into an almost 'empty' world market. The argument now arose that small nations must therefore be integrated 'federally or otherwise, with or without some as yet undetermined autonomy, into viable nation states'.[9] It was with this in view that President Wilson pressed for the unification of small states in Central Europe after the First World War. But Wilson forgot that this was a new era — the era of modern imperialism.

All theories of customs unions and regional integration have been based on these premises. Without paying attention to the specific history and politics of colonial developments, they have argued from first principles for economic integration of 'small states'. Yet the introduction of capitalism in its moribund form into the colonies by the European dominant imperialist nations was itself responsible for stirring up the national feeling and sentiment which resulted in national movements led by local petty bourgeoisies and 'national' bourgeoisies. But the independence won by these national forces did not lead to an independent development of capitalism based on the economic strength of these 'national' bourgeoisies. The dominant imperialist bourgeoisies still continued to exploit and dominate the economic resources of those countries, with the result that the capitalism that prevailed in the neo-colonies was not founded upon those national markets as such. Indeed these 'national' markets themselves constituted only a small segment of the markets of these dominant bourgeoisies who by now were operating globally, taking the whole world as their market.

It follows that the economistic arguments about 'economies of scale' put forward by imperialist economists only applied to economies on the world scale and not on the national scale. As Marx observed over a century ago, but which applies even more to today's monopoly bourgeoisie: 'The industrialist always has a world market before him, he compares and must continue to compare his cost price and those of the whole world, and not only with those of the home market.'[10]

Today the monopoly capitalist does not just compare costs in the Third World, he can actually determine them more and more through the monopoly hold he has over the entire world's markets, determining wages, interest rates, rents and prices. As the popular saying goes today: 'When the imperialist bourgeoisies catch an economic cold in the imperialist centres, it is the "national" bourgeoisies in the neo-colonies who sneeze!' Spiralling inflation the world over proves this beyond doubt.

The upshot of all this is to bring home the point that any theoretical formulations that harp on the market question as the rationale for regional integration, on arguments of regional economies of scale or trade creation, beg the question. This has been amply demonstrated in the previous chapters. The crucial issue is, therefore, not one of smallness or largeness of market, but one of *national* exploitation and domination of those markets by the monopolies.

The Only Solution

There is only one real solution to the basic problem: The call for the continuation of the class struggle on an international scale, on the basis of a *national* programme uniting all the national forces, under the leadership of the working class. It is only after the new democratic revolution is won that the question of *national economic development* can be faced. What then, it may be asked? Will the mere removal of imperialist domination do away with all the constraints posed by small segmented markets? Does the question of cost and the law of value not feature in a small-sized socialist state, particularly a backward one with little or no industrialization?

To these arguments we say in reply: Down with economism! For indeed what is economic development? To us it is the release of the full human and material potential of a country from the fetters imposed by international monopoly capitalism. Only then can the national forces come into full play on the basis of a national plan. Then there can be development. Such development can and has taken place in a number of small countries such as North Korea and Albania. Despite the fact that these countries still are backward compared to the more developed imperialist countries who exploit others, the achievements of such small countries developing by their own efforts with mutual assistance between themselves and on the basis of only mutually advantageous economic relationships with other countries has improved the general standard of living of the people overall, which has not happened in the neo-colonial Third World.

It is to the credit of Clive Thomas, a Guyanese who was Professor of Economics at the University of Dar es Salaam, Tanzania, that he has pointed to the importance of this possibility.[12] Professor Thomas has pointed out that, as soon as nationalism and self-determination constituted a major historical force, and as soon as socialist thought recognized the progressive character of this development, the facts of a small national market and some nations' limited size were built into their analyses by both capitalism and socialism.[13]

In the case of capitalism, according to Thomas, smallness of size was seen as a constraint on economic development. Yet many of the arguments about economies of scale, measuring the ratio of physical input and output factors, simply failed to explain the relationships between costs of production, output levels, and prices at which the output became available. Professor Thomas does not bring up the point, but implicit in the argument is the fact that it is monopolistic competition in the capitalist economies which explains the anarchy in the economies of undeveloped countries (a fact that questions the real significance of the economies of scale theory).

He pointed out that high unit costs of production in many lines of manufacturing in these countries were brought about by competition, resulting in a proliferation of plants in which high costs are compensated for by the high levels of local protection. Without understanding this, he argues, it could not be explained why, for instance, in 1967, the total number of cars and trucks produced in the Latin American Free Trade Area was 650,000 units from as many as 67 production plants.

> In this confusing situation not only are the output capacities of individual plants very small, but the level of utilization of this capacity is also a very small proportion of its potential. And, despite

this, the levels of private profitability of these operations are very high indeed. Thus we can show how complex and unclear is the effect of economies of scale on production costs, selling prices, and social and private rates of return.[14]

It follows, Thomas argued, that prices can only be rational — and therefore useful in guiding production decisions — insofar as they reflect domestic demand priorities, etc. The optimum scale of operation will be a useful indicator of efficiency in the context of a realistic and practicable 'critical minimum level', if 'we are to operate effectively within the context of size constraints'. In this case the critical minimum can be described as 'the range of the cost function over the rate of inversion (i.e. rates of cost changes). In such a situation cost savings are greatest, and the social costs of industrialization are rapidly reduced, at the point where the level of production reaches a "critical minimum". '

It is for this reason, Thomas argues, that all the customary arguments about and reliance on optimal output considerations to determine decisions are very misleading in their implications for the industrialization of small countries in the undeveloped world, for how could it be otherwise when all these concepts of optima are derived from the preoccupations of firms operating in industrialized countries 'which are in a position to serve the whole globe'.[15]

These arguments of Professor Clive Thomas support the right of nations — small and large — to *economic* self-determination and are consistent with the Marxist-Leninst thesis on the *political* right of nations to self-determination, Regrettably, however, Thomas backslides when, in his latest attempt at formulating a 'Marxist theory of regional integration', he seems to suggest that regional economic integration among small countries is justifiable if their relations of production have been changed and are 'progressive'. This is made conditional upon the 'development of the productive forces'.[16] But it can be asked how are the productive forces to develop under conditions of neo-colonial economic domination? Possibly Clive Thomas would answer that this is possible under his economics of transitional transformation, with respect to small-sized economies of the 'Tanzania type'. However this notion of economies of the 'Tanzania type' is confusing. He correctly maintains that one cannot judge whether a country is in transition to socialism on a basis that the leaders claim to be socialist.[17] A policy is socialist only if:

a political revolution has been initiated and has succeeded in transferring state power to a worker/peasant alliance, thereby fundamentally altering productive forces under control and direction, to disengage from international capitalism, and to raise the material levels of the welfare of the population are the central economic issues at a stage in constructing socialism.[18]

Yet Thomas categorizes Tanzania along with North Korea, Cuba and Vietnam[19] as belonging to this type of country!

Thomas is able to do this because he is careful to exclude the leadership of the proletariat from his definition of 'political revolution' spelt out above. In his view it is adequate if the revolution 'transfers' power to the worker/peasant alliance. It is for this reason that his theoretical thrust falls to the ground despite its partial consistency with the Marxist-Leninist thesis on the right of nations to self-determination. But this only partial consistency establishes a dualism which eventually leads back to idealism, and therefore Thomas's theory becomes a basis for the petty-bourgeois economism of economic transformation under petty-bourgeois leadership. Instead of disposing of and disengaging from international capitalism, the small nation will slip back into the fold of Western imperialism.

Professor Thomas's theory also lends itself to the aims of the Soviet Union – which does not always act in a disinterested way. This is because in his 'Marxist theory' of regional integration he puts forward a defence of so-called 'socialist integration'. He states that the 'rise of the socialist world system, and the successful prosecution of the national liberation struggles also help to determine the nature of the regional process'. He argues further that, 'to the extent socialism genuinely prevails', the socialist division of labour carries the process of regional integration to a higher stage. He adds:

> This is possible because socialism eliminates the fundamental contradiction of capitalism, through socializing and collectivizing the appropriation of the product, and so bringing the social relations which govern production into a closer correspondence to the rapid development of the process of internationalization of production. [Under these conditions] socialism makes it possible for regional integration to proceed without discontinuities derived from antagonistic conflicts.[20]

This, Thomas is careful to point out, is only good when 'socialism genuinely prevails'. He does not say whether the socialism that exists in the Comecom arrangement in Eastern Europe is 'genuine' or not, but since he favours the developments under this sort of integration, it would appear that he supports this institution.

In our view, whether or not socialism 'genuinely' exists in a number of socialist countries or not, regional economic integration among such countries does not necessarily bring about an equal development of the productive forces in each country. Even development between socialist countries cannot be brought about by a 'socialist division of labour' but on the basis of the mobilization of the national energies and resources of each particular country on the basis of full national sovereignty. This does not mean autarchy for it is possible for genuine mutual support and assistance to be extended by the more developed socialist states to the less developed ones, provided each less developed socialist state retains full responsibility for all development lying within its territory.

This principle is what characterized the Comecom in principle. In the statement issued by the countries of Eastern Europe in January 1949, when Comecon was formed, the national sovereignty of each of the member-states was the keynote. The communique noted that these countries had rejected the hegemony of one country implied in the Marshall Plan for Europe, 'which would have violated their sovereignty and the interests of their national economies'. It added:

> In the light of these circumstances, the meeting studied the question of the possibility of organizing a wider economic co-operation between the countries of the people's democracies and the U.S.S.R. To establish this wider economic co-operation between the people's democracies and the U.S.S.R., the conference considered it necessary to create the Council for Mutual Economic Assistance between the countries represented — on the basis of equal representation and with the *task of exchanging economic experience, extending technical aid to one another and rendering mutual assistance* with respect to raw materials, foodstuffs, machines, equipment, etc.[21]

This emphasis on each country being responsible for its own development was recognition of the fact that uneven development between countries could only be avoided by the pooling of resources on a national scale. This implied, first, economic development without an inevitable growth in trade between these countries; the stress had to be the development of the national productive forces, particularly heavy industry and engineering, alongside light industry to provide consumer goods within the country,

This emphasis on each Eastern European country's national sovereignty was changed, in my view, immediately after Stalin's death and efforts were now made to create a supra-national institutionalization of Comecon. In the words of Krushchev in a Leipzig speech in 1959:

> If we speak of the future, it seems to me that the further development of the socialist countries will in all probability proceed along lines of reinforcing a single world system of socialist economy. . . . Not a single sovereign socialist state is able to shut itself up within its own frontiers and rely exclusively upon its own potential, or its own wealth. If the contrary were true, we would not be communist internationalists but national socialists.[22]

This vulgar 'communism' of Krushchev opened the doors to Soviet economic hegemony in Eastern Europe. From now on, a real integration of the countries of Eastern Europe into a Soviet-dominated 'international socialist division of labour' began which had — it could be argued — nothing in common with 'genuine socialism'. One unintended result was that it enhanced national feeling in Eastern Europe and correctly earned itself the wrath of the people of those countries. National development in our view was still a valid issue in these countries and something they increasingly demanded.

Our Political Programme

If support of sovereign development of each country ought to be the position for socialist countries, it is even more so for the countries of the Third World dominated as they are by capitalist imperialism. They ought to assert their national independence and throw off the yoke of foreign domination as a prerequisite of genuine national development. The throwing off of foreign domination is itself a task that can only be accomplished by all the national forces, and requires today the leadership of the working class. Despite its internationalism in terms of economic interest, the working class must play a *national* role in mobilizing national forces against foreign exploitation and domination, and by developing these forces, both socially and materially. This is a precondition for removing distinctions between nations and hence establishing a true internationalism based on relatively even development of all nations devoid of exploitation and domination.

The experience of economic integration, whether under bilateral or multilateral imperialism — the so-called regional integration of countries — was nothing but an aspect of the vertical integration of these countries with imperialist economies, in which East Africa was but a component market. Such integration therefore cannot but be exploitative and oppressive of the national forces whose unity becomes essential in repulsing these forces of domination. Only on the basis of a new democratic revolution in which the working class plays a leading role can imperialism be contested.

Absence of working-class organization merely prolongs the exploitation of these countries, for the 'national' bourgeoisie and petty bourgeoisie cannot provide the leadership to eliminate such exploitation since their economic interests are purely temporary in today's epoch of a world transition to socialism, and their own hopes of improving their position in the world market in which they play their part is unachievable. But precisely because they cannot achieve this, the 'national' bourgeoisie does remain in permanent contradiction with imperialism, and to that extent they can play a progressive role in the anti-imperialist struggle, but only when guided and led by the revolutionary line of the working class in each country. Only by assuring national independence to the peoples of Kenya, Uganda and Tanzania can real economic transformation take place in these countries.

References

1. John H. Hertz, *International Politics in the Atomic Age,* (New York, 1959), see also his *Nation-State and the Crisis of World Politics.*

(New York, McKay, 1976), pp.99-124, esp. p.101.
2. Ibid., p.118.
3. Ibid., pp.122-3.
4. H.J. Morgenthau *Politics Among Nations* (New York, Knapf, 1967).
5. John G. Stoessinger, *The Might of Nations* (New York, Random House, 1975), p.7.
6. Ibid., p.9.
7. Mao Tse-tung, *New Democracy*.
8. E.J. Hobsbawm, *The Age of Capital* (London, Abacus, 1975), p.107.
9. Ibid., p.108.
10. K. Marx, *Capital*, Vol. III, p.390.
11. See C.P. Kindleberger, *International Economics* (Irwin, 1973), p.263.
12. C. Thomas, *Dependence and Transformation* (New York, Monthly Review, 1974).
13. Ibid., pp.43-4.
14. Ibid., pp.208-9.
15. Ibid., pp.210-2.
16. C. Thomas, 'On Formulating a Marxist Theory of Regional Integration', *Transition*, Vol. 1, No. 1, University of Guyana.
17. Op. cit., pp.27-8.
18. Ibid., p.29.
19. Ibid., p.34.
20. Thomas, op. cit., p.68.
21. Quoted in Michael Kaser, *COMECON: Integration Problems of the Planned Economies* (Oxford, R.I.I.A., 1967), pp.11-2.
22. Quoted in Kaser, op. cit., p.201.